Abortion: The Development of the Roman Catholic Perspective

John Connery, S.J.

Loyola University Press

LOYOLA UNIVERSITY PRESS

Printed in the United States of America

LIBRARY OF CONGRESS

CATALOGING IN PUBLICATION DATA

Connery, John R., 1913-
   Abortion: the development of the Roman Catholic perspective.

   Includes bibliographical references.
   1. Abortion—Religious aspects—Catholic Church. I. Title.
HQ767.3.c66   261.8'3   76-51217
ISBN 0-8294-0257-8

Cover design by Deborah Brown Callahan

About this book

Abortion: The Development of the Roman Catholic Perspective was set by Black Dot Typographers, Inc. The text is 12/14 Bodoni Book; the reduced matter, 10/12; the notes, 10/12; and the cover display type, Bembo.

It was printed by Photopress, Inc., on Warren Olde Style 60-pound paper and bound by The Engdahl Company.

The reduced price of this book was made possible by a generous grant from The Joseph P. Kennedy, Jr. Foundation.

CONTENTS

viii

Abortion:
The Development
of the
Roman Catholic
Perspective

INTRODUCTION

Almost ten years ago when the author decided to undertake the present study, his purpose was to supply what was a real need. At that time there were only two works in print dealing with the development of the Roman Catholic perspective on abortion: *Ius fetus ad vitam,* a monograph written in Latin by Joseph Palazzini; and *The Crime of Abortion in Canon Law* by Roger J. Huser. But neither of these treatises brought the development up to modern times and both of them were more interested in the canonical than in the moral development. Although these two perspectives are intimately related, they are different, and a study that concentrates on one will not supply the need for the other. In 1970 John Noonan's historical treatment of abortion appeared as a chapter in a book he edited on *The Morality of Abortion* (Cambridge, 1970). This treatment of the issue brought it up to modern times and was broader than a strictly canonical approach. Similar chapters on the historical perspective were included in Daniel Callahan's *Abortion: Law, Choice and Morality* (London, 1970) and Germaine Grisez's *Abortion: The Myths, The Realities and The Arguments* (New York, 1970). At that time the author of the present work began to wonder whether the need he started out to supply was already provided for. But with further consideration it became increasingly clear that a two-thousand-year development could hardly be presented adequately in a single chapter of a book; it would call for a presentation of at least booksize proportions. Also, none of the above named authors was a professional moral theologian, and although they did a generally competent job of researching the historical facts, they were not in a position to deal with them from a theological background and with a technical understanding of the language involved. The author concluded that there was still need for a study that would show the development of the tradition in more detail and with greater sensitivity to the theological dimension.

It was shortly after that time (1972-73) that the author had the good fortune of receiving an invitation to spend a year at the Kennedy Institute, Center for Bioethics, at Georgetown University as a senior research scholar. Work on the manuscript for the present book was taken up again seriously at that time and was completed in a second year spent at the center in 1975-76. During the first year at the center added incentive to continue the project was provided by the abortion decision of the U.S. Supreme Court. The Court decided that it was unconstitutional to give the fetus any protection against abortion decisions by the mother during the first six months of pregnancy or anything resembling full protection after that time. Although the present study deals only peripherally with the legal aspect of abortion, it is hoped that it will set the record straight regarding the history behind abortion legislation of the past. The historical parts of Roe versus Wade were so garbled and the history so misused that this seemed imperative. From the viewpoint of eighteen hundred years of legal tradition the decision has to be considered a complete *volte face*.

The present study was not meant to be a comprehensive history of abortion, recording everything that any Father, canonist, or theologian of the Church wrote on the subject. There may be a need for this type of comprehensive work, but the present study was never intended to satisfy this need. Some of the authors defending craniotomy and embryotomy in the nineteenth century accused moral theologians over the centuries of copying and following one another *ad instar avium et ovium* (like birds and sheep). Although anyone acquainted with the history of moral theology will know that this is an exaggeration, it is understandable that not every moral theologian would make a contribution in every area of moral theology he treated. But in the present work authors and theologians who just repeated what their predecessors had said are not cited. The purpose of this work is to give a sufficient sampling to provide a clear picture of the development of thought that took place regarding the morality of abortion, and so to concentrate on those authors who contributed to it. It was necessary, of course, to point out whether an opinion became common or failed to win support, so some attention had to be given to numbers.

The scope of the book is limited to the development of opinion that took place within the Roman Catholic Church. During the first fifteen centuries this was not a real limitation, at least in reference to Christian thought, since the tradition was common. But it did become a limitation in the post-Reformation period. No effort was made to follow the development of thought among Protestant theologians after the Reformation. This still needs to be done, but the author of the present study could not claim the competence or the acquaintance with Protestant theology necessary for such a project. From the little acquaintance he has he would hazard a guess that the thinking among Protestant theologians, at least until very recent times, was not too different.

The ambition of the author was to present as objective a picture as possible of the development that took place, and to situate it in as much of a context as necessary to explain it. A serious effort was made not to inject personal bias or to distort the historical development in any way. One is never as successful at this sort of thing as he would like, but the author hopes that he has kept the personal intrusions to a minimum.

The reader may find some of the medical concepts underlying the discussion of the morality of abortion rather naive. This will not be surprising to anyone acquainted with the history of medicine. Medicine has come of age only in relatively recent times, and it is only since the discovery of the ovum by Von Baer in 1827 that our knowledge of the process of conception and generation has been at all accurate. Even the discovery of sperm in the semen, although looked upon sceptically in the beginning, served only to confirm the errors of the past regarding the exclusive role of the male contribution as an active agent in generation.

A writer dealing with the past always runs into problems regarding names of people and places. Most of the sources the author dealt with were written in the Latin language. It was usually easy enough to substitute the English equivalent of the Latin name of some city or town; it would be recognized easily. But many of the authors, and especially the more modern ones, while they belonged to modern European countries and had modern language names, are better known by their Latin names. To use their modern language names, and especially to anglicise them, would have made recognition difficult. Although it is not easy to follow a consistent policy in this sort of thing, the author generally used the Latin name of the author unless he was better known by his modern language name or its English equivalent. The name on the title page of his work was ordinarily the one chosen.

Another decision had to be made regarding the use of the many texts consulted in the course of the work. The author decided that lengthy quotations in Latin (or other languages) would have been of little use to the ordinary reader and would have expanded the book to prohibitive proportions. He also decided that even an attempt to offer these texts in translation would have called for a disproportionate investment of time. The final conclusion was that perhaps the best procedure would be to digest them or paraphrase them for the most part in the body of the book. The more scholarly reader may not be satisfied with this conclusion, but he will always have the option of comparing these renditions with the original texts through the references given at the end of the book. An exception to the general policy was made in favor of texts and expressions of special importance; these were cited in the original Latin. But unless the meaning of the Latin was obvious from the context or its similarity to English, an English translation was added either in the text of the book or in the notes.

It is often difficult for a reader to put together and retain all the facts and lines of argument that make up an historical development as compact as this had to be. As an aid to the reader in this task, the author tried to recapitulate and summarize with some frequency the development that took place. Most of these summaries will be found at the end of the individual chapters, but some of them were inserted elsewhere. It is hoped that the reader will not find them repetitious. It would be risky, of course, to rely solely on these summaries for an overall understanding of the development. They will be properly understood only if read in conjunction with the previous history.

In this type of publication in which one is dealing with innumerable names, dates, facts, and opinions, immunity from error is hard to come by. The most an author can do is keep the number of errors to a minimum. Having experienced the frustration of being misled by erroneous references, the author would like to promise the reader that he will not have a similar experience. But he knows that it would not be realistic to do so. His only hope is that his own frustrations have made him more careful.

The cutoff point for the study is the middle of the present century. There may be a rare reference to more recent developments, but the author had no intention of entering into the current debate. This would take another publication of at least equal proportions and the time is certainly not yet ripe for such an undertaking. Thought needs the test of time to assess its validity, and not enough time has elapsed as yet to provide this test of current opinions.

There remains the pleasant, although somewhat risky, task of thanking personally all those who not only responded to but even anticipated calls for help. I am indebted above all to Andre F. Hellegers and Richard A. McCormick, S. J., for the part they played in making it possible for me to spend two years at the Kennedy Institute, Center for Bioethics, Georgetown University as a senior research scholar. Without this opportunity this publication might never have seen the light of day. I am indebted also to the staff at the center, particularly to Pat Schifferli, Mary Baker, Rijnep Moskey, and Carol Hetler. Thanks are due also to the staffs of the many libraries used in doing the research for the book. Many of these must remain anonymous, but Doris Goldstein of the library at the center, Arlene Feiner of the library of the Jesuit School of Theology in Chicago, Caroline Lee of the Mullen Library at the Catholic University of America, and Henry Bertels, S.J., of the Woodstock Library at Georgetown University can be named especially. Thanks must go again to Andre Hellegers and to Joseph F. Mangan, S.J., for their generosity in reading the manuscript and offering valuable suggestions. I owe a debt of gratitude also to Father Vincent Horrigan, S.J., director of the Loyola University Press, both for accepting the manuscript for publication and assisting in the actual editing. And lest the first be last, I want to offer heartfelt gratitude to Sargent and Eunice Kennedy Shriver for their encouragement and support. They went far beyond the call of any duty, bioethical or otherwise. My only hope is that their generosity has not gone beyond the limits of prudence and that the book will prove worthy of the confidence and interest they have shown. My last vote of thanks is to all those who helped in so many ways to bring this project to term, especially those who would have and should have been named here except for an unfaithful memory.

CHAPTER ONE

The Jewish Background

Any history of the development of theological opinion regarding abortion during the Christian era must begin
with an account of the context into which Christianity was
introduced. It would indeed be quite impossible to provide
a comprehensive review of all pre-Christian thought and
practice regarding abortion, and it would not be advisable,
even if it were possible, since the scope of the present work
is to account for the Christian era rather than the pre-
Christian era. It also seems preferable to reserve some
background material relating to specific problems to the
treatment of those problems when they occur. But it will be
helpful to preface the main discussion with a brief account
of two very important influences on the Christian tradition:
the Jewish tradition regarding abortion and Roman law and
practice. Some acquaintance with both of these influences
will be important for an understanding of the Christian
tradition, although it would be a mistake, as several authors rightly advise,[1] to expect to find a complete explanation of the Christian tradition either in Roman or even
Jewish law as such. On the other hand the Christian attitude toward abortion will be in general continuity with the
tradition of the Jews of the pre-Christian and early Christian era.

The fundamental law of the Jews is found in the Pentateuch, the first five books of the Old Testament, known to the Jews as the Torah, the law. One would expect to discover there the source, or at least the expression, of Jewish tradition regarding abortion. It may seem curious to the modern reader, but an examination of the Pentateuch yields only one text that deals clearly and explicitly with this issue. The text comes from the Book of Exodus, more specifically from that part of Exodus known as the book of the covenant (20:22-23:19), which contains a Jewish legal code. In its present form it does not go back beyond the ninth century before Christ, but much of the material in the book has an earlier origin and shows the influence of such earlier codes as that of Hammurabi, the Hittites, and the Assyrians, not to mention even earlier sources.[2] Although it contains much that would look like mere civil (penal) legislation, it must be remembered that to the Hebrew it was a covenant with God. The distinction between law, morality, and religion was not all that sharply drawn, so one must not conclude from the fact that civil penalties are prescribed in the code that one is dealing merely with civil law. It is in this covenant that one finds the only text in the Old Testament explicitly dealing with abortion. It reads as follows:

> When men have a fight and hurt a pregnant woman, so that she suffers a miscarriage, but no further injury, the guilty one shall be fined as much as the woman's husband demands of him, and he shall pay in the presence of judges. But if injury ensues, you shall give life for life, eye for eye, tooth for tooth, hand for hand, foot for foot, burn for burn, wound for wound, stripe for stripe.[3]

This is an example of what is called casuistic law, a model used frequently in the book of the covenant.[4] In all likelihood the woman in the case was the wife of one of the combatants. Some evidence for this assumption may be found in Deuteronomy, where the law imposes certain limits on the tactics to which a wife may resort "to save her husband from the blows of his opponent."[5] More important for this study, however, is the fact that the book of the covenant differs from other near eastern codes in setting the

offense in the context of a quarrel between two men. In the
code of Hammurabi, as well as in that of the Assyrians and
the Hittites, the case simply involves a man striking a
woman or causing her to miscarry.[6] Why is a different setting used in the Hebrew code? A previous statute in the
covenant had dealt with a quarrel between two men,[7] but
the statute immediately preceding the one under discussion dealt with a man striking a slave,[8] so the lawmaker
was aware of both models. Why did he not use what seems
to be the simpler model of the man striking a woman?

Perhaps no certain answer is available from this distance. But since in the covenant case the main target of the
blows was the male opponent, the relationship with the
abortion and the damage to the woman seem less direct.
There is less likelihood, perhaps, that at least the abortion
would be intentional. The Hebrew statute then could more
easily cover an abortion that was in some sense accidental.
But even in the Hebrew statute the person causing the
damage must be somehow blameworthy. This is quite clear
from the previous statute on homicide where a distinction
is made between a death deliberately pursued and one resulting from an act of God. If the death resulted from an act
of God, asylum is provided the human agent until the wrath
of the avenger of blood subsides.[9] Exodus itself does not
elaborate on this distinction, but some clarification can be
found in Deuteronomy.[10] There the law states that if a man
is chopping down a tree and the head of the axe flies off and
hits his neighbor, striking him a mortal blow, the
woodsman is entitled to asylum. The implication here is
that this was an act of God and the woodsman was not
blameworthy. What he was doing was entirely legitimate,
and the damage to the neighbor was altogether unforeseen
and unblameworthy. Similarly, in the abortion case, no
penalty could be legitimately imposed if the human agent
was in no way to be blamed for the damage. But it is entirely conceivable in the covenant case that even if the
abortion was not intended, the one causing it was considered blameworthy because he was doing something

wrong in fighting; he was therefore liable for damage resulting from the fight. The whole question of liability for unintended damage resulting from wrongful conduct will be discussed thoroughly during the Christian era. But perhaps all that can be said of the covenant statute is that it does not seem to require that the damage be intentional to be imputable. On the other hand, it will not hold a human agent liable for an act of God. But there is a gray area in between that will need more refinement.

What is of special interest to the present study is the distinction in the statute between the penalty imposed for the miscarriage and that imposed for injury to the mother. A fine is imposed for causing the miscarriage; the *lex talionis*, which calls for a punishment in kind, is applied to injury to the mother. Punishment by fine or indemnity generally represents a less primitive approach to penalties than the *lex talionis*, and is more characteristic of agricultural than nomadic societies.[11] Since the Hebrews of the time were moving from a nomadic society to a more agricultural type, the "composition" penalty which is legislated here may represent this changing situation. Yet it should be admitted that a punishment in kind, which the *lex talionis* calls for, would be difficult to apply to the crime of causing a miscarriage. Also, if Hebrew society was moving toward a more sophisticated approach to punishment, how does one explain the reversion to the *lex talionis* in punishing damage to the mother? Actually, this is the first full expression of the *lex talionis* in the Old Testament, and although it may sound primitive and harsh to modern ears, it did offer a safeguard against and set a limit to the more severe penalties to which uncontrolled vengeance might easily lead.[12] Although more primitive than punishment by fine, the *lex talionis* does show some respect, however crude, for the limits of justice. Nor has modern society completely outgrown this law. Corporal punishment has largely disappeared from modern penal codes, but many of them still call for "life for life," that is, capital punishment for some crimes.

The question this distinction in penalties poses is whether it implies anything regarding the status of the fetus. It is easy to see that the prescription "eye for eye" or "tooth for tooth" would not apply to the miscarriage. But the penalty "life for life" does seem pertinent. If a capital sentence is imposed for the life of the mother, why not for the life of the fetus? Even though it might not be feasible to arrange "miscarriage for miscarriage," some reasonable equivalent might be provided. Or is one to presume that the indemnity arranged by the husband (father) is the equivalent of the "life for life" penalty? Since there is no way of knowing what indemnity would be decided upon, and even if there were, no way of comparing it with the value of a life, it would seem quite impossible to argue that the penalties, although different in nature, are equivalent. It is really more likely that the penalty for causing the miscarriage is a lesser penalty. This is quite clear, for instance, in the code of Hammurabi where the penalty for causing a miscarriage never goes beyond ten shekels, whereas the penalty for the death of the woman herself (if she was a slave) was one third of a mina of silver (which would be worth twenty shekels.)[13] The same is true of the Assyrian code, although the penalties there were generally more severe. It seems reasonable to conclude that even in the Hebrew code the penalty for abortion was less than that imposed for the death of the mother. It is generally accepted also that this implies that the fetus did not have the same status as the mother in Hebrew law.

For a clear statement of the status of the fetus in Jewish thought, one must go to the Talmud rather than the Torah. The Talmud is a collection of Jewish rabbinical literature built up around the law. There it is stated explicitly that the fetus is not a separate entity but part of the mother until it is born, in much the same way as it is stated in Roman law that the fetus is *pars viscerum mulieris*.[14] Depriving the fetus of a juridical personality of its own and considering it part of the mother, the law certainly gives it a status inferior to that of a person already born. In doing so it offers a reason why miscarriage should be considered a lesser crime than causing the death of the mother.[15] It also explains the response in the Talmud, to be discussed later, allowing dismemberment of the fetus to save the life of the mother. But this judgment about the status of the fetus should not be over interpreted. Apart from the uses mentioned above, the dependent status of the fetus was appealed to more to settle problems of ownership, especially on the subhuman level, for example, to decide the ownership of an embryo found in the womb of a newly purchased animal.[16] It was also used to deny to the fetus the right of ownership enjoyed by independent juridical persons. But it was never appealed to in pre-Christian times to justify any general right to abortion by the mother or any kind of liberal policy in this area. In fact, it is undoubtedly reading history backwards to project the concept of woman's right to abortion back into those times. Even in Roman society whatever right was allowed in this area belonged to the *paterfamilias* rather than the mother herself. It should be pointed out also that the Talmud was not put into writing until the early Christian era, so one cannot be sure that it represents the thought of the writers of the Torah. But it would be generally admitted that the concept of the fetus as part of the mother until birth is of earlier origin than that, for instance, of Aristotle who considered the fetus a human being in the full sense of the term when it was formed.

The text from Exodus under discussion deals explicitly only with abortion caused by a third party; it says nothing about abortion caused by the mother herself. Nor is there any other explicit reference to abortion in the book of the covenant. How is one to interpret this silence? Of the other near eastern codes mentioned earlier, only the Assyrian code explicitly condemns abortion by the mother herself, but it imposes on her what everyone would consider a very severe punishment, impalement and denial of burial.[17] Did this type of abortion go unpunished among the Jews? One might wish to extend the statute already discussed to cover abortion caused by the mother herself, arguing that if abortion (perhaps even unintentional) by a third party was punished, intentional abortion by the mother herself must also be condemned. But it is at least conceivable that the law was more concerned with the rights of the husband and the mother than the rights of the fetus, since the statute was dealing with a crime committed by a third party, and presumably against the wishes of the husband or the woman herself. If this is true, it could hardly be stretched to include an abortion caused by the mother herself, at least if done with the consent of her husband. Their rights would not be at stake. Moreover, it would be difficult to apply this statute to an abortion committed by the mother herself. There would certainly be no application of the *lex talionis*, since if the mother suffered any injury, it would be self-inflicted. And if the husband consented, there could hardly be any question of indemnification. If the husband did not consent, indemnification would be in order, but the idea of collecting damages from a wife, if at all practical, sounds somewhat alien to the culture of the time. So it is not clear how this statute could be applied to abortion caused by the mother herself.

There is another text in the Old Testament that would more easily apply to abortion caused by the mother herself, that is, if it can be applied to abortion at all. It occurs in Genesis 9:6 and reads as follows: "If anyone sheds the blood of man, by man shall his blood be shed; for in the image of God has man been made."[18] This text, which seems to be an abbreviated statement of the *lex talionis*, allows for the reading *in man* as well as *by man*. If the version *in man* is used and the comma is placed after it rather than before it, the reference might be to abortion, the fetus being considered a *man in man*. Since the law reads more generally than the text in Exodus, it could more easily cover an abortion committed by the mother as well as by a third party. Also, it seems to consider it a capital crime, calling for the blood of the one responsible.

In taking this stance, it is, of course, in direct opposition to that taken in the book of the covenant, which prescribed only a fine for abortion. But since the words were addressed to Noah and his sons, the Jews applied it to the non-Jewish world. Hard put to explain why abortion should be a capital crime for the non-Jewish world and not for the Jew, some admitted that it was not really murder for either but by special dispensation capital liability was attached to the non-Jew causing abortion. It was also explained as the reaction of the Jews against the frequent abortion and infanticide practiced among the heathens.[19] Whatever may be the explanation of the text, there is no explicit reference to it by the early Fathers in connection with abortion, although, as will be seen, several of them speak of abortion as homicide and parricide.

In the absence of any law explicitly penalizing abortion caused by the mother herself, it might be tempting to conclude to a permissive attitude toward self-induced abortion. If there were no other explanation for this silence, this conclusion might be warranted. But other explanations suggest themselves. The danger to the woman herself associated with abortion may have been a very effective deterrent to self-induced abortion. It is also possible, and there is more evidence for this, that the thought of intentionally causing an abortion was so foreign to the mind of the Jewish woman that there was no felt need for penal legislation against it. There are actually many indications that the idea of abortion was totally alien to the Jewish mentality. The attitude of the Jews toward barrenness as a curse, the regard for fertility as one of God's greatest blessings, the mandate to increase and multiply, the hope of the Jewish maiden that she might bear the Messiah, all militated against any easy attitude toward self-induced abortion, or even any deliberate abortion. And there is no positive evidence of such an attitude. All the available evidence points to a wholesome acceptance of and respect for the life which God was making "in his own image," even though it was not yet completed. Indeed, it would seem somewhat presumptuous to suggest an easy attitude toward self-induced abortion on the part of the Jews, given the severe attitude manifested by their neighbors, the Assyrians. The religious and moral standards of the Jews were at least as high as that of their neighbors, and generally considered higher.

In the whole early tradition of the Jews there is only one case in which taking prenatal life is explicitly allowed. This case is discussed in the Mishna, which forms the core of Talmudic literature. This literature is a commentary on the law and represents an oral tradition built up around the law. But it was not put into writing until well into the Christian era (A.D. c. 200) so it is not certain how far back the origin of the opinions it represents may go. But it does present a case in which taking the life of the fetus is explicitly allowed to save the mother. Here is the case:

> If a woman has difficulty in childbirth, one dismembers the embryo within her limb from limb because her life takes precedence over its life. Once its head (or the greater part) has emerged, it may not be touched, for we do not set aside one life for another.[20]

This response deals openly with a case in which the life of the fetus is sacrificed to save the life of the mother. Although this procedure, since the fetus presumably is viable, might not strictly be classified as abortion, the moral issue is the same. It seems obvious also that it is the prenatal status of the fetus that is the decisive factor in permitting this kind of destructive procedure. As long as this status continues, the life of the mother has priority in any situation where it is threatened. But once the head is delivered, or the greater part of the body, the status of the fetus changes. It becomes a human person, equal to any other human person, and may not be sacrificed for another. Even in a conflict or threatening situation "we do not set aside one life for another." It is interesting to note that some wanted to permit dismemberment even in this case, considering the fetus a "pursuer" of the mother or, in scholastic terminology, an unjust aggressor.[21] An attack on the fetus in such circumstances would become just self-defense and would be allowed even if the aggressor were a mature adult. But their opponents refused to consider the child an unjust aggressor. If the mother was being pursued, she was being pursued "from Heaven."[22]

There is no doubt that according to this opinion it was permissible to sacrifice the fetus to save the life of the mother. But this is the only case in which taking the life of the fetus is explicitly allowed in the early written tradition of the Jews. The fact that it is singled out for justification argues in favor of a tradition in which abortion even by the mother was considered wrong. If abortion were generally accepted, there would hardly be need to justify it in extreme need of this kind. So in addition to the silent testimony to this tradition already mentioned, there is here another indication of an antiabortion mentality. Further evidence of this will appear in the discussion of the *Didache* in the early Christian era.

It might be helpful at this juncture to raise the question about the commandment against killing in the Decalogue.[23] Can it be appealed to as a comdemnation of self-induced abortion? Contrary to what many may think, since there is no explicit reference to abortion in the commandment, a certain answer to this question may not be discernible. Abortion could be considered wrong without being a violation of the commandment against killing. A strong argument for this position can be gathered from the penalty imposed on abortion caused by a third party; it was not the penalty usually attached to homicide. There might indeed have been other reasons for not imposing the penalty of homicide on this crime even though it was considered homicide, but it is generally agreed that it was not imposed precisely because it was not considered homicide, and this because the fetus was not considered a full human being before it was born. And if the fetus was not considered a human being, it is not certain that the Jews would have applied the commandment against killing even to self-induced abortion.

The tradition under discussion up to the present has been that based on the Hebrew text of the code of the covenant. This came to be known as the Palestinian tradition. More important for the development of subsequent Christian tradition than the Hebrew text is the Septuagint version of the same text. This Greek translation of the bible produced in Alexandria in the third century before Christ carries a version of the text on abortion quite different from the Hebrew text discussed above. The difference will be seen immediately in the following translation:

> If two men strive and smite a woman, and her child is imperfectly formed, he shall be forced to pay a penalty; as the woman's husband shall lay upon him, he shall pay with a valuation. But if he be perfectly formed, he shall give life for life . . . [24]

Apart from other verbal variations the basic distinction made here regarding penalties differs considerably from that of the Hebrew text.[25] There the line was drawn between the death of the fetus (miscarriage) and the death of the mother (or other injury). In the Greek text the distinction is between the perfectly formed and imperfectly formed fetus. There is no reference to injury to the mother. The death penalty is imposed if the fetus is perfectly formed; otherwise an indemnity to be decided by the husband is prescribed. The implication here is that the abortion of the formed fetus is considered homicide, whereas the abortion of the unformed fetus is penalized as something less than homicide. According to this version, then, the fetus is treated as a human being in the eyes of the law as soon as it is formed, not when it is born, as seemed to be the case in the Hebrew text.

The first question that naturally arises regarding this version has to do with its departure from the Hebrew text. Is it simply a mistranslation?[26] Or is it a translation from some Hebrew text that has been lost? Or does it represent a deliberate ideological change? Scripture scholars have not definitely ruled out any of these possibilities. But whatever may account for the change in the Septuagint version, there is no doubt that in putting the emphasis on formation it coincides noticeably with Greek, and particularly Aristotelian, thought on the status of the fetus. According to Aristotle the fetus became a full human being when it was formed because at that time the human soul was infused.[27] Before formation it was not properly disposed to receive a human soul. Initially it had only a vegetative soul and then a sensitive soul.[28] Hebrew thought had never divided man into body and soul, and it is not clear even in the Septuagint that the translators are subscribing to an Aristotelian metaphysics of man. But in imposing the penalty for homicide on causing the death of the formed fetus, it is treating it as a full human being. Aristotle maintained that formation took place forty days after conception in the male fetus and ninety days in the female fetus.[29] The Septuagint, however, made no time estimate, let alone a distinction between the male and female fetus. But in treating the formed fetus as a full human being, the Septuagint is obviously departing from the Hebrew text which limited the penalty for homicide to the death of the mother, thus implying that even the formed fetus is not considered a human being in the full sense of the term as long as it is in the womb.

It is also easier to argue from the Septuagint text that self-induced abortion, at least of the formed fetus, was considered wrong. Even though the case still deals with abortion caused by a third party, in imposing the penalty for homicide on the abortion of the formed fetus, the law makes the life of the fetus the real issue rather than any possible violation of the rights of the parents. If this is so, even though the penal legislation of the Jews may not deal with self-induced abortion, there is no reason why the moral judgment should not be the same, at least for the formed fetus. If it is homicide in the one case, it must be in the other as well. The fetus does not cease to be a human being vis-à-vis the mother.

The Septuagint version became the basis of the teaching of the Alexandrian Jews on abortion. It was this text rather than the Hebrew text that seems to have had the greatest influence on the Christian tradition. This was undoubtedly due to the fact that Greek was the common language of the time. The early Christians, and even many of the Jews of the Diaspora, were not sufficiently conversant with the Hebrew language to handle the Hebrew text, so the Septuagint was much more accessible to them. This does not mean that the Hebrew text was unknown to early Christianity; St. Jerome, for instance, followed it in producing his Latin translation. But there is no evidence to show that the early Christians ever accepted the position that the fetus is not a human being until it is born.

Before going on to the Christian tradition, mention should be made of two important voices in the Jewish tradition, one a philosopher named Philo (25 B.C.-A.D. c. 41), the other a historian, Josephus Flavius (37-c. 100). Their lives coincided with the early Christian era, so they can shed important light on Jewish thought of that period regarding abortion. Philo was an Alexandrian Jew and a philosopher. In his treatise *De specialibus legibus* he states that if one fights with a pregnant woman and strikes her in the belly, causing an abortion, he will be punished by a fine, if the child is still unformed, both for the assault and for the fact that he has prevented nature from bringing into existence a human being.[30] But if the child is formed, the aggressor shall die. He compares the formed fetus in the womb to a completed statue in the sculptor's workshop waiting only to be released to the outside world.

Although Philo presents a slightly different version of the case, one will recognize here the distinction of the Septuagint between the formed and unformed fetus. Even in dealing with the unformed fetus, however, he is concerned with more than the rights of the mother (or father). The culprit will pay the penalty also for preventing nature from bringing a human being into existence. But if the fetus is formed, he will die because he has slain what is really a man, even though it is still lying in the workshop of nature. Philo is appealing to this text in a passage where he is condemning exposure of children. He argues that even though Moses said nothing explicitly about this, in imposing the death sentence on killing the formed fetus he was implicitly forbidding the murder of children after birth. Philo admits that some philosophers and physicians consider the fetus a part of the mother until it is born (and therefore might not admit his *a fortiori* argument against exposure), but even they would have to admit that once the child is brought forth and separated from the mother, it becomes a living animal lacking nothing to make it a human being. But Philo's own sympathies seem to be more with what he considers to be the Mosaic opinion regarding the status of the fetus in the womb.

Josephus was a Jewish historian who wrote apologetically on behalf of the Jews. In dealing with abortion in his *Antiquitates*, like Philo, he varies the case from Exodus but differs from him in using the Hebrew rather than the Septuagint text. He says that one who kicks a woman with child and causes a miscarriage shall pay a fine, as the judge decides, for having diminished the multitude. But if the woman dies, he will also be put to death.[31] Josephus' dependence on the Hebrew text here is unmistakable, although in justifying the penalty for causing the miscarriage, he shows, like Philo, a concern for more than the rights of the parents. The penalty is imposed for having "diminished the multitude." But if one judges by the penalty, the fetus is still not treated as a human being in the full sense. In the *Contra Apionem*, however, when he speaks of abortion and infanticide, he says without distinction that if a woman is responsible for either of these "she will be a murderer of her child by destroying a living creature and diminishing human kind."[32] It is not easy to reconcile this passage with that quoted above. If abortion is not punished with the death sentence, it is difficult to understand how Josephus can call abortion "murder." As pointed out before, even if abortion is considered murder, there may be reasons for not imposing the penalty for murder. But the implication in the law seems to be that abortion is not punished as murder precisely because it was not considered murder. And it was not considered murder because the fetus was not looked upon as a human being in the full sense until it was born. If one accepts this, he can hardly turn around and call the one who causes an abortion a murderess, as Josephus seems to have done. But this ambiguity will continue to plague the abortion issue for many centuries to come.

An examination of the Jewish tradition in pre-Christian and early Christian times reveals an attitude which recognizes abortion as wrong. This recognition is explicated in the law in reference to abortion caused by a third party. Although abortion attempted by the mother herself was not penalized in the book of the covenant, at least explicitly, there is no reason to believe that it was any more acceptable to the Hebrew people. The earliest tradition did not consider the fetus a human being in the full sense of the term as long as it remained in the womb. But even on the basis of this tradition, abortion—or rather dismemberment—was allowed only when necessary to save the life of the mother. There is no evidence for any other exception. A later tradition represented in the Septuagint version of the Exodus text seemed to consider the fetus a full human being from the time it was formed, and therefore considerably before birth. It consequently penalized the abortion of the formed fetus with a capital sentence. The early Christians inherited from the Jews their general respect for human life at all stages, an attitude which put them in conflict, as were the Jews themselves, with the surrounding Roman world, where both abortion and infanticide were widely accepted.

CHAPTER TWO

The Roman Background

When one moves from the pre-Christian Jewish world to the Roman world, he discovers certain similarities in the attitude of the law toward the fetus. For instance, in the Roman law the fetus was never considered a subject of rights in the full sense, since it did not enjoy the autonomy necessary to be considered a human person; it could not be called a man, but only *spes animantis*,[1] and was looked upon as part of the mother, as it was in Jewish law. *Partus enim antequam edatur mulieris portio est vel viscerum.*[2] But the Roman law, perhaps more than the Jewish law, recognized the ambiguity of the situation of the fetus. Although it was not yet considered a human being in its own right, since it would eventually be such, certain juridical effects were attached to it, for example, the right to inherit, and this goes back to early Roman times.[3]

Two factors were influential in determining and maintaining this judgment of the law that the fetus was part of the mother, the one legal itself, the other philosophical. The legal factor was the *jus gentium*. It has already been seen that Jewish law considered the fetus part of the mother until birth. This judgment was shared by other peoples as well, to the extent that it could be considered a common opinion, and therefore the *jus gentium*. The beginning of a person's juridical capacity was generally identified with the date of his birth. A philosophical basis for this position was provided by Stoicism, a very influential philosophy during the period of the Roman republic. According to Stoic philosophy the child did not receive an *anima* until birth, or more precisely, when it began to breathe.[4] Until that time it was considered part of the mother, and often compared to fruit growing on a tree; it was part of the tree until it fell or was plucked.

In spite of these two influences, however, there was a pull in the opposite direction, that is, to attribute more and more rights to the fetus. It was not, however, until well into the Christian era that some kind of reconciliation between these two tendencies was effected. During the rule of Hadrian a principle was worked out whereby the fetus was considered like a child already born whenever it would be to his advantage (*conceptus pro iam nato habetur quotiens de eis commodis agitur*).[5] As the law moved more and more in this direction, that is, to treat the fetus more like a child already born, the way was being prepared for the imposition of a legal penalty against abortion. Unlike Jewish law, early Roman law had no penal statute against abortion. But before it would be ready for such a statute, another development in Roman legal thinking would have to take place. This was the thinking regarding the position and authority of the *paterfamilias* in Roman society. It was the attitude of the law toward the authority of the *paterfamilias* more than its attitude toward the fetus that explained the lack of abortion legislation in early Roman history.

The Roman legal system did not deal with problems within the family.[6] The *paterfamilias* was the one who governed the family, and within the family he wielded what was for all practical purposes political authority. It even extended to life and death (*jus vitae necisque*). It was to the *paterfamilias* rather than to the civil authority that one would have to look for a judgment regarding abortion. And the father of the family was not governed by civil laws in regulating the ethical life of his family, but rather by the *mos maiorum*, the customs that had been handed down from his ancestors. The civil law governed the relationships between the different families that made up the state, but it did not govern life within the individual family. So the violation of the *mores* within the family would be subject to a domestic tribunal, where the father was the judicial authority. If a question of abortion came up, it was up to the *paterfamilias* to command it or forbid it according to the *mos maiorum*.

Just what the *mos maiorum* might have been in regard to abortion is not readily ascertainable. It can undoubtedly be assumed that the father did not have arbitrary power of life and death over his children, at least those already born. But Westermarck observes that in Rome, whether by custom or law, the father could dispose of deformed children.[7] And Seneca states explicitly that "we destroy our monstrous children and also drown our children if they are weak or unnaturally formed," adding that this is a reasonable thing to do.[8] Whether a child was deformed or weak could not indeed be known until after birth, so this mentality would not generally lead to abortion. But given this attitude, it seems safe to presume that the *mos maiorum* would tolerate abortion in certain circumstances, even though it might not condone an indiscriminate practice.

Originally there seems to have been no outside control over the *paterfamilias* in the event of a violation of the *mos maiorum*. But once the office of censor was set up, the father of the family fell under the supervision of the censors.[9] If he permitted or ordered an abortion without justifying cause, he was subject to severe criticism, with all the adverse impact this would have on his social and political life. In the course of Roman history the authority of the censor grew beyond all measure, even to the point where it reacted with great severity to the slightest moral infraction. This would have meant a tight control over the *paterfamilias*.

The only abortion that would fall under the law in a system where the *paterfamilias* had full authority over his family was one performed by a member of one family on a member of another. This was subject to a legal settlement agreeable to the *paterfamilias* of the woman on whom it was performed. But if the woman were outside the authority of any *paterfamilias*, as was often the case with prostitutes, an abortion would not be covered by the law. [10]

This system, in which authority was concentrated in the *paterfamilias*, worked reasonably well as long as the Roman family remained intact. But when the family began to break down, morality, which depended so heavily on family authority, also broke down, and an era of moral licentiousness began. This statement does not pretend to exhaust the reasons behind the breakdown of moral life in Roman society, but it would be beyond the purpose of this study to pursue them. It is sufficient to point out that the breakdown in family life and the authority of the *paterfamilias* left a vacuum into which the civil law would move.

There is nothing to indicate that abortion was common or a problem in early Rome. But it did become problematic toward the end of the Republic and continued to be such into the Empire. This is attested to both by pagan writers and Christian apologetes. Complaints by pagan authors should not, of course, be interpreted as blanket opposition to abortion. Cicero, for instance, complains to Atticus about an abortion committed by Tertulla, wife of Cassius and sister of Brutus, but at the same time says that he wanted to see the destruction of the hated offspring of Caesar by an abortion of Cleopatra. [11] But there were complaints against abortion and the number of complaints began to grow from the beginning of the Empire. On the occasion of the difficulties of a certain Corinna who lay in serious danger because of an attempt at self-induced abortion, Ovid delivered himself of an impassionate plea against abortion. [12] He asks what good it is for a woman to be free from the perils of war if she is to use weapons against herself. The woman who plucks the tender life within her deserves to die in the warfare she began. What she has done, not even the tigress in the jungles of Armenia has done; nor has the lioness had the heart to destroy her unborn young; yet tender woman does it, but not unpunished: she herself dies in the attempt. At about the same time Seneca pays tribute to his mother for never having destroyed *"conceptas spes liberorum"* (future children) in her womb.[13] Tacitus says that Nero exiled Octavia for an abortion,[14] and Juvenal accuses noble women of abortion, as well as trying to hide their lust by other crimes which would make abortion unnecessary.[15] As an example of a noble woman given to abortion he names Julia, the daughter of Augustus. He complains that one scarcely ever sees a noble woman give birth to a child, so many sterilizing drugs are available, and so many drugs to destroy *homines in ventre*. Finally, Seutonius tells the tragic story of another Julia, the daughter of Titus and niece of Domitian.[16] After being seduced by her uncle she died in an attempt at abortion to which he himself forced her. All these references point to a practice of abortion widespread enough to attract the attention and criticism of the leading writers of the time.[17]

Abortion was not as frequent in Rome as infanticide. The author of the article in Hastings' Encyclopedia maintains that the destruction of the embryo never became a social habit among any peoples, something he could not say of infanticide.[18] This did happen, and he names ancient Italy as one of the places where it did. The *paterfamilias*, as already seen, had absolute power over the family and this extended to accepting or rejecting newborn children. Seneca said that it was reasonable to reject deformed or weak children, and it seems that female children often fell into the latter category. Raising a female child in ancient societies was considered an expensive luxury. That infanticide was widespread and was not limited to deformed or weak children is testified to by both pagan and Christian authors. But the term *infanticide* would have to include another method of getting rid of unwanted children, exposure or abandonment. Parents who could not bring themselves to "drowning" newborn children might be less reluctant to choose this method of ridding themselves of unwanted children. The classical example of exposure to which they could point with hope was the mythical story of Romulus and Remus. But there is no reason to believe that other children received any better treatment from the animal world than they received from their parents. Many of them were devoured by animals, a way of death hardly less awful than a death a parent might inflict. Even those who were abandoned in places where they could be picked up by other human beings were not always able to look to their rescuers as benefactors. They were often selfishly motivated and only interested in using these youngsters for illegitimate purposes.

One might have been inclined to conclude that, given the judgment regarding the legal status of the fetus, abortion would have been more common than infanticide. But if one considers the power and the practice of the *paterfamilias* regarding newborn children, it is not clear that the latter enjoyed any greater legal protection. Other reasons would also tend to make infanticide more common than abortion. Abortion, of course, would not offer a solution to the problem of weak or deformed children, since these defects would be apparent only after birth. It would conceal, if done early enough, such irregularities as adultery and fornication. It would also prevent the anxiety that might arise from the disfigurement caused by pregnancy. But the danger to the mother associated with abortion, as well as uncertainty regarding the effectiveness of the methods used, would incline women to a postnatal solution of their problems whenever this was feasible. All of these factors taken together would make for more frequent infanticide and exposure of children.

Attempts were made in the early days of the Empire to strengthen the family by bolstering up the authority of the *paterfamilias*, but they were ineffective, at least as an answer to the problem of abortion and infanticide. Yet the state even under the early emperors seemed reluctant to legislate penalties against abortion. Actually, according to Plutarch legislation relating to abortion went back to the time of the kings.[19] Abortion was one of the causes recognized, along with others, as reason for divorce by the husband. The legislators also showed a certain concern for the fetus in prohibiting the burial of a pregnant woman who had died, until the fetus was removed. Pliny traces this back to Numa Pompilius.[20] Cicero even tells of a Milesian woman who was sentenced to death because of an abortion.[21] But the punishment in this case was not for the abortion itself, but rather because the mother accepted a bribe from the other heirs to commit it. If the child had been born, the will which made them heirs would have been invalidated. Another piece of legislation relating to abortion came from Hadrian, who forbade a pregnant woman condemned to death to be executed until she had delivered the child.[22] Such legislation showed a concern by the state for the husband, and even for the fetus. But the state imposed no direct sanction on abortion itself until well into the second century of Christianity. When, however, it did begin to move directly against abortion as a crime, it was not necessary to create new legislation but merely to extend laws already in use. Legal precedent could be found not only to penalize abortion caused by a third party, but also abortion caused by the mother herself. This was an historic development and affected the law of Western society for many centuries to come.

Iulius Paulus, an eminent jurist of the early third century, was the first to state expressly that the *Lex Cornelia de sicariis et veneficis* (Cornelian law against brigands and poisoners) included those who gave poisonous drugs to others to cause abortion or stimulate an amatory reaction. The law itself dated from 81 B.C., the time of the Dictator Sulla, and was enacted in general against murderers and poisoners. Poisoning was a common way of taking the life of another person at the time, and the problem was sufficiently serious to call for legislation. Those who engaged in

poisoning were called *venefici*,[23] although the term included also those who sold drugs publicly, as well as those
who prepared them or kept them for lethal purposes. Actually, the Latin word for drugs is *venena* which literally
means poisons. But Marcian, another jurist at the time,
explains that there are good and bad *venena*, and that the
term also includes a *poculum amatorium*, a love potion.[24]
He notes that the *Lex Cornelia* itself is dealing only with
those drugs which are given to cause death. But the law
was extended, he admits, by a *senatusconsultus* even to
include drugs to cause conception if the woman who took
them died as a result; even if these were not given with evil
intent, they did give bad example. Iulius Paulus himself
says that if a man died of a drug, even if given for purposes
of health or as a cure for some disease, the one who administered the drug would be penalized either by exile or
death, according to his social status.[25] It can be gathered
from all this that therapy with drugs even though well-
intentioned was surrounded with great suspicion in ancient
times.

Here is the way Paulus applies the *Lex Cornelia* to
abortion:

> Qui abortionis aut amatorium poculum dant, etsi dolo non faciant,
> tamen quia res mali exempli est, humiliores in metallum, hones-
> tiores in insulam, amissa parte bonorum, relegantur. Quodsi
> mulier aut homo perierit, summo supplicio adficitur.[26]

This is usually referred to as the *Qui abortionis*. The
poculum amatorium is generally understood to mean a
love-philter, a potion to excite love. Whether it involved a
sterilizing factor is a question that will be discussed later.
But even if it was no more than an aphrodisiac, the concern
was that it might also produce insanity, and in this sense
carry with it the danger of serious harm to the woman. If
these drugs were given maliciously *(dolo)*, that is, with evil
intent or by deception, they were covered by the law. But
even if this was not the case and the intention was good,
with no deception involved, the law would still cover them
because the act would be a source of bad example. This

might even have been the case in giving the *poculum abortionis*. It might have been given, for example, to save the life of the mother, and in this sense, with a good intention. Provision for this case where there was no evil intent is undoubtedly based on the extension of the Cornelian law by the *senatusconsultus* to the case where a drug was given to cause conception. The reasoning behind this position is evidently based on the danger associated with such drugs, even though the intention in giving them may be good, and the other party consents. At any rate, a very severe penalty is attached to giving such potions, and it seems, independently of any consideration of the damage done. If the other party died, a capital sentence was imposed.

The wording of this last part of the statute has caused some controversy. It reads that if the *mulier aut homo* perishes, the death penalty is imposed. The meaning of the word *mulier* needs no explanation since a woman might be the victim of either a *poculum abortionis* or a *poculum amatorium*. But what is the meaning of the word *homo* in the decree? It would refer at least to the *poculum amatorium*, since a love-philter might be given to a man as well as to a woman. The question raised by later authors was whether it might refer also to the *poculum abortionis*, and apply to the formed fetus. One may not be able to rule out this possibility, but it seems more likely that this is a later development. If it did refer to the formed fetus, it would be very difficult to explain the discrepancy between this penalty and the penalty imposed on the mother in the decree of Severus and Antoninus discussed below; no death penalty is imposed there. If the penalty is the death sentence in the one law, it should also be in the other, at least when the fetus becomes a *homo*.

This interpretation of the *Lex Cornelia* does not seem to implicate the pregnant woman herself, even if she willingly took the potion; it penalizes only the one who gives it. But Marcian, the jurist already mentioned, who lived under the emperor Severus, says that this emperor together with Antoninus enacted a decree which imposed the penalty of exile on a woman who caused an abortion on herself.[27] The reason they gave was that it did not seem right for a woman who deprived her husband of children in this way to go unpunished. Triphoninus Claudius, another jurist of the time, maintained that this penalty extended even to an abortion caused by a woman after she divorced her husband.[28] It has been seen that concern for the rights of the husband goes back to early Roman history when, according to Plutarch, the husband had a right to divorce a wife who committed an abortion. The legislation of Severus and Antoninus may have merely substituted for a penalty the *paterfamilias* might have imposed at an earlier date. Even this legislation, however, might not have had any application where the woman had no marital relationship. But Ulpian, a contemporary of both Paulus and Claudius, simply presented the statute without any qualifying or limiting reason as follows.

Si mulierem visceribus suis vim intulisse quo partum abigerit constiterit eam in exilium praeses provinciae exiget.[29]

Worded in this way the *Si mulierem*, as it is called, would have a much broader scope, including an abortion even by an unmarried woman, or one to which the husband consented. It would seem to be motivated more by concern for the fetus than for the husband. But the penalty for the abortion was simply exile, which implies that the abortion was not considered homicide no matter when it was performed.

———————————————

To sum up, it seems clear from what has been said that the Roman penal law did not move into the area of abortion until the end of the second century of the Christian era. Before this time it fell under the authority of the *paterfamilias* who looked to the *mos maiorum* rather than civil legislation for his guidelines. To what extent the civil law moved in under the influence of Christianity is not clear. Some authors see a strong Christian influence in this

development. But it is also possible that the law was attempting to restore the balance that had been lost due to
the decline of the family and the authority of the *paterfamilias*. But even when the law began to penalize abortion, there is little or no evidence that it considered abortion homicide. This was a later development, at least on the
level of civil law.

CHAPTER THREE

—◆—

The Early Christian Era
(to 300)

Passing from the Old Testament to the Christian era one finds a somewhat different approach to moral failures and wrongdoing. The Jewish community functioned as a political as well as a religious community. The code of the covenant, as has been seen, reflected this complexity in its statutes, attaching civil penalties to the wrongdoing it proscribed. Since the Christian community as such is not a civil community, this whole aspect of the law of Moses will fall into disuse. The position of the Church vis-à-vis the use of civil penalties may have been somewhat ambiguous in certain periods of its history, but certainly during the early centuries, even if it wanted to, it was in no position to exercise any kind of civil authority. The penalties that do appear in the early Church are spiritual or religious, not civil penalties, and are related to the reconciliation of sinners. Even this type of penance will not appear as official church legislation until the beginning of the fourth century. This is not to imply, however, that penances for sins were not imposed before that time by individual bishops. It is only to say that local synodal or conciliar legislation dates from the early fourth century.

This lack of interest in civil penalties may well account for an initial disregard for those distinctions, particularly the Septuagint distinction between the formed and unformed fetus, which were used to grade such penalties. Abortion was wrong to the early Christians, and this was what concerned them, not what penalty it deserved. They were not interested in comparing one abortion with another for penal purposes. Abortion was wrong whether the fetus was formed or not. One finds in the early Church, then, simple, clear condemnations of abortion without any attempt to distinguish or classify.

If anyone expects to find an explicit condemnation of abortion in the New Testament, he will be disappointed. The silence of the New Testament regarding abortion surpasses even that of the Old Testament. For the reasons mentioned above, the absence of any reference to the penal statute of Exodus is understandable. It has also been pointed out that the relevance to abortion of the command against killing in the Decalogue can be questioned, at least in the Hebrew text. The penalty for abortion was not the penalty for homicide. In the Sermon on the Mount Christ enlarges on the meaning of this commandment but more to bring out its implications for one's internal dispositions and attitudes. He says nothing that would relate the commandment more explicitly to abortion.

Some have seen in Paul's condemnation of *pharmakeia* in his epistle to the Galatians a possible reference to abortion.[1] *Pharmakeia*, which is translated into English, somewhat inadequately, as sorcery, is the practice of giving poisonous drugs to others with evil intent. Because of largely inadequate knowledge of the properties and effectiveness of such drugs in themselves, the practice of *pharmakeia* was associated with magic and superstitious appeals to evil spirits to achieve the desired effect, which is undoubtedly the reason for the use of the English word *sorcery*. The practice of poisoning has already been discussed in connection with the Roman background to the abortion question. The Latin word for this practice was *veneficium*, and as has been seen, it was condemned by the *Lex Cornelia de sicariis et veneficis*. While the law was aimed at those who gave drugs to others with evil intent, it was extended to cover those cases in which bad example was given, even if there was no evil intent. It was even applied to the practice of medicine, when the patient died from the drug.

The practice of *pharmakeia* went far beyond the use of abortifacient drugs. In fact, the Cornelian law was not explicitly interpreted to include abortion until the end of the second century after Christ, long after Paul wrote his letters. It might have been applied to abortion before this, but there is no juridical evidence that it was. Even if it were, however, the penalty was imposed on the one who gave the *poculum abortionis*, not on the woman who took it. If Paul was thinking in terms of abortion at all, he may not, indeed, have had in mind the limitations of the Cornelian law and may have included in this condemnation a mother who took the *poculum abortionis*. But a condemnation of *pharmakeia*, while it might have included an abortion caused by drugs, would not affect one caused by some other means. So, a condemnation of *pharmakeia* is at the same time much broader and much more limited than a condemnation of abortion. If Paul wanted to condemn abortion as such, this was a very confusing and ineffective way of doing it.

In spite of the silence of the New Testament, the incompatibility of abortion, as well as infanticide, with the Christian message came through quite clearly. An explicit condemnation of both abortion and infanticide is found in the *Didache*, or *Teachings of the Apostles*, a work probably published in apostolic times which was intended for the instruction of converts to Christianity. Although it is a document of the early Christian Church, it is not all original with that Church. Audet argues that the first part of the instruction, commonly known as the *Duae viae (Two Ways)*, belonged originally to the Jewish community and was used for proselytizing among the pagans.[2] It is entitled *Instruction of the Lord to the Gentiles*, and if Audet is correct, the Lord in the title is Jahweh, not the Lord

Jesus. Also, if he is correct, the *Duae viae* is as representative of the moral standards of the Jews of the pre-Christian era as it is of the early Christians.

In presenting the precepts of the *Via vitae (The Way of Life)*, the *Didache* includes specific condemnations of abortion and infanticide. *You shall not kill the fetus by abortion, or destroy the infant already born.*[3] The commandment is given generally, so it can hardly be limited to abortion caused by a third party. Moreover, it refers to those who do these things as destroyers of the work or image of God,[4] thus showing a concern for the fetus as a work of God rather than the property of the parents. In this respect it goes beyond both the penal law of Exodus (Hebrew text) and the *Lex Cornelia*.

A similar condemnation of abortion and infanticide is found in the *Epistle of Pseudo-Barnabas*[5]. It is not known who Barnabas was, but it is certain that he was not the apostle of that name. Some think he was an Alexandrian. His *Epistle*, like the *Didache*, was an attempt to explain the demands of the Christian life to prospective converts from paganism. Like the *Didache* also it makes use of the *Duae viae*. The relationship between the *Epistle* and the *Didache* has been the subject of much controversy. The best opinion seems to be that the *Didache* precedes the *Epistle* in time, and is consequently not dependent on it. As already mentioned, Audet also suggests, and with valid supporting reasons, that the *Duae viae* was a document of earlier Jewish origin and that both may have drawn on it independently of each other[6]. But the wording of the condemnation of abortion and infanticide in the *Epistle* is almost identical with that of the *Didache*. After the silence of the New Testament the appearance of such explicit condemnations of abortion and infanticide in Christian documents that were almost contemporary may seem surprising. The explanation may well be found in the fact that these two documents were addressed to gentiles, people coming from a culture where both abortion and infanticide were practiced with frequency, and to a large extent, even condoned. For the most part the New

Testament was addressed to a Jewish audience who did not have this practice or tradition.

The next explicit reference to abortion in early Christian documents will be found in a *Plea for Christians* by Athenagoras, a Greek philosopher from Athens, in the second half of the second century.[7] By this time a body of apologetic literature to defend Christians against attacks and charges made by outsiders began to build up. Athenagoras is defending the Christians against the charge of cannibalism. The charge arose from misinformation about the eucharistic gatherings of the Christians. Athenagoras bases his defense on the Christian condemnation of infanticide and abortion as murder. The person who regards even the fetus in the womb as a created being, and therefore, the object of God's care, can hardly take its life after it is born. Nor can the person who thinks it is wrong to expose infants and charges those who do this with murder, consistently take the life of a person at a later date. In other words, those who show such respect for life, even fetal life, can hardly indulge in human sacrifice or cannibalism. According to Athenagoras then Christians condemn both abortion and infanticide. In this respect he is in the tradition of the *Didache* and the *Epistle*, and in classifying both as homicide, he is perhaps speaking even more explicitly.

Another condemnation of abortion may be found in the *Paedagogue* or *Teacher* of Clement of Alexandria.[8] In the *Paedagogue*, which was written to instruct new converts on how to lead their Christian lives, Clement calls for confidence in Divine Providence. He says that life will go on as it should if people do not destroy by wicked means the offspring which Divine Providence gives them. Women who have recourse to lethal drugs to conceal fornication destroy not only the fetus within them but their own humanity. The emphasis here is on the dehumanizing effect of destroying offspring.

The *Refutation of All Heresies*, or *Philosophoumena*, a work which dates from the first half of the second century and is generally attributed to Hippolytus, also refers to the problem of abortion, but this time within the Christian community.[9] It comes in the course of a vicious attack on Callistus, Roman pontiff from 217 to 222, whom Hippolytus considered a bitter enemy. He accuses Callistus of great laxity and blames him among other things for the fact that women, considered believers, began to resort to drugs to cause sterility and to bind themselves tightly to cause abortion. The reason behind all this was that Callistus, contrary to Roman law, allowed them to marry slaves and men of inferior social status. They resorted to these practices out of fear of offending their families; they did not want to give birth to the child of a slave or person of inferior status. While he was critical of Callistus for allowing such marriages, his main complaint was that Callistus readmitted these women to communion with the Church. In so doing he was teaching both adultery and homicide.

What was at issue here was a supposed relaxation of penitential discipline for which Hippolytus was blaming Callistus. The controversy over penitential discipline cropped up several times during the first three centuries and was basically a conflict between holiness and the exercise of mercy in the early Church. Some, opting more for holiness, were opposed to a *secunda penitentia* (second forgiveness or reconciliation) in the Church, that is, forgiveness of sins committed after baptism. They feared that this would compromise the holiness of the Church and lead to a lowering of moral practice if not moral standards. The issue was particularly acute in the case of the *lapsi*, those who had succumbed to pressure to apostatize during times of persecution. Less acute, but still problematic, were cases of adultery and homicide. These are the concern of Hippolytus and he accuses Callistus of introducing a relaxation into penitential discipline that would allow those guilty of these sins back into communion with the faithful. The implication is that prior to the time of Callistus the Church did not forgive serious sins of this kind if committed after baptism.

Whether this relaxation originated with Callistus, as Hippolytus charges, has been widely disputed. When the first reference to such an official relaxation came to light (Tertullian, *De Pudicitia*, I, 6-9), it was traced to Pope Zephyrinus, who preceded Callistus in the papacy.[10] He is alleged to have issued a decree that he would forgive sins of adultery and fornication after those who had committed them did penance. It was only when the *Refutation of All Heresies* was discovered in the nineteenth century that the author of the edict was identified as Callistus rather than Zephyrinus. More recently, scholars do not consider it a papal edict at all, but the work of Agrippinus, bishop of Carthage, which would make the relaxation a local one, rather than an official relaxation of the whole Church.

The so-called "edict" referred to by Tertullian provided forgiveness only for sins of the flesh. Hippolytus, however, accused Callistus of introducing a relaxation regarding homicide as well. Whether Callistus deserves the blame or credit for this may be questioned, but at least by the time of the Council of Ancyra (314) forgiveness was no longer denied for homicide, although it was given only at the time of death.

It must be admitted that the rigid discipline favored by Hippolytus existed in the early Church, but the universality of this discipline either in time or in place can be, and has been, seriously questioned. It is impossible to reconcile it with New Testament Christianity, which is a message of mercy as well as holiness. But it did plague the early Church and gave rise to two heresies, Montanism and Novatianism, which even denied that the Church had the power to forgive serious sin committed after baptism. But for the present study the important consideration is that Hippolytus classified abortion as homicide. It is precisely because it is in this category that he is opposed to forgiveness.

Perhaps the most familiar reference to abortion in this early period is found in Tertullian (160-240) a Carthaginian and one of the first Latin Fathers. In his *Apologetics*, in which he is defending Christians against the accusation that they sacrifice children, he charges that the Romans themselves are guilty of the very acts for which they criticize the Christians.[11] He mentions specifically ritual sacrifice of children, and what is worse, drowning children and exposing them to cold, hunger, and dogs. In contrast to this Christians hold that homicide is always wrong. For them it is not permissible to destroy even the conceptus in the uterus, as long as it is still living. To keep someone from being born is anticipated homicide, nor does the fact that he is not yet born make any difference. He is a man who will be a man, since the fruit is already contained in the seed. So, Tertullian appeals to the Christian respect for the unborn child and its condemnation of abortion as anticipated homicide as a response to the charge that they practice infanticide. The statement that the fruit is contained in the seed is, of course, based on a very inadequate understanding of the process of human generation.[12]

He returns to the subject of abortion again in his *De anima*, where he is attacking various pagan theories about the soul.[13] He argues particularly against those who maintained either that the soul preexists the body or that the fetus is not animated until birth, that is, when it begins to breathe. His own theory is that the soul begins to exist simultaneously with the body. He conceives of the soul as a corporeal substance, though different from the body, which also originates in the *semen*. The seed of the soul is planted in the uterus at the same time as the seed of the body. In the course of this discussion he makes the statement that the fetus in the womb is a man from the time its form is completed. To back this up he appeals to the Septuagint version of the Exodus text on abortion and says that according to Moses one who commits abortion after the fetus is formed is liable to the *lex talionis* because it is then a man. In taking this stand he seems to be arguing that although the seed of the soul is planted at the same time as the seed of the body, some development has to take place before this composite can be called man. But once its form is completed, it is a man. If this interpretation is correct, however, it is not easy to reconcile with the statement already cited from the *Apologetics*, which seems to say that the conceptus is a man right from the time the seed is planted in the womb. Perhaps the solution is contained in the somewhat enigmatic statement: *Homo est, et qui futurus est*. This might be interpreted to mean that the implanted seed is a man or *homo* because it will be a man when it is formed. But it must be admitted that the passage in the *Apologetics* seems to make birth rather than formation the dividing line.[14]

There is another passage in the *De anima* in which abortion, or rather dismemberment of a fetus, to save the life of the mother is discussed.[15] In this passage, however, Tertullian is not primarily interested in the morality of the procedure he is discussing. He is trying rather to prove against the Stoics that fetuses are alive, and therefore have a soul, before birth. He argues first from the fact of stillbirths, that is, that some children are born dead. One could not speak properly of a fetus being born dead unless it was previously alive. More persuasive is his appeal to the practice of embryotomy, when doctors find it necessary to dismember a fetus in order to deliver it. He is speaking of a case where normal delivery is impossible, more specifically, of a transverse presentation of the fetus. Unless an embryotomy is performed, the fetus will be a *matricida* (killer of the mother) and the mother will die. He goes on to describe the instruments used in this procedure, one of which is a sharp pointed instrument used to bring about the death of the fetus before the dismemberment and extraction take place. The obvious purpose of this part of the procedure is to make it painless for the fetus, as Tertullian says, "...*ne viva lanietur*" (lest it be dissected while still alive). If the fetus was not alive, such a precaution would not be necessary.

The obvious question this passage poses for the present study is whether Tertullian is approving embryotomy to save the life of the mother. A response must begin with the preliminary comment that he was not really concerned in this passage with the morality of craniotomy. He was simply trying to prove that the fetus was alive before it was born. To do this, it was enough to call attention to the assumption underlying the initial part of the procedure. There was no need for any moral judgment, and it may not be realistic to look for one. Yet, he does use expressions which might imply a justification of the procedure in his mind. For instance, he speaks of the whole procedure as a *crudelitas necessaria* (necessary cruelty), since otherwise the fetus would be a *matricida* (killer of the mother), causing the death of the mother. This could be interpreted as a justification of the procedure as self-defense against unjust aggression. But he also uses words such as *scelus* (crime), *trucidatur* (it is slaughtered), *caeco latrocinio* (unseen damaging) which imply a critical judgment of the practice. So, if there is a value judgment in the passage regarding the morality of embryotomy, it would not be easy to draw it out of the conflicting evidence. But even if Tertullian were speaking with approval of the procedure, it would be the only explicit approval of an exception to the condemnation of abortion to be found in the first millenium. It will be seen when the controversy over craniotomy comes up in the second half of the nineteenth century that some authors will refuse to accept the silence of the rest of the Christian writers of the first millenium as an argument against the procedure. But it will be better to comment on this at that time.

There is one other passage where Tertullian refers to abortion. This is in his treatise on the *Veiling of Virgins* where he complains about what happens when girls are forced into virginity against their wills.[16] To cover up their failures, that is, to conceal a pregnancy, there is no limit to what they will do, even attempting abortion. Whatever one may say about his judgment of embryotomy to save the life of the mother, Tertullian's disapproval of abortion here is unambiguous, although the primary object of criticism is the underlying cause of this evil, forced virginity.

Another expression of the Christian attitude can be found in the *Octavius* of Minucius Felix, also an early Latin Father.[17] Like Tertullian, he is defending the Christians against charges made by the pagans, this time the accusation of engaging in initiation rites which include the slaughter of infants. Minucius retorts that no one would believe these charges unless he had a mind to do such things himself. He then points out that the Romans were doing the very things for which they were criticizing the Christians. Thus, they were exposing their children to wild birds and beasts to be devoured, or strangling them to death. Their women were taking drugs to destroy nascent life within their wombs, committing parricide even before birth. The worst part of all this is that they learned all these practices from their gods. Saturn, for instance, devoured his children. This is indeed a severe indictment of the Romans and their religion for their easy attitude toward infanticide and abortion. Minucius' use of the term *parricidium* in speaking of abortion reveals a judgment that it is even worse than homicide. The parental relationship gives it a special malice.

St. Cyprian (c. 200-258), bishop of Carthage, also uses the word *parricidium* in speaking of an abortion.[18] In a letter to Pope Cornelius he is complaining of Novatus, an African priest who joined the Novatian heresy. Among other charges against Novatus, Cyprian writes that he caused his wife to abort by kicking her in the stomach, thus making himself guilty of parricide. In very rhetorical fashion Cyprian asks how he can condemn the hands of those who offered sacrifice to idols when he has done far worse damage with his feet. The reference, of course, is to those who under torture offered sacrifices to pagan idols and thus apostatized. The Novatians strongly opposed receiving them back into the Church. Cyprian points out the gross inconsistency of Novatus' attitude, considering his own conduct far worse than that of the so-called *sacrificantes*. Whether he is arguing theoretically that parricide and the other things of which he accuses Novatus are worse than apostasy, or merely contrasting a sin of weakness with sins of malice is not certain. But in speaking of abortion as parricide, he is judging it even more evil than homicide. Cyprian then goes on to add that Novatus, conscious of his crimes, was afraid that he would not only be removed from the priesthood but even from communion with the faithful. Actually, the day for the trial was set, but it never came off because of the Decian persecution. This seems to be the first reference to ecclesiastical penalties connected with abortion. Since Novatus was guilty of other serious crimes, the penalties might not have been for abortion alone. But there can be no doubt that it was a primary consideration.

The word *parricidium* also appears in Lactantius (250-c. 317), a Latin Father who was born in Numidia but spent most of his life in Nicomedia, but it is not clear whether he is speaking of abortion or only of infanticide.[19] He says that some, lest there be a crime with which they have not soiled their hands, will deprive of the light of life *"rudibus adhuc et simplicibus animis."* He refuses to accept poverty or a lack of resources to support such children as a justification of these actions. These people are arguing as though it was not God who made the rich poor and the poor rich.

However uncertain the application of this statement to abortion may be, there is no doubt about Lactantius' opinion regarding the time of infusion of the human soul in the fetus. In his *De opificio dei* he says that formation is completed on the fortieth day and it is at this time that the soul is infused, not after birth as some philosophers think.[20] He is referring, of course, to the Stoics who believed the fetus began to live only when it began to breathe, that is, after birth. But with this opinion he would be no more tolerant of abortion, at least of the formed fetus, than of infanticide.

Finally, Eusebius (255-339-340) in his *Praeparatio evangelica* quotes from the *Contra Apionem* of Josephus the law against abortion and homicide which the latter attributed to Moses. According to Josephus, as already seen, this law forbids abortion and infanticide and regards the

woman who commits them a murderess.[21] What is noteworthy in this citation is the continuity it shows between
the moral standards of the early Christians and represen-
tatives of the Jewish community.

With Eusebius one comes to an end of the Christian
writers of the first three centuries who take up the question
of abortion. Anyone reading this testimony must see in it an
unequivocal condemnation of abortion. Many of these
writers condemn abortion as homicide, and where the
parent-child relationship is involved, parricide. While
such language may go beyond what seems to be the mentality behind the abortion statute in the Hebrew text, it is not
out of continuity with the attitude of pre-Christian Jews.
Statements such as that of Josephus in the *Contra Apionem*
as well as the apodictic condemnations of the *Duae viae* are
indicative of such continuity. Indeed without it the Christian attitude can hardly be explained. In the absence of any
specific condemnation of abortion in the New Testament,
it could hardly be considered a Christian innovation. And
there is no other likely source. At the same time, however,
the influence of the Septuagint text also begins to show
itself in such writers as Tertullian and Lactantius, although
the latter seems more dependent on Aristotle. But this
influence will not surface on the level of law for some time
to come.

CHAPTER FOUR

———————◆———————

Early Legislation
and Patristic Thought
(300-600)

There is no trace of any official legislation of the Church dealing with abortion during the first three centuries. The condemnations cited in the last chapter all came from individuals, many of them speaking with authority and undoubtedly reflecting the teaching of the Church itself, but none of them constituted church legislation. The first piece of legislation that has come to light dates from the first part of the fourth century and originates in a local council held at Elvira in Spain about the year 305. It is the first appearance also of what might be called penal legislation, if one understands this in the sense of spiritual penalties associated with the reconciliation of sinners. Elvira devoted two of its canons to the penitential discipline of the Church regarding abortion, canons 63 and 68. According to canon 63, if a woman who was baptized committed adultery in the absence of her husband and then destroyed the child, she was not to be restored to communion with the faithful even at the end of her life, since she has committed a double sin.[1] Canon 68 prescribes that if a catechumen does the same thing, she may be baptized at the end of her life.[2] Since the two canons do not speak explicitly of abortion, it might be urged that they are referring only to infanticide. But they have generally been interpreted by subsequent authors and councils to include abortion as well. It might also be added that abortion would be a more likely means of concealing adultery than infanticide.

Canon 63 legislates a very severe discipline, one of which Hippolytus would certainly approve. It seems to defend this severity by appealing to the fact that a double sin has been committed, adultery and abortion. In another canon, however, it prescribes a much less severe penalty for adultery, which apparently implies that the severity of the penance is due largely to the abortion. Then too, since canon 68 allows baptism at the end of her life to a catechumen who has committed the same two crimes, the status of the sinner must be a decisive factor. Penitential discipline differs from baptismal discipline. In other words, the council is denying a *secunda penitentia*, that is, forgiveness of serious sins committed after baptism. Permanent and irrevocable excommunications of this kind were meted out by the Council of Elvira with great frequency, even to the point that some accuse it of being tainted with Novatianism.[3] This would be difficult to prove. The council represents a severe penitential discipline, but there is no indication that it thought the Church did not have the power to forgive sins committed after baptism, which is the heresy of Novatianism.

The severe discipline of Elvira gave way to a less rigorous penitential legislation in a council held only a few years later at the other end of the Mediterranean. This was the Council of Ancyra, capital of Galatia, held in 314, which was attended by bishops from the whole of Asia Minor, as well as other parts of the eastern Mediterranean. Canon 21 of the council prescribes the penance for a woman who has fornicated and destroyed the fetus in her womb, as well as those who prepare drugs lethal to fetuses.[4] While admitting that an earlier official statement (probably Elvira) denied communion to these people even at the end of their lives, and that some still agree with this discipline, Ancyra in a more humane spirit allows them to be received back after ten years of penance. The process of reconciliation is to be a gradual one, involving the prescribed steps.

The prescribed *gradus* (steps) of reconciliation the council speaks of were known as *stationes* (stations).[5] Those in the first stage of reconciliation or penitence were known as the *flentes* (mourners), and they were completely excluded from the church while they were in this stage. The next class of penitents, the *audientes* (hearers), were allowed into the vestibule of the church. Only those in the final two stages, the *prostrati* (the prostrate) and the *adstantes* (bystanders) were allowed inside the church, but the former only for the first part of the liturgy. The *adstantes* were excluded only from the offering and the reception of the eucharist.

Although Ancyra dealt more leniently with abortion, it did not show the same leniency in dealing with homicide as such. It did not, indeed, consider homicide a sin that should not be forgiven at any time, as the old discipline seemed to demand, but it did delay reconciliation to the end of the penitent's life.[6] After Ancyra the penance for homicide will be further reduced, but not to the point where it will equal the penance for abortion. Yet abortion will continue to be considered a form of homicide. Is the difference in penance based on some objective gradation of the two sins? This is a possibility. But it is also possible that abortion is not dealt with as severely as homicide because of a concern for the special pressures a pregnant woman may be under to commit abortion.

The Councils of Elvira and Ancyra were only local councils, but the legislation of Ancyra, particularly, was accepted by the other Churches and made its way into many of the so-called canonical collections. It became an accepted norm for most of the Churches, at least for the next few centuries. On the contrary, the abortion legislation of Elvira seems to have had very little influence, at least after the Council of Ancyra. The next conciliar legislation on abortion will not come until the year 524 in the Council of Lerida, Spain. In the meanwhile, however, abortion will be discussed from many different angles both in the eastern and western Churches.

The most important discussion of abortion in the eastern Church after Ancyra is that of Basil the Great (330-379). It occurs in a series of letters to Amphilochius, bishop of Iconium, in which he describes the discipline of the Church. They are referred to as canonical letters because some unknown author after Basil divided them up into canons. The first reference to abortion is in canon 2 where Basil says that anyone who purposely destroys a fetus will pay the penalty of homicide.[7] This holds without any attention to subtle distinctions like that between the formed and unformed fetus. The penalty will vindicate the death not only of the fetus but also the mother herself, since women who attempt abortions often die themselves in the attempt. He does not think, however, that the penance should go on for the rest of the sinner's life, but only for ten years. In a somewhat apologetic tone he protests that it is not so much the amount of time spent that should be counted as the way in which one spends his penitential period.

Basil in adopting a ten-year period of penance for abortion is definitely following Ancyra. But what is most interesting is his reference to what he calls the subtle distinction between the formed and unformed fetus. This is the first time this issue has come up in connection with penitential discipline. Neither Elvira nor Ancyra made any provision for it. Basil apparently feels that he should mention it, even though he reveals a certain impatience with it. He does not think it operative in this case because the mother herself often dies in the attempt of abortion. This leaves open at least the theoretical possibility that it would be pertinent if only the fetus died. But Basil does not consider this possibility. It seems a little incongruous to set up a penance which assumes the death of the person for whom it was meant. It would make much more sense if it was intended for a third party, but this interpretation would hardly fit in with the wording of the canon. A later canon refers more properly to those who give abortifacients to others.[8] There Basil makes it clear that those who give abortifacients as well as those who take them are guilty of homicide.

Basil reduces the length of the penance for voluntary homicide assigned by Ancyra (until just before death) to twenty years, but this still leaves a gap between the penance for homicide and the penance for abortion. The penance for abortion is the same as that which he assigns to involuntary homicide. Balsamon, commenting on Basil several centuries later, says that women who commit abortion are not subject to the full penance of homicide because they act out of fear and shame.[9] This would indeed be a valid reason for mitigating the penance, but one cannot be sure that Balsamon is reflecting the mind of Basil from such a distance in time.

The distinction between the formed and unformed fetus, which Basil found so subtle, will become an important factor in the theological discussion of abortion for many centuries to come. It will be recalled that it appeared first in the Septuagint translation of the text on abortion in Exodus. To what extent it was related to Aristotle's views about the time of infusion of the rational soul is uncertain. The first reference to the distinction in the Christian era was seen in Tertullian. Lactantius said that the fetus was formed after forty days and it was at this time that the soul was infused. Cyril of Alexandria (d. 444), commenting on the Septuagint text from Exodus, says that the fetus does not belong to the human species until after forty days, that is, until it is formed, but he says nothing explicitly about the time of animation, that is, the time when the human soul is infused.[10] What is of interest in both Lactantius and Cyril is their failure to make any distinction between the male and female fetus. The Aristotelian distinction will not reappear, at least explicitly, until Aristotle is rediscovered by the scholastic theologians of the middle ages. But it might be presumptive to interpret the omission of the distinction in the meanwhile as a denial of it.

Whether the time of formation is also the time when the fetus is informed with a rational soul will be a subject of controversy for several centuries. Theodoret (c. 393-457), bishop of Cyrus, a small town near Antioch, in a work in which he relates the philosophy of the pagans to the gospels, clearly identifies the time of formation with the time of animation.[11] For this identification, however, he does not rely on philosophy but the scriptures. He argues that in the creation of Adam God did not breathe in a human soul until the body was formed. He also uses the well-known Septuagint text of Exodus, interpreting it to mean that animation with a rational soul takes place at the time of formation. This is why, he adds, Moses decreed that if the abortion took place after formation, it was considered homicide. If the fetus was not formed, it was not considered homicide, because the fetus was not yet animated.

A similiar identification of the time of animation with formation may be found in the so-called *Constitutio apostolorum*.[12] Both the authorship and date of publication of this work are unknown, but it certainly does not go back to the apostles or apostolic times. In dealing with the question of abortion it cites the precept of the *Duae viae*, but then adds as a reason for the precept that every formed fetus has been endowed by God with a soul, and so, if it is destroyed, the one responsible will pay the penalty for unjust killing. The *Constitutio* says nothing explicitly about the unformed fetus, but the reason it gives for the precept also seems to limit it. Was this limitation implicitly in the precept itself as it appeared in the *Duae viae*? There seems to be no valid reason for assuming this.

The identification of the time of animation with formation did not go undisputed. St. Maximus (580-662), in his *Ambiguorum liber*, argues for the infusion of the human soul at the moment of conception.[13] He claims that those who argue from Exodus to the identification of animation with formation are misinterpreting the text. He says that Moses is not speaking of the time of infusion of the soul into the body, but only of the time when the figuration of the body has been completed. Maximus in adopting the position of immediate animation seems to be concerned largely with the incarnation. He says that this took place at conception, and not at some later time. If one holds a theory of delayed animation, the incarnation would have to be considered an exception. At a much later date this was precisely what St. Thomas and his followers held. [14]

The writers cited since Ancyra all belonged to the Eastern Church. If one turns to the Latin Church, he will find even greater attention being paid to the issue of abortion and related questions. The canons of Ancyra exerted a strong influence in the West as well as in the East, and were either adopted explicitly or at least used as a basis for official statements of the Western Church. But before considering official statements, serious attention should be given to some of the great fathers of the Latin Church. The opinions of some of these fathers were very influential for several centuries to come even in forming official opinion.

These authors continue to condemn abortion. A simple but somewhat dramatic condemnation comes from Zeno, bishop of Verona. [15] In a treatise on greed he complains that among other evils it leads to a new kind of madness which causes a mother to bury a fetus in the womb, thereby making it a tomb and preventing the fetus from ever experiencing either a legitimate life or a legitimate death. Greed is involved because the fetus is destroyed to avoid the expense of supporting a child or else to gain an inheritance.

More attention is given to the question of abortion by Jerome (347-419), one of the most important Fathers of the Western Church. He is in agreement with all his predecessors in condemning it. In his letter to Eustochium *De virginitate* he complains of widows who try to protect their consciences by throwing a cloak of deceit over their violations of chastity. [16] Some do this by making themselves sterile, thus destroying the human being before it is even conceived.[17] Others attempt abortion and frequently lose their own lives in the attempt, thus committing three sins, violating chastity, taking the life of the child, and taking their own lives in the attempt. In another letter in which he is commenting on the epistle to the Ephesians, he has St. Paul paraphrasing himself and explaining why he encourages men to marry and have children.[18] He does not want them to commit adultery and be forced to destroy their offspring out of fear.

Although Jerome's opposition to abortion is strong and clear, there are elements of unclarity in his treatment of it. For instance, in his letter to Eustochium he accuses even a woman who makes herself sterile of homicide.[19] But in his letter to Algasius he seems to imply that only the abortion of the formed fetus is homicide.[20] There he says that the seed develops gradually in the uterus and is not considered a man until the elements have taken on the figure and the members of a human being. If homicide is defined as taking the life of a human being, it should be limited to the abortion of the formed fetus. In fact, Gratian several centuries later uses this text to support the thesis that abortion does not constitute homicide until the fetus is formed, that is, animated with a human soul.

This brings up another element of unclarity in Jerome, his opinion of the time of animation. Authors already discussed have been seen to differ on this point. Some, like Theodoret and the writer of the *Constitutio*, held that the body is animated with a rational soul when it is formed. Others, like Tertullian, held that the seed of the soul was implanted at the same time as the seed of the body. But before the issue of the time of animation is pursued further, it should be separated from a different, although related, question, that of the origin of the soul. There were two schools of thought regarding the origin of the human soul, creationist and traducianist. The traducianists maintained that the soul, like the body, was transmitted through the parents. Tertullian, for instance, was a traducianist, holding that the seed of the soul was implanted by the parents at the same time as the seed of the body. It is easily seen that

traducianism commits one to a theory of immediate animation. The same would not be true of creationism, a theory
that held the independent creation of the individual soul by
God. Theoretically, this could occur before, during, or
after conception. Christian writers did not hold the precre-
ation of the soul, but some creationists held that the soul
was infused at the time of conception; others, that it was
not infused until the body was formed. Jerome was inclined
toward the creationism of the Greek Fathers, but he was
somewhat shaken in this position by Augustine and his
problem with the transmission of original sin. Augustine
himself, as will be seen, was never sure of himself on this
question, but inclined toward a kind of spiritual
traducianism, a somewhat more subtle approach than that
of Tertullian, but one which, to him, also made it easy to
explain the transmission of original sin through the parents. Perhaps the most one can say about Jerome is that he
too never decided the question for himself.

Even if Jerome held a theory of immediate animation, it
might still be possible for him to maintain that the *conceptus* should not be considered a human being until a certain
amount of development had taken place, that is, until it
was formed. Tertullian seems to have taken a position similar to this. So Jerome's statement that the fetus is not a man
until it is formed does not necessarily commit him to hold
delayed animation. Nor, it seems, did it commit him to a
position that abortion would not be considered homicide
before the fetus was formed. If he was able to refer even to
sterilization as homicide, he must have been using that
term in reference to any interference in the transmission of
life, even though what was destroyed was not yet a man. It
was perhaps easier to take this position regarding sterilization at a time when so little was known about the process of
generation and conception. If conception involves nothing
more than planting, it does not seem to make much difference whether the seed is destroyed by being planted in
sterile soil or removed from fertile soil.

The most authoritative writer of this period is certainly St. Augustine (354-430). He discusses abortion in many of his writings, but perhaps the best known and most pertinent statement is taken from his work *De nuptiis et concupiscentiis* and is referred to universally as the *Aliquando*, the introductory word of the passage.[21] Early condemnations of abortion were directed largely at pagans, and the practice of abortion was highlighted as one of the differences between the Christian and the pagan. As the Church began to grow, however, and particularly when the masses began to be converted to Christianity, some of these pagan practices began to make their way into the Christian community. Later condemnations of abortion, therefore, are addressed to Christians, but mostly against those who resort to abortion after fornication or adultery. Augustine is the first to speak in general of birth control measures within marriage, although he says that married people who engage in intercourse and attempt to prevent offspring are like fornicators and adulterers. He complains that lust for pleasure mixed with cruelty drives some people to the point where they use sterilizing drugs, and if these do not work, in one way or another destroy the fetus while still in the womb, willing its destruction before it begins life, or if it is already alive, putting it to death before it is born. If both partners act this way, they are really not acting like married people. And if they were this way from the beginning, they did not come together for marital union, but rather for concubinage. If only one or the other acts this way, either the woman is the mistress of the man, or the man is the adulterer of the woman.

This is certainly a forceful condemnation of married couples who try to prevent birth by abortion, or even by sterilization. Augustine considers both a violation of the marital bond, actually reducing married partners to the status of fornicators or adulterers. It is adulterers and fornicators who usually resort to this type of sin, not those who enter into a union aimed at procreation. But apart from considering sterilization and abortion a violation of the marriage bond, there is no attempt in this passage to classify them otherwise, or grade them in any way. For further clarification one will have to look to other passages from his work.

Clarification of the status of the fetus will be found in his attack on Julian, the Pelagian.[22] There he asserts that Christians never considered the fetus part of the mother while it is in the womb. If a conceptus were merely part of the mother, one would not baptize a child whose mother was baptized while she was carrying it. But it is the practice to baptize such children, and it is not considered a second baptism. This rests on the belief that when the child is conceived, it is a son of Adam, and hence subject to original sin. It is therefore in need of the saving waters of baptism.

He takes up the subject of the fetus again in *The City of God* where he inquires about the resurrection of aborted fetuses.[23] He is somewhat hesitant on the point, but his inclinations seem to be all in favor of resurrection. He sees no reason why fetuses should be excepted if it is true that all who have died will rise again. Yet, when he takes up the same question in the *Enchiridion*, he distinguishes between the formed and unformed fetus.[24] He thinks that the opinion which allows for the resurrection of the formed fetus can be at least tolerated. As for the unformed fetus, he is more inclined to think that it will perish just like semen that has not been conceived. His difficulty, however, did not seem to be so much that the unformed fetus did not have a soul, but rather that it should arise unformed. But then he suggests that in the resurrection whatever is lacking in the way of form may be supplied. One can sympathize indeed with the difficulty of conceiving the risen body as unformed, or even partially formed.

Augustine looks into the question when life begins, but admits to some despair about man's ability to answer it.[25] In his mind it all hinges on whether life can be present without movement, even though in some hidden way. In what seems to be a reference to the argument of Tertullian

drawn from the practice of embryotomy he does conclude
that it is quite rash to maintain that the fetus is not alive the
whole time it is in the womb. But he goes no further in this
discussion, so one could not argue from this passage in the
Enchiridion when during uterine existence life begins. It is
possible, however, that his commentary on the Septuagint
version of the passage in Exodus on abortion may throw
some light on the question.[26] He says there that the Mosaic
law did not want to consider the unformed fetus a man, and
therefore, did not look upon the abortion of such a fetus
homicide. Was this because it did not consider the unformed fetus animated? This is a large question, he says,
and one not to be decided precipitously. He himself leaves
open the possibility that even the unformed fetus might be
animated, although he admits that the law did not think
that one could speak of a living soul in a body that lacked
sense organs.

Augustine shows some hesitancy about identifying the
time of animation with the time of formation. Is the question of the time of animation the same question he was raising above about the beginning of life? It would seem so,
even though in the one case the criterion about which he
was concerned was the presence of motion, in the other,
formation or the presence of sense organs. It was seen that
according to Aristotle movement could be detected in the
fetus at the same time as the formation was completed, so
practically speaking the two criteria would not differ. If one
held that animation took place on the basis of either criterion, it would be forty to ninety days after conception. But
Augustine was asking whether life or a living soul could be
present even before that time. According to the Stoics, life
or a living soul was not present in the child until after birth.
Before birth the fetus grew and developed in the mother's
body like any of her other organs or members. Aristotle on
the other hand held that life was present in the embryo
from conception, but it was only vegetative life. The rational soul was infused only when the fetus was formed (or
began to move). Since there is no evidence that Augustine
thought in terms of a succession of souls, it would seem to

follow that to him life would begin with animation, that is, the introduction of the human soul. The question he found difficult to decide was whether this happened at the time of formation (or when movement began) or earlier. Although he saw difficulties about holding earlier animation, he did not want to close out the possibility.

Whether animation occured at the time of formation was still an open question to Augustine, and not to be decided hastily. At a much later date Gratian, in establishing the thesis that the time of formation and animation were the same, cited not only the above test but also one from pseudo-Augustine (really Ambrosiaster), which makes a clear identification of the two.[27] This author says that Moses made the distinction between the formed and unformed fetus to show that no soul is present before the body is formed. To prove his case, he points to the creation of Adam whose soul was infused into the body only after the latter was formed. He admits that the soul might have been united to the dust and the body formed afterwards, but this goes against reason. He argues that the house has to be built before it can be inhabited. And the soul, since it is spirit, cannot inhabit dust; it is said to dwell in the blood system. So how can there be a soul until the lineaments of the body have been defined? Whatever one may think of this reasoning, it is introduced to support the belief that animation takes place at the time of formation, and not before. But it is the opinion of some writer other than Augustine.

If Augustine was uncertain regarding the time of animation he seemed to have no doubts about the length of time formation took. He takes up the question in connection with the passage in St. John (John 2:18-22) where Christ predicts that he will rebuild the temple in three days if anyone destroys it.[28] Since he was speaking of the temple of his own body, Augustine compares the forty-six years it took to construct the temple with the number of days it takes to form the human body. He describes and computes the time of development of the human body in this way. For six days after conception the semen continues to have the appearance of milk. After that it takes nine days for it to turn into blood. Twelve days are consumed in solidifying the mass, and then in eighteen more days it is perfectly formed with all its members. All this comes to forty-five days, but if you add one, you get the number forty-six. For the rest of the time the fetus is in the womb, it just increases in size. Multiplying forty-six by six, he gets the total number of days (276) which Christ spent in the womb of his mother. If one prescinds from Augustine's numerology, he still gets an estimate close to that of Aristotle for the formation of the male fetus. The embryology, however, is quite primitive and seems based on the assumption that the deposit of semen itself gradually develops into the human being. This, of course, is a false assumption, but knowledge of the existence of sperm would only come centuries later. And knowledge of the ovum is an even later acquisition.

Some time after Augustine one finds in the sermons of Caesarius of Arles (470-543) frequent condemnations of abortion and infanticide. Many of these sermons were at one time attributed to Augustine, but they definitely belong to Caesarius. Since they are sermons, the treatment of both these subjects is more pastoral than speculative. In one of these sermons he urges women to accept both their sterility and their fertility.[29] If they are sterile, they should not appeal to the devil to make them fertile. If they are fertile, they should accept their children. Abortion and infanticide are both homicide. Caesarius is also in the tradition of Jerome and those who condemn even sterilization as homicide. Those who take "sterilizing" potions to prevent conception are destroying the fertility God wants them to have. If they do this, they will surely commit as many homicides as the number of children they might have conceived. This last statement will be found in several of Caesarius' sermons and will be quoted often by later authors.

He returns to the subject of abortion and infanticide in another sermon.[30] Here he says that the devil deceives women who have two or three children to kill the rest or take a *poculum aborsionis*, because otherwise they will not get rich. He warns them that they may be taking the lives of those who would serve God better or love their parents more than children who are actually born. If they do not want children, there is a more salutary way of going about it—make a religious pact with their husbands. Chastity should be the only sterility of the faithful wife.

It was about this time (524), two hundred years after Elvira, that the Spanish bishops again met in council, this time at Lerida, and in addition to other legislation issued another penitential canon regarding abortion and infanticide.[31] This canon, like that of Elvira, is dealing with children conceived in adultery whose lives parents attempt to take, either before or after birth. The canon makes a distinction between the adulterers and the *venefici* (the poisoners), and in this respect differs from Elvira. It will be remembered that the penance set by Elvira covered or included both sins. According to Lerida, the adulterers themselves, whether male or female, could be received back into the Church after seven years, although the council demanded that they spend the rest of their lives in sorrow for their sins.[5] The *venefici*, the poisoners, will be received back at the end of their lives if they have lived lives of repentance. The adulterers themselves might, of course, also have been the *venefici*. If so, they would be subject to the more severe penance, but while the exclusion from communion with the faithful went way beyond the time length prescribed by Ancyra, it was still less severe than that of Elvira. They would be received back into communion at least at the end of their lives. In the same canon Lerida makes what seems to be the first official statement about a cleric involved in this type of sin. He may never return to his ministry, but after he has been received back into communion, he may take his place again in the choir.

Not too long after Lerida, and apparently in conjunction with the Third Council of Braga (Portugal), Martin, bishop of Braga, and the whole synod made up a list of

canons from the Greek councils and translated them into
Latin. One of these canons dealt with abortion, and in the
Mansi edition of the councils it is listed as the canon of
Ancyra. But anyone reading Martin's canon will recognize
that it is much more than a translation of Ancyra.[32] The
Bragan version states that if a woman committed fornication and tried to kill the child after birth or abort it beforehand, or if she tried to prevent conception, whether
married or not, she and anyone cooperating with her would
do penance for ten years. It adds that this penance is prompted by mercy, earlier canons having decreed
that she could not be received back into communion until
the end of her life.

It is possible that this is a translation of a canon of some
other council that never came to light in the original, but it
is not a simple translation of Ancyra. Even though it speaks
of women who commit fornication, it addresses itself
explicitly to married women as well. This may be a reflection of the Augustinian accusation that married women
who try to prevent or destroy offspring are really acting like
fornicators. The most striking departure from Ancyra,
however, is the inclusion of an attempt to prevent conception among the sins mentioned. Ancyra says nothing about efforts to prevent conception. Braga is obviously
not the first to condemn such efforts, so it is not innovating
in this sense, but it cannot point to Ancyra as the source of
the condemnation. The ten-year period of penance is that
of Ancyra, but the reference to the previous practice which
received these people back into communion only at the end
of their lives is not at all accurate. It will be remembered
that Ancyra was referring to a practice which did not allow
those guilty of abortion back into communion even at the
end of their lives. The penance referred to in the Bragan
canon sounds much more like that prescribed by Lerida for
the *venefici* themselves. But in making this canon, whatever may be its origin, available to his people and those of
the other bishops of the synod, Martin was tempering the
discipline not only of Elvira, but also of Lerida.

Although it was not made during the first six centuries, attention should be called here to a statement on abortion issuing from the Council of Trulla.[33] This council, sometimes called Quinisextum, was an ecumenical council of the Greek Church and was held in Constantinople in 692. Canon 91 of the council imposed the penance for homicide both on those who give abortifacients and on those who take them. This is really taken from Basil's canons, more precisely canon 8. The council itself does not say what the penance for homicide is, but it may also be following Basil in this as well. Basil himself actually adopted the penance of Ancyra.

All of the canons on abortion seen this far have come from local councils. Although, strictly speaking, these canons affect only those areas over which the bishops of the council had authority, many of them were accepted by other local Churches, and often became general church discipline. This was particularly true of the canon of Ancyra on abortion. The general diffusion of these authoritative statements was achieved through what are known as canonical collections, that is, collections of local ecclesiastical legislation. These collections began to appear about the middle of the fifth century and continued to appear for the next several centuries.

One of the earliest of these collections, known as the *Prisca* or *Itala*, gathered the decrees and canons of several Eastern councils and made them available in a Latin version to the Roman Church. The canon on abortion was taken from Ancyra.[34] The same canon was also included in the more influential collection of *Dionysius Exiguus*.[35] This collection enjoyed great respect throughout the Western Church for the next several centuries. This is undoubtedly attributable to the interest in it taken by Pope Hadrian. It was sent by him to Charlemagne and actually became the semiofficial law of the Frankish Church. Another collection of the same period, the *Quesnelliana*, also included the canon from Ancyra,[36] as did two African collections, the *Breviatio canonum* of Fulgentius Ferrandus

(Carthage)[37] and the *Concordia canonum Cresconii*.[38] The latter seems to have been the work of some African bishop around the year 600. So it can easily be seen how and why the canon of Ancyra on abortion from local beginnings became legislation that was virtually universal throughout the Church. As a matter of fact, the only collection that included the legislation of the Spanish councils on abortion was the *Collectio Hispana*, but even this collection contained the canon of Ancyra.[39] In the Eastern Church the canons of Ancyra, St. Basil, and the Council of Trulla were all gathered in a collection made by Photius called the *Syntagma canonum*.[40] As already seen, there is a dependence among these canons that ultimately goes back to Ancyra, which points to the influence the canon had also in the Eastern Church.

In this second period (300 to 600) of the Christian era there is a twofold development, one legal, the other more philosophical and theological. The period witnessed the appearance of the first conciliar legislation regarding abortion. It appeared in relation with penitential discipline. The initial penance set by Elvira, severe by any standards, presumably represented an earlier discipline, but it was soon tempered by Ancyra, and this latter penance was generally accepted throughout the Church. A later condemnation of abortion by Martin, bishop of Braga, and alleged to be a translation of an oriental canon, included a condemnation of attempts aimed at preventing conception as well as abortion, and classified these as homicide. The philosophical and theological discussion centered around the distinction between the formed and the unformed fetus, particularly in reference to the time of animation and the beginning of life. A tradition was forming which looked upon only the abortion of the formed fetus as homicide. Abortion of the unformed fetus, although universally condemned, was not classified as homicide. But not all the writers who considered only the abortion of the formed fetus homicide identified the time of formation with the time of animation, or the beginning of life. Parallel with this tradition was another which considered not only the abortion of the unformed fetus, but even sterilization, as homicide. These two traditions will continue to grow side by side for some centuries to come, and many attempts will be made to reconcile them.

CHAPTER FIVE

Private Penance
and Abortion
(600-c. 1100)

Up to the present the official position of the Church regarding abortion has been revealed largely through canonical legislation regulating the practice of penance in the Church. According to these canons a person responsible for abortion was excluded from communion with the faithful, which was the penalty for all such serious sins. According to Elvira this exclusion was permanent, but Ancyra and other local councils allowed for eventual reconciliation. It seems that ultimately the ten-year period of exclusion imposed by the Council of Ancyra was generally accepted by other Churches in the Mediterranean area. But in this tradition the emphasis was clearly on exclusion or excommunication from the Church. What other forms of penance would be done during this period were prescribed locally. In some Eastern Churches also the process of reconciliation was a gradual one, involving prescribed stages of penance, the concluding step being participation in the eucharist itself.

All of this occured on what appeared to be a very legal level and was quite public except perhaps for the confession of the sin itself.[1] But there was only one reconciliation for very serious sins committed after baptism, a tradition which Poschmann traces back to Hermas in the early second century and which was rigidly adhered to during these early centuries.[2] Moreover, from the beginning of the fourth century the person who had once undertaken public penance could never be restored to his prepenitential status.[3] He could never be admitted into the clerical state and he must live within very strict limitations. He could not hold public office, he could not serve in the military forces, and, most important of all, he could not engage in marital intercourse.[4] In other words, his status as a reconciled penitent called for a renunciation of the world not unlike that made by the person who entered the religious state. Also, failure to live up to these restrictions was equivalent to relapse into sin. So, even with the relaxation of Ancyra, the penitential discipline for a woman who committed an abortion after fornication was by any standards very severe. But this was public penance as it was known and practiced in the early Church.

While this development was taking place in the Mediterranean Church, another penitential tradition was forming in a more remote corner of the Church, particularly Ireland and England. This was the tradition of private penance. It would be a mistake to look upon this development as totally unrelated to the tradition of canonical or public penance, but there were significant differences, enough to cause serious conflict when the two traditions eventually met on the Continent. Part of the explanation for these differences will be found in the different religious structure of these insular Churches. The religious life of the people was built more around the monasteries than it was around a diocesan organization. It was not regulated so much then by legislation arising from local councils as it was by the religious practices of the monasteries themselves. The penitential practices of the people were as a result influenced largely by the penitential practices of the monks, particularly the practice of manisfesting their consciences and of confessing to the abbot. Just as in the practice of public penance, the penances assigned were of some duration, but generally not as long as public penances. Although reconciliation was not granted ordinarily until after the penance was completed, the penance itself was not expressed in terms of a period of exclusion from the eucharist, but rather in terms of fasting and abstinence. Nor was the penitent put in a penitential class during this period; it was private penance. A more important difference, however, was the absence of any limitation on private penance; it could be received any number of times. Significant also was the fact that the status of the penitent was no different after reconciliation than it was before he committed the sin. Briefly, the practice of private penance, which resembles much more closely modern penitential practice, was a much less severe discipline in many respects than its Mediterranean counterpart.

Private penance developed in Ireland and England, and then through the missionary efforts of the monks spread to the Continent. As it developed, a penitential literature built up around it as an aid to priests in assigning penances for different sins. These were simply called penitential books, and they became very common throughout the whole Western Church during the second half of the first millenium. As already intimated, the approach of these books to penance was quite different from that of the councils both regarding the nature of the penance and its duration. Generally speaking, the approach was more ascetical than legal. No explicit mention was made of exclusion from the Church, although even in this system reconciliation was generally granted only after the penance was completed. The actual penance assigned usually involved fasting and abstinence. The duration of the period of penance was ordinarily not as long as that of public penance, but because of its severity it was considered the equivalent of these penances. The penitential books were also far more detailed than the canons and made meticulous provision for differences in circumstances surrounding the sin, for the intention of the sinner and for his ability to perform the assigned penance. A whole list of redemptions or commutations was provided for those who for reasons of health or otherwise were not able to fast or abstain.

One great drawback of the penitential books was their individualism. The author of each book made his own judgment about the appropriate penance for a particular sin. This resulted in a great variety of penances attached to the same sin. The arbitrariness of these penances did not appear as long as these books were limited to local use, but as they began to be more broadly circulated, it became quite apparent and caused considerable confusion. It has already been seen that there was some variety in the penances attached to abortion by local councils, but that general acceptance was given to the ten-year penance of Ancyra. Given the proliferation of penitential books that occurred on the Continent, there was no possibility of reconciling the great variety of penances they assigned for the same sin, especially since most of them originated from unknown authorship, and hence lacked any kind of authority.

But before going on to the penitential books themselves, attention should be given to one of the few Irish canonical documents that have come to light. The so-called *Canones Hibernenses*, which date from the second half of the seventh century (c. 675) cannot be connected with any particular Irish synod, but a teaching of such a synod is cited as the source of the section in which the canons on abortion are found.[5] Canons 6 to 8 refer to the sin of abortion. In canon 6 a penance of three and a half years, presumably on bread and water, is imposed for the destruction of *liquoris materiae filii in utero*. McNeill translates this as "the embryo of a child in the mother's womb,"[6] but this translation does not seem to bring out adequately the distinction between this canon and canon 7. There a penance of seven years on bread and water, and in continence, is imposed on the destruction of the body and soul in the uterus of the mother. This distinction may or may not coincide with the distinction already seen between the formed and unformed fetus, but it seems clear that destruction of the conceptus while still in the "liquid" state is not considered as serious a sin as destruction of the conceptus after it has become flesh and spirit, whenever the latter occurs.[7] But this represents the first appearance of a distinction in canonical penances based on the stage of development of the fetus.

The most unusual canon, however, is canon 8, which says that the life price *(pretium animae)* for the destruction of the "liquid" and the mother is twelve female slaves.[8] This sounds more like a civil penalty than a spiritual penance. Penalties of this kind were found in the book of the covenant, but there they were obviously of a civil nature. Undoubtedly, a close connection existed between the civil and ecclesiastical authorities in Ireland at the time, and it may be that the synod here is merely presenting the civil law. On the other hand, the penance could conceivably be a commutation of a fasting penalty.

Some clarification of these canons may be found in the penances for causing a miscarriage listed in the *Old Irish Penitential* (c. 800).[9] It prescribes that if a woman causes a miscarriage of that which she has conceived after it has become established in the womb, the penance will be three and a half years. If the flesh is formed, the penance is seven years. If the soul has entered it, fourteen years. If the woman dies of the miscarriage, that is, the death of body and soul, fourteen cumals (female slaves) are offered to God as the price of her soul *(pretium animae)*, or fourteen years' penance.

There are recognizable similarities between these prescriptions and those of the *Canones*. The difference between canons 6 and 7 and the above prescriptions is that a third stage in fetal development is introduced, resulting presumably in a "liquid" stage, a carnal stage, and finally an animated stage. The implication, of course, is that the soul is not infused or does not "enter" the body until sometime after the liquid turns to flesh.[10] A similar, if not identical, distinction will appear in a few other penitentials. Of comparative interest also is the *pretium animae* referred to in the last part of the prescription. The so-called "price" is fourteen female slaves rather than the twelve of the *Canones*, but here it seems to represent some kind of redemption of the poor woman's soul, and a fasting alternative is allowed for those who might not have the price of fourteen female slaves. What kind of eschatology was behind this kind of prescription is not at all clear. Nor is it clear that the prescription in the *Canones* reflects the same kind of thinking. It seems obvious that in the *Old Irish Penitential* the woman is both the cause and the victim of the abortion. In the *Canones* the cause of both deaths may have been a third party, so what was prescribed in canon 8 may well have been a penance in the strict sense, or at least a commutation, although one cannot rule out entirely the possibillity that it is a civil penalty. If it is a penance, the prescribed duration, at least for the loss of the animated fetus, comes closer to canonical penances than to those of the penitential books.

The penitential of Finnian is of much earlier origin than the *Hibernenses*, dating from the first half of the sixth century. The identity of Finnian is not certain, but the extensive use of his penitential by Columban shows that his work was respected. Finnian deals with what seems to be the sin of abortion under the heading of *maleficium*.[11] *Maleficium* appears to be closely related to, if not identical with, the sin of *veneficium* condemned by St. Paul, and penalized by Roman law. Later penitentials will use both words, and sometimes indiscriminately, but the preference seems to be for *maleficium*. What is common to both is the factor of doing harm to others, although in both *maleficium* and *veneficium* one also finds an association with superstitious appeals to evil spirits. If there is any difference between the two practices, it is that *veneficium* speaks explicitly of the use of drugs. *Maleficium* would seem to allow for other means to cause the harm or perhaps just an appeal to evil spirits.

The reason for the doubt about the reference to abortion is that the penitential uses the word *partum* in dealing with the sin. This word might be used of a child already born or one not yet born, but there is sufficient evidence in the penitentials of its use to designate a child not yet born to warrant this assumption here. The canon is speaking of someone other than the mother as the source of the harm; it has no canon prescribing for an abortion caused by the mother herself. The Finnian prescribes as a penance for a woman who causes another woman to abort by some *maleficium* a half year on measured bread and water, a two-year fast from wine and meat, and an additional six fasts of forty days duration on bread and water. While very severe, this penance was less than that for causing homicide (seven years). The reason for the difference, which is clear in the later penitential of Columban, may be that the *maleficium* was aimed more at stimulating sex than at the abortion itself.[12] That Columban associates the sin with homicide, however, is clear from the reason he gives for the additional penance when abortion occurs—*ne reus sit homicidii*. The meaning of this clause is not entirely clear, but it does connect the sin of abortion with homicide.

The penitential of Columban, which follows the Finnian quite closely in prescribing for abortion caused by *maleficium*, dates from the end of the sixth or the beginning of the seventh century and is attributed with good reason to the Irish missionary monk of that name. Like the Finnian also it does not prescribe a penance for an abortion caused by the mother herself, but deals only with an abortion caused by someone else. Mention should be made also of the *Cummean Penitential*, for which Irish origin is claimed, which was published about the middle of the seventh century.[13] Although it contains no canon on abortion, it was the basis for several later European penitentials. But the canons on abortion for its European offspring had to be taken from other sources. Finally, Irish origin is often claimed for the so-called *Bigotian Penitential*, associated with the beginning of the eighth century.[14] The canons of this penitential which deal with abortion will be recognized for their similarity with the *Canones Hibernenses*. But the *Bigotianum* prescribes different penances: three years for the destruction of the "liquid," but fourteen years (rather than seven) for the destruction of the flesh and spirit in the womb. This sounds more like the *Old Irish Penitential*. The *pretium animae* for the loss of both mother and fetus is fourteen female slaves.

By way of summary, then, there seem to be two Irish sources for penitential prescriptions regarding abortion, the *Canones Hibernenses* and the Finnian. The Finnian prescribes only for abortion caused by a third party and makes no distinction in the penances based on the development of the fetus. The penance in the *Hibernenses* seems to include abortion caused by the mother, at least if interpreted according to the *Old Irish Penitential*, and grades the penances according to the stage of development of the *conceptus*. The other penitentials, namely, the Columban, Cummean, and Bigotian, depend on previous Irish sources for their treatment of abortion or on other sources.

The earliest set of Anglo-Saxon penitentials are derived from Theodore, archbishop of Canterbury (668-690). There were three such penitentials: *Capitula Dacheriana*, *Canones Gregorii*, and the *Penitentiale* of the so-called *Discipulus Umbrensium*. There is no reason to believe that Theodore was the actual author of any of these penitentials, but all of them reflect his *judicia*. Theodore himself came originally from Tarsus, so his theological thinking is more that of the Eastern Church, a factor which was to make for conflict when his penitentials appeared on the Continent. For instance, his *judicia* regarding clerical celibacy and the indissolubility of marriage conflicted with the thought of the Western Church on these subjects. Unlike the Finnian and Columban penitentials, those of Theodore do not deal with the subject of abortion under the heading *maleficium* but rather in the general category of sins of married people. What is characteristic of these penitentials is the distinction they make between an abortion before and after forty days from conception. All three penitentials make this distinction and assign the same penances, so it will be sufficient to cite the *Penitentiale*, since it is the most detailed.[15] It says that if a woman performs an abortion before the fetus has a soul, the penance will be a year or three forty-day periods according to the nature of the fault. If she does this afterwards, that is, after forty days *accepti seminis* (forty days after insemination), she will do the penance for homicide, that is, three years on Wednesdays and Fridays, and three forty-day periods. The concern of the *Penitentiale* for conformity with the canonical penances is evidenced in the statement it makes that the above penances are the equivalent to a *decennium*. The reference is obviously to the penance of Ancyra.

Although the *Penitentiale* does not speak explicitly of the time of formation of the fetus, it can be assumed that this is what is understood by the forty-day dividing line. But it is explicitly stated that the fetus receives a soul at this time. The *Canones Hibernenses* made no explicit time estimate, but it was undoubtedly dealing with the same distinction. In both Irish and English penitential sources, then, the opinion of delayed animation seems to be accepted and utilized to grade penances for abortion.

While the *Penitentiale* tries to show continuity with the rest of the Church regarding the duration of assigned penances, it is expressly aware of differences in the two traditions. In speaking of reconciliation, for instance, it says that it takes place on Holy Thursday, and after the penance is performed. But it then goes on to say that it is not public *in hac provincia*, since penance itself is not public.[16] Although it shows this awareness of the difference between the two traditions, there is an underlying assurance that it is substantially the same reality.

There are two other Anglo-Saxon penitentials, one attributed to Bede and the other to Egbert, archbishop of York, but only the *Bedae* prescribes for abortion. The penance it prescribes is the one- or three-year penance of the Theodore penitentials based on the forty-day dividing line.[17] But Bede allows for some variation of this depending on the situation of the woman. As he says, it makes a big difference whether the woman commits the sin because she is poor and cannot support the child or whether she is trying to conceal a sin of fornication. This distinction is taken up by many later penitentials.

As private penance spread to the Continent, penitential books written on the Continent also began to appear. In general, these penitentials show great dependence on their Irish and Anglo-Saxon ancestors. Thus the penitentials of Columban and Theodore, as well as the *Cummean Penitential*, were the source of many continental penitentials. In dealing with abortion those penitentials which depended on the Cummean prototype had to borrow their prescriptions from some other penitential. Those which depended on Columban, and this seems to be the largest group, added to the Columban canon on *maleficium* a canon on abortion caused by the mother herself. But these penitentials generally make no distinction between the animated and unanimated fetus and prescribe a three-year penance. Those penitentials, however, which follow Theodore in their penitential regulations for abortion do make the one-three year distinction. In the penitentials which were in use on the Continent the range of penance for abortion went all the way from fourteen years to one year, depending on the Irish or English source from which they drew.

When the practice of private penance spread to the Continent, it was bound for reasons already mentioned to come into conflict with the system of public penance. Initially, however, it moved into what was largely a vacuum, at least in many parts of the European Church.[18] After the fall of Rome at the end of the fifth century, conciliar and synodal activity in the Church became almost nonexistent. It continued for a while in the Church of Arles and remained quite vigorous in the Spanish Church, but for the rest of the European Church legislation came largely to a standstill. Contact with Rome also became less and less frequent. The spread of private penance then would not meet with much active opposition. And even though the legislative foundation for public penance was long established, the practice of public penance, because of the severity of the discipline, had either disappeared or was put off until the end of one's life.[19] So whatever conflict arose was more with the theory of public penance than its practice.

As might have been expected in a country where local conciliar activity was still vigorous, private penance did not receive any cordial welcome in Spain. The Third Council of Toledo (589) branded it as an abuse.[20] But in France the Synod of Chalon issued a statement which Poschmann interprets as a commendation of private penance, and there seemed to be general acceptance of the practice in the Church north of the Alps.[21] Perhaps the best testimony of the popularity of private penance in this part of the Church is the proliferation of penitential books that occurred. There would have been little need of such books if the practice had not been generally accepted. But once accepted, the practice deepened its roots and spread through Europe, apparently without serious opposition until the middle of the eighth century. At that time the Carolingian reform set in and among other goals attempted to restore the ancient discipline of public penance.[22]

In their effort to restore order and discipline to the Church the reformers aimed at restoring contact with the ancient law, which for all practical purposes meant restoring contact with the Roman Church. One of the most influential instruments in this reform was the collection of canons made by *Dionysius Exiguus* which was given by Pope Hadrian to Charlemagne in 774. It became known then as the *Hadriana* and was the authentic text of the reform.[23] The more conscious the Frankish Church became through the reform of the old discipline of public penance, the more apparent became the conflict with the practice of private penance that was then widespread. By the beginning of the ninth century synodal opposition to the penitential books began to crystallize.

The Council of Tours (813), attempting to dispel the confusion caused by the great variety of penitential practices originating in the various penitential books, urged the

selection of just one of these books for the diocese.[24] The
Council of Chalon, held in the same year, was not satisfied
with any kind of compromise between the two traditions,
but urged the restoration of the old public discipline as well
as the elimination of all the penitential books *"quorum sunt
certi errores, incerti auctores."*[25] The same attitude was
taken by the Council of Paris (829), which advocated burn-
ing all penitential books.[26] A short time later, however, the
Council of Mayence seemed willing to accept a compromise stand, distinguishing between private sins and
public sins.[27] It will be seen that this position was eventually adopted in the Frankish Church.

The opposition movement was effective, if not in end-
ing the practice of private penance, at least in putting an
end to the old type of penitential book. From the beginning
of the ninth century penitentials of this type no longer appeared. Penitentials which did begin to appear at this time
all had the character of the reform. Perhaps the most
celebrated of these was that written by Halitgar, bishop of
Cambrai (c. 829). It was written at the request of Ebbo,
bishop of Rheims, who complained that the penitentials in
circulation were so confusing and so lacking in authority
that they were of no help to confessors or penitents. But
Halitgar seemed to have no intention of ignoring the penitentials completely. Although in Books III to V he collects
canons and decretals relative to public penance, he goes on
to add a sixth book, a penitential which according to him
came from a *scrinio Romanae ecclesiae* (literally "a book-
chest of the Roman Church").[28] His reason for adding this
sixth book was to provide for those who might find the contents of the first five books superfluous or who would not
find in them the treatment of certain sins. He says in
another place that one will find in this penitential many
things not found in the canons, and that this book may be
helpful to priests not sufficiently sophisticated to deal with
the canons.

Books III to V would certainly have been superfluous in
those areas where public penance had fallen into de-
suetude. But even in those parts of Europe where local

councils were making heroic, but not always successful, efforts to restore it, a compromise situation was developing which allowed for both practices: public penance for public sins, private penance for private sins. A work such as Halitgar's would certainly be helpful in this situation, since it was providing for both practices. As an authoritative penitential also, the Sixth Book would take precedence over the innumerable penitentials then current and do away with the confusion these gave rise to. It was evidently with this in mind that Halitgar explicitly pointed to the Roman origin of his penitential. This would give it an authority which the other penitentials, mostly of unknown authorship, could not claim. Halitgar then would be accomplishing what the Council of Tours urged the bishops to do.

In truth Halitgar may have done nothing more than choose one of the then current penitentials to incorporate into his own work. Whatever is meant by getting this penitential from the *scrinium* of the Roman Church is not clear, but there seems little doubt that the penitential is not of Roman origin. Wasserschleben lists it as a Frankish penitential dependent upon the penitential of Columban. In dealing with abortion Halitgar is certainly dependent upon Columban when prescribing for an abortion caused by *maleficium*.[29] But he shows dependence upon other sources as well. For instance, for an abortion or infanticide after fornication he cites the canon of Ancyra with its ten-year penance.[30] For an abortion caused by a woman on herself without reference to any previous sin, he prescribes a penance of three years.[31] Since the Columban penitential had no such penance, he must have had some other source for it. It will be remembered that this is the penance the penitentials derived from Theodore prescribe for the abortion of a fetus after forty days, which these books considered homicide. The penitential of Halitgar may simply have taken over this penance without the distinction. The distinction of the Theodorean penitentials could hardly have been adopted by this penitential unless it also was made in the other two canons on abortion. Actually, the distinction is not that commonly found in the continental penitentials.

It may come as a shock to the modern reader to find an author making a false claim regarding the origin of his work. But an acquaintance with the writers of the period will reveal a certain freedom in claiming sources and in dealing with texts that would not be countenanced today. One simply does not find in those days the same concern for fidelity and authenticity in transmitting works of the past that is expected today. Ample evidence of this is the existence of the many apocryphal works that appeared during the first millenium. In the area of abortion attention has already been called to the freedom with which Martin of Braga dealt with the canon of Ancyra. It must be remembered also that the period of Halitgar coincided with that of the false decretals and the false capitulars, when attempts were made to establish the independence of the Church from the civil authority by deliberately appealing to false decretals and capitular decrees of the past.[32] One gets the general impression in dealing with these works that as long as the falsifications served a good purpose, they were considered acceptable. Since it was only by appealing to Roman authority that Halitgar could insure an authoritative status for his penitential book and thus put an end to the confusion arising from a multiplicity of anonymous books, it seemed reasonable to do this. It is frequently possible, of course, to reduce apparent falsifications to copyist mistakes, but even granting that the copyists made many mistakes, such mistakes will not explain all the errors found in these works. At a later date Cardinal Atton challenged specifically the Roman origin of Halitgar's penitential.[33]

Shortly before Halitgar, Theodulph (d. 824), bishop of Orleans, wrote a *Capitulare*, which is also in the tradition of the reform movement.[34] He lists the canon of Ancyra and another of unknown origin prescribing a seven-year penance for a woman who causes an abortion on herself without reference to adultery or any previous sin. What is

most interesting, however, is that Theodulph, like Halitgar, seems willing to compromise somewhat with the system of public penance. After dividing the penitential
periods up into two stages, he says that the penitent will be
allowed to receive communion only after he has completed
the whole period. But then he gives the priest the option of
allowing the penitent to receive communion before that
time according to the spirit of repentance he shows. As for
actual fasting, again he leaves it up to the priest to adjust it
to the repentance and needs of the individual person.
Strictly speaking, the tradition of private penance also allowed reconciliation only after the penance was completed, but in practice both the *Praefatio Gildae* and the
Penitentiale (Theodore) permitted priests to anticipate the
completion of the penance. The *Praefatio* allowed this
after a year and a half.[35] The *Penitentiale, pro misericor-
dia*, permitted communion after a year or six months.[36]
The gradual contraction of the period of exclusion from the
eucharist continued until the whole penitential procedure
was reduced to one act, reconciliation preceding the actual
performance of the penance. From about the year 1000 this
became the traditional practice of the Church.[37]

Other efforts to restore canonical penance were less
compromising. Thus, for instance, the *Penitentiale* of
Pseudo-Gregorii presents a canon on abortion and infanticide which draws on much previous legislation and penitential literature yet really represents none of them. But
the approach is clearly canonical rather then penitential.[38]
Similarly, the so-called *Penitential* of Rabanus Maurus did
nothing more than recall the canons of Ancyra, Elvira, and
Lerida.[39] The same concentration on the early canons is
found in the *Collectio* of the False Isidore (841-859)[40] as
well as the *Capitula Angilramni* (c. 850).[41] A set of
Capitula, the work of Rodulphus, bishop of Biturica (d.
866), included the version of Ancyra broadcast by Martin of
Braga.[42]

The period also saw conciliar efforts to restore the canonical penances. Thus, the Council of Mainz, held in 847,
under Rabanus Maurus, who was then archbishop of

Mainz, again promulgated the decrees of Ancyra, Lerida, and Elvira. [43] At about the same time the Council of Worms (848) prescribed that a woman who aborted a fetus before term was to be considered a homicide. [44] Neither of these councils, however, were offering any new legislation, although the declaration of Worms may be the first explicit classification of abortion as homicide by a council in the Western Church.

One of the most important collections of this period was the *Libri synodales* (c. 906), published by Regino of Prum, at one time abbot of the monastery in that city. [45] His concern seemed to be to provide those who attended synods with a legislative background regarding causes that would likely be brought before such synods. Like some of his predecessors he drew not only on canonical legislation but also on the penitentials. In dealing with abortion, after citing the canons of Ancyra, Lerida, and Elvira, he goes on to present a canon from Pseudo-Bede. According to this canon, if a woman destroys a fetus before forty days, she must do penance for one year. If she destroys it after forty days, the penance is three years. But if she causes the abortion after the soul has been infused, she must do penance for homicide. A double distinction similar to this was seen in the *Old Irish Penitential*, but this was the only other use of it that has been seen. What is seems to imply is that animation does not necessarily take place at the time of formation, that is, after forty days, Generally speaking, the penitentials we have seen, if they make a distinction at all, seem to identify animation with the time of formation.

What is most important for the whole future discussion of abortion is canon 89 of Book II, a canon which as Regino presents it, does not even seem to refer explicitly to abortion. According to this canon, if anyone out of lust or premeditated hatred, to prevent the person from having children, does anything to a man or woman, or gives them some potion to keep them either from generating or conceiving, he must be held as a murderer. [46] This canon will become known in the discussion of abortion for the next ten centuries or more by the first two words of the Latin original, *Si aliquis.* It would be possible to read the canon in such a way that it refers explicitly to abortion but a more natural reading would limit the explicit reference to sterilization. Even in this reading, however, abortion would be at least implicitly included. If a person who causes sterility in another must be considered a murderer, there is more reason to make the same charge against one who causes another to abort. But the canon deals with the act of an outside agent, not with an abortion caused by the mother herself. So there is question of harming another, and one who does this kind of harm to another must be held as a murderer. In the canon immediately preceding (canon 88) Regino says the same thing about castrating another.

Regino says that he took these canons from the Roman law, more specifically from the *Sententiae Iulii Pauli.* Generally speaking, Regino shows great respect for the civil law, particularly the Roman law, and in a note following canon 89 he says that canon law is generally in agreement with the civil law. The law in question here is the *Lex Cornelia de sicariis et veneficis* and Paulus deals with it in the Fifth Book of his *Sententiae,* Title XXIII. The canon on castration is clearly there,[47] but there is no canon like the *Si aliquis* in that section of Paulus. The canon following the one on castration in Paulus is the canon *(Qui abortionis)* on abortion.[48] If this is the model for Regio's canon, it was certainly altered in the transmission. If the *poculum amatorium* in Paulus could be interpreted as a sterilizing potion, one might argue that Regino merely made it more explicit in his canon. But even if this were true, there would still be a great difference between Regino's canon and Paulus. In Paulus, the guilty party will be charged with murder only if some one dies. Regino says nothing about the death of the other party but charges the person with murder without qualification. Another possibility to be considered is that canon 89 is nothing more than a further refinement of the canon on castration and therefore dependent on Paulus' canon on castration. The parallel here would be much closer, that is, if in those times giving someone something to prevent generation or conception would have been considered as serious a crime as castration. Paulus does impose the death sentence for castration, so the punishment would be the same. But the canon in Regino as it stands does not have a literal parallel in Paulus. It may well be that Regino, like many of his contemporaries, did not scruple about tampering with his sources or even claiming a false source to give his canons authority. Whatever its origin, the *Si aliquis* expresses a tradition that goes back at least to Jerome and will occupy a central position in the discussion of abortion for many centuries in the future.

At about this time also those condemning abortion and sterilizing procedures begin to appeal neither to the ecclesiastical canons nor the penitential books, but to the Fathers. For instance, Ratherius, bishop of Verona (d. 974), cites St. Augustine's *De nuptiis et concupiscentiis*, and particularly the text that later became a byword in this whole discussion, the so-called *Aliquando* text.[49] What made appeal to the Fathers more popular at this time was the appearance of many so-called *florilegia*, collections of passages from the early Fathers.[50] It is possible, of course, that the authors mentioned above used the Fathers themselves, but it seems more likely that they took advantage of these *florilegia*. What is important, though, is that this appeal to the Fathers reflects a move away from a strictly canonical or penitential approach and marks the beginnings of an interest in *sententiae* (opinions) rather than canons. This interest was destined to flourish, and eventually reach its peak in the *Sententiae* of Peter Lombard.

The next work of importance appeared at the beginning of the eleventh century and was authored by Burchard, bishop of Worms. His *Decretum* (1012-1022) was a collection of ecclesiastical and penitential canons, probably the most complete collection up to his time. He deals with abortion in Book XVII under the heading *De fornicatione*.[51] The councils he cites are the usual ones, Elvira, Ancyra, and Lerida, and from the penitentials he chooses the so-called *Roman Penitential* of Halitgar. It will be remembered that this dealt with an abortion caused by the mother without reference to any previous sin and the penance was three years. But what is of more interest is that he includes Regino's *Si aliquis*, and apparently in reference to abortion, but without Regino's inscription. Burchard, like a number of his contemporaries, exercises great freedom in dealing with his sources. For instance, he removed all those inscriptions which related legislation in any way to the civil authority, apparently for the reason that he refused to recognize the competence of any civil authority in reference to ecclesiastical matters. In this respect he was just the opposite of Regino himself, who seemed to feel that there was a close relationship between the two. Burchard presented the *Si aliquis* as a canon of a Council of Worms, his own diocese. It is certainly not the canon on abortion of the council of 868, which has already been cited, and there is no such canon on record from any other Council of Worms up to his time. It is possible that the canon was picked up from Regino by a Council of Worms of which there is no record, but it seems more likely that this is just another example of the liberty which Burchard took with his sources.

Burchard takes up the question of abortion again in Book XIX called the *Corrector*. This book which provided an interrogatory for confessors was circulated widely as a separate work for their benefit. Here again one finds a mixture of ecclesiastical canons and canons from penitentials, but strangely enough, the canons cited in Book XVII do not appear. The ecclesiastical canon he uses is Martin of Braga's version of Ancyra which extended the decree of Ancyra to cover sterilization. In support of this extension he quotes Caesarius of Arles' dictum that as often as one resorts to such things as sterilization, he is guilty of as many homicides as there might have been children. But with Bede he says that it makes a difference whether this is done by a poor woman because she cannot afford to feed another child. The penance for her will be three years. After this he cites the canon of Lerida, at least to the extent that it reduces the penance (for the ordinary sinner) to sev-

en years. This is also the penance he imposes on one who
gives something to another to cause abortion. For the
woman who causes an abortion on herself he abandons the
Roman Penitential for one that distinguishes between an
abortion before the fetus has been animated and one after
the *spiritus*.

The *Decretum* of Burchard, and particularly the *Corrector*, exercised great influence, but apparently for only a
short time. In the middle of the eleventh century the Gregorian reform movement, initiated by Leo IX, started a
new trend.[52] Like many previous movements it aimed at
restoring the ancient discipline and strengthening the bond
with the Holy See. The old collections, the *Hadriana* and
the *Hispana*, were still available, but new and more
methodic collections were needed. The collection of Burchard, which had replaced that of Regino, was sufficiently
recent, but for many reasons was not a suitable document
to promote the ideas of the reform. The partisans of reform
saw clearly the defects of many penitentials and collections, as well as their manipulation of texts. Peter Damian
condemned these works severely for mixing "fables" with
the sacred canons.[53] He also questioned their authorship
and the Roman origin of those for which it is claimed. Cardinal Atton, an aide of Gregory VII, complains of the multiplicity of apocryphal texts beginning with the famous
Roman Penitential. He charges that the claim of Roman
origin for this work is totally unfounded.[54] The first duty of
the canonists of the reform is to rid the Church of all these
apocryphal texts. To do this a very simple but effective way
offers itself: to accept as canonical only those texts approved, at least tacitly, by the Holy See.

The most important collections of this period were
those attributed to Ivo, bishop of Chartres. The *Decretum*
of Burchard, as already pointed out, was not able to satisfy
the demands created by the reform. On the other hand,
collections produced in Rome according to this spirit were
inspired by a mentality too exclusively Roman to satisfy
clergy north of the Alps. While these clergy were imbued
with the spirit of the reform, they were still unwilling to

turn their backs on the mass of texts produced since the Carolingian reform. It was up to Ivo somehow to replace the *Decretum* of Burchard with a collection that would reflect the reform without abandoning the work of the last few centuries.

In his *Decretum* Ivo takes up abortion under the heading *De homicidio*.[55] A movement away from the penitential books is easily detected here, since Ivo does no more than cite Ancyra, Lerida, and the canon of Martin of Braga; there is no reference to any prescriptions from the penitential books. But more important for the future discussion of abortion is his use of the Fathers, particularly Augustine and Jerome. In his *Decretum* he cites the familiar *Aliquando* in which Augustine charges that those who take sterilizing potions or cause abortion are not acting like husbands and wives but fornicators.[56] The other texts deal with the classification of abortion as homicide.[57] In his *Panormia* these latter texts are all cited under the heading: One who procures an abortion before the soul is infused into the body is not a homicide.[58] Augustine himself was uncertain whether to identify this with the time of formation, but the second text ascribed to him, which was really authored by Ambrosiaster, does this clearly, and this was certainly a long-standing tradition by the time of Ivo. This same set of texts collected under the same heading would later be taken over by Gratian and Peter Lombard, and from this vantage point would exercise a great influence on the thinking about abortion from the beginning of the second millenium until the middle of the nineteenth century. The identification of the time of infusion with the time of formation would be reinforced by the rediscovery of Aristotle in the West.

———————————◄———————————

During this period private penance which originated in Ireland and England spread to the Continent. Generally speaking, although the penance itself seemed more severe than public penance, the period of penance was shorter. In dealing with abortion the penitential books ordinarily prescribe a penance of about three years duration, or if they make a distinction, a one-three year penance based on a forty-day dividing line. Although these penitentials do not speak explicitly of the time of formation or animation, it seems safe to assume that the penances are graded on this basis. Only two Irish penitentials bring in a third stage of development, speaking of the change of liquid into flesh and then into animated flesh, but these did not enjoy much of a following. Although the penalty for abortion was generally less than that for ordinary homicide, many of these penitentials classified abortion, at least after forty days, as homicide.

Since public penance fell largely into disuse by the year 600, private penance spread rapidly on the Continent, due largely to the missionary efforts of the Irish monks, and until the middle of the eighth century, met with little opposition. At that time the so-called Carolingian reform movement attempted to restore the ancient discipline. It did this by reviving some of the old collections, particularly the *Dionysiana* and the *Hispana*, as well as by the publication of new collections. For many reasons, however, efforts to stamp out the practice of private penance were unsuccessful. Some of the new collections, for example, that of Halitgar, represented a willingness to compromise with private penance. Eventually a solution which prescribed public penance only for public sins, allowing private penance for private sins, was accepted. In this situation the penances for abortion legislated by the councils would be imposed only for abortions that were public. Abortions that did not come to the public attention would be subject to private penance, that is, the penances prescribed in the penitential books.

The most important collection after Halitgar was that of Regino of Prum. Like Halitgar he made use not only of the canonical legislation of the past, but also of the penitential books. The most important contribution Regino made was the famous canon *Si aliquis*, which was to play an important part in the treatment of abortion for centuries to come. Like Halitgar, who falsely claimed a Roman (ecclesiastical) source for his penitential, Regino claimed, just as falsely, the Roman civil law as the source of his canon. Later Burchard, using the same kind of liberty, claimed a Council of Worms as the source of this canon. The canon, which seemed to refer more explicitly to sterilization than abortion, charged anyone who caused another to be sterile with homicide. This charge had been made several times in patristic literature, but on the legislative level attempts to prevent conception were not put in the same category as abortion except in the version of Ancyra published by Martin of Braga.

Shortly after Burchard, in the middle of the eleventh century, another reform movement began, this time under Hildebrand, who later became Gregory VII. The reform was aimed at restoring the ancient discipline and union with the Holy See. To this end it stimulated new collections, with the particular goal of ridding the Church of all the apocryphal works of the past centuries. The false claims of Halitgar and Regino were just samples of a practice that was somewhat widespread. The most important representative of this movement was Ivo, bishop of Chartres, to whom is attributed three very influential works of the period. He is important in the discussion of abortion because of his apparent acceptance of the opinion that abortion does not constitute homicide until the soul is infused into the body. What is chiefly significant is his appeal to the Fathers rather than the penitential books, as the source of this position. The position was adopted by Gratian and eventually was given official acceptance by Innocent III.

CHAPTER SIX

Canonical Development
from Gratian to 1300

From the beginning of the fourth century one has witnessed an accumulation of local legislation regarding abortion. This legislation was related to penitential discipline and was part of a general pattern. Universal legislation in dealing with moral matters simply did not exist. Even on the level of public penance the norms set down by Ancyra, Elvira, Lerida, and Martin of Braga regarding abortion differed considerably. It is quite true that the norm of Ancyra was generally accepted, but it was never legislated as a general norm for all to abide by. With the introduction of the penitential books new norms were introduced and without benefit even of local legislative authority. They were norms based on the prudent judgment of pious and holy men, the authors of the penitential books, and there was a multiplicity of them. The Carolingian reform of the middle of the eighth century and the Gregorian reform of the eleventh century both attempted to bring order and even unity into penitential discipline, but neither of these movements met with complete success. The Roman Church was obviously interested and involved in both of these reforms, but perhaps too concerned with dogmatic disputes and unity in belief to give attention to unity in penitential practice. Had the difference been on the level of doctrine, the Roman Church might well have played a more decisive role.

Whatever may have been the reason, the Roman Church during this period did not see fit to legislate a unified practice in penitential discipline but allowed considerable local freedom. Some in the Church did not see any difficulty in allowing the great variety of local practices to continue, even though they had long since passed beyond local boundaries and were causing considerable confusion. They saw these practices as different, but not necessarily opposed to one another. Others felt that some kind of reconciliation of all these practices was needed to eliminate the confusion to which they were giving rise. The revival of interest in Roman civil law also encouraged this desire for unification of the law. Someone was needed to do for church law what Justinian had done for Roman civil law. It was undoubtedly this desire for some kind of codification and unification that led Gratian (d. c. 1160) to project his *Concordia canonum discordantium*.[1] He was trying to bring some order into the chaos brought about by the multiplicity of canonical collections in existence with their catalogs of different and, perhaps, even opposing disciplinary practices.

Very little is known about the life of Gratian except that he was a Camaldolese monk and belonged to the school of Bologna. There is no doubt that his *Concordia* is a classical work in the area of church law, and this in spite of the fact that Gratian himself enjoyed no authoritative position in the Church. Although it had no ecclesiastical authority, it became known as the *Decretum Gratiani*. Benedict XIV was to state later that it did not have the force of law and that its contents had only whatever authority they would have had if they were never published in the *Decretum*. For instance, it contains some of the false decrees of Isidore. These decrees would not gain any authority because they were in the *Concordia*.

When he took up the subject of abortion, Gratian had three sources from which to draw, the early canons, the penitential books, and the Fathers. Curiously enough, he made use neither of the early canons nor the penitential books, but only the Fathers. Actually the source of the basic theses he chose on abortion was the *Decretum* and the *Panormia* of Ivo of Chartres.[2] The first thesis was that of the familiar *Aliquando* text of Augustine; namely, that married people who use drugs to cause sterility are not acting like marriage partners but fornicators.[3] The *Aliquando*, of course, was speaking of abortion as well as sterilization, but looked upon both of these as violations of the marital bond. The second thesis speaks only of abortion, and in reference to the question of homicide rather than the marital bond.[4] The thesis is that before the human soul is infused abortion does not constitute homicide. Presumably, this statement condenses the thought found in the passages cited from Augustine and Jerome. It says nothing explicitly about the time of infusion of the human soul. As already mentioned, Augustine himself was not ready to delay this until the time of formation, although he seemed willing to go along with the Mosaic law that abortion would not be considered homicide until the fetus was formed. The author of the second text attributed to Augustine, really Ambrosiaster, clearly identifies the time of infusion with the time of formation. Even though the summary statement mentioned above does not do this, there seems to be no doubt that this is the tradition.

Gratian refers in passing to abortion in two other sections. In the one he is really dealing with infanticide. He quotes Pope Stephen VI (885-891) who is arguing that if abortion is considered homicide, there is more reason to classify the slaughter of a two- or three-day-old infant under the same heading.[5] Some have tried to maintain that since no distinction is made here between abortion before the soul is infused and abortion after infusion, Gratian is not being consistent with himself.[6] But the absence of such a distinction in this text should not be overinterpreted.

Stephen, after all, was not talking primarily about abortion, but infanticide. Moreover, his argument would have been valid even if abortion was considered homicide only during the latter part of pregnancy. And there was general agreement on this point. It would have served no purpose to bring in the distinction regarding early pregnancy.

In another section Gratian takes up a case presented in a decretal falsely attributed to Pope Gelasius.[7] The question is one of imputability rather than classification and it deals with a certain Placidus whose wife is run down by a team of horses and suffers an abortion. Since Placidus was driving the team, which was apparently out of control, the question of his culpability was brought up. The response was that if Placidus was stealing the horses, he would be at fault. But if his wife was run down by accident, he should not be held by the law.

In treating abortion, then, Gratian bypassed all the penitential legislation of the past, not to mention the prescriptions of the penitential books. It was certainly simpler to do this than to attempt to reconcile the confusing mass of prescriptions from the past confronting him. Moreover, at that time the task of prescribing penance was moving from the external (legal) forum into the hands and judgment of the priest confessor. It must be admitted, of course, that the *Decretum* does include penitential legislation in other areas, so this cannot be the whole explanation. Whatever may have been his reason for bypassing past penitential legislation, he did not succeed totally in burying it. The *Si aliquis*, in particular, with its more extensive concept of homicide will reappear in the *Decretals* of Gregory IX and continue to compete with Gratian's more restrictive definition.

The glossators of the *Decretum* concentrated to a large extent on the case of Placidus. The abortion in the case was in some sense accidental, and the question concerned Placidus' responsibility. The question of responsibility for accidental abortion was not a new one. The original law in Exodus seemed to cover a case of accidental abortion and appeared to presume the culpability of the person who struck the woman. But in Deuteronomy it was stated that damage would not be imputed if it resulted from an act of God, even though a human agent was involved. So not all accidental damage was imputed to the human agent. The original Roman law *(Lex Cornelia de sicariis et veneficis)* dealing with homicide called for *dolus* (evil intent) which would have ruled out a penalty for accidental homicide, but a *senatusconsultus* extended the law to cover a case where there was no *dolus* but only *malum exemplum* (bad example). With this extension the law would also apply to accidental homicide. The response in the present case said that if the wife was trampled accidentally and there was no evidence of bad will on the part of the husband, he should not be held by the law. But if he had taken someone else's team of horses, he would be held responsible.

It was because of the ambiguity of the response that the glossators gave their attention to the case. One of the glossators interpreted the response to mean that if Placidus were driving someone else's team, he should have warned his wife of the danger, which would not have been necessary if he had been driving his own horses.[8] In the latter case, he could have assumed that his wife would know the horses well enough to avoid the danger. It was because he failed to warn his wife of the danger that he was culpable. Another argued that if he was stealing the horses he would be responsible precisely because he was doing something illicit.[9] Still others argued that even if he was stealing the horses, although he would be guilty of theft, he would not be responsible for the subsequent abortion if it were accidental.[10] As authority for this stand Ioannes Teutonicus (d.c. 1240) cites Pope Nicholas in a reply to Bishop Osbald regarding a priest who had struck a deacon on horseback. The deacon fell off the horse and died of a broken neck. Was the priest guilty of homicide, and therefore excluded from the exercise of his priesthood? The response of Nicholas was that if the deacon died directly from the blow, the priest would be deprived permanently of his office. But if the deacon died from the fall rather than the blow, the priest would not be held guilty of homicide.

This would imply that even though one is doing something illicit, he will not be responsible for resulting damage unless he himself is the real cause of the damage. Applying this to the case of Placidus, one would have to conclude that he would not have been held responsible for the abortion simply because he was doing something wrong (stealing the horses) when it occurred.

Teutonicus cited the reply of Nicholas in response to the position taken by Huguccio.[11] Huguccio argued in the case that Placidus would not be held by the *Lex Cornelia*, since it called for *dolus*. But he claimed that he would be bound by the canons which make one who is doing something illicit responsible for whatever damage follows upon his illicit act. Eventually, the norm represented in the response of Nicholas would be generally accepted, but for the time being the requirements for responsibility for accidental damage would continue to be debated.

A much more important discussion built up around Gratian's distinction between the fetus before and after the infusion of the soul in classifying abortion as homicide. Roland Bandinelli (d. 1181), who later became Alexander III, seemed to be in sympathy with the distinction, arguing that homicide means killing a *man (homo)*, and that therefore procuring an abortion before the fetus is formed should not be classified as homicide.[12] But he goes on to add that even the will to kill is considered homicide, whether the effect follows or not, and that in this sense one who destroys a fetus to keep it from being animated or born can be called a murderer, in the same way as one who prevents crime can be called an *extirpator vitiorum* (preventer of crime) as much as one who stamps it out.

A similar approach is taken by Magister Rufinus (d. 1190) in his *Summa decretorum*. In commenting on the *Aliquando* in the *Decretum*, he says that sterility can be brought about in two ways: either by preventing conception or by destroying the fetus in the womb. In the latter case it is called abortion.[13] In dealing with the first way of causing sterility he has recourse to Burchard *(Si aliquis)* and the Council of Worms, and says that one who does something to another to prevent conception should be considered a homicide. But his penance will be less than the regular seven-year penance for homicide and the judgment will be left up to the priest. As for abortion, if it was not voluntary, the woman will not be held responsible. But she should do some penance *propter habundantem cautelam*.[14] Similarly, if someone causes a woman to abort accidentally, he should do some penance. But if the abortion is voluntary, whether caused by the woman herself or someone else, if the fetus is not formed, the penance will be three years. But if the fetus is formed, since the soul is infused at this time, the person causing the abortion will do the regular penance for homicide because this is actual homicide.

In commenting on the next chapter (Chapter 8) of the *Decretum*, Rufinus claims that here Augustine was arguing against the traducianists who maintained that the soul was "created" at the same time as the body.[15] He comments that Augustine, in making the distinction between the formed fetus and the unformed fetus and limiting the classification of homicide to the former, was speaking of actual homicide, that is, *quantum ad actum, non quantum ad reatum* (relative to the act, not to the guilt). If one causes the abortion of an unformed fetus, although he has not killed a man *(homo)*, he is *reus homicidii*. To establish this point, he argues that if even a person who does something to prevent conception must be considered a homicide, for a greater reason the one who causes the abortion of an unformed fetus should be so considered. He then argues like Roland that if one has the will to kill someone, whether the effect follows or not, he is a homicide. He will be guilty of homicide before God, but he will not be punished by the Church as much as one who is guilty of actual homicide, since greater punishment is meted out for actual homicide than intentional homicide.

What is significant in the commentary of both Roland and Rufinus is the reservation both make in Gratian's thesis regarding abortion and homicide. Both want to extend the category of homicide, at least in some sense, beyond the destruction of the animated or formed fetus. Roland extends it to the abortion of the unformed fetus, and Rufinus, appealing to the *Si aliquis*, extends it even to contraception. They do this by distinguishing between actual homicide and *reatus homicidii*, by which they mean the intention of homicide. While they admit some difference between the two, and allow for a lighter penance for the latter, they would want to put both of these actions in the general category of homicide. A quite similar approach was taken by Gandulphus, a professor of Bologna, toward the end of the twelfth century. So while all these authors accept Gratian's thesis, they all feel the need to reconcile it with a more inclusive understanding of homicide. These efforts will continue for some time to come.

Ioannes Teutonicus in dealing with this issue observes that even though the law of Moses does not consider abortion of the unformed fetus homicide, the Cornelian law as well as the Aquilian law both punish it.[16] He cites the *Si mulierem* of Ulpian which imposes exile on a woman who causes the abortion of her own child. The Aquilian law penalizes one who strikes a pregnant (slave) woman or a pregnant mare.[17] Much more interesting, however, is his observation that the civil law also distinguishes between the unanimated and the animated fetus, imposing the death penalty on the abortion of an animated fetus.[18] He cites here the *Qui abortionis* of Iulius Paulus. It will be seen later that Accursius, a glossator of the *Corpus iuris civilis*, in his gloss on the *Divus* says that it holds only for the first forty days. After that there is question of homicide and hence the *Lex Pompeia de parricidiis*. And this would also apply to the *Qui abortionis*. But the distinction is found neither in Paulus himself nor in the later *Digest* of Justinian. It has to be considered the result of a medieval effort to bring canon law and civil law into accord. It appears that Teutonicus is reading this distinction into the *Qui abortionis*.

The *Concordia* of Gratian by no means put an end to the collections of canons that were so common before it was published. The *Concordia* did not contain all the church legislation of the previous centuries and ecclesiastical legislation did not stop with it. Besides studying the glosses and commentaries on Gratian, then, one must continue to follow the work of the collectors or compilers. The most important of these *compilationes* was the work of Bernard of Pavia (d. 1215). Unlike Gratian, who dealt with abortion under the general heading of sins of married people, Bernard, more in the tradition of Ivo, deals with it under the heading *De homicidio*. Another characteristic of his treatment is his recourse to scripture as well as law as a source.[19] In discussing abortion he uses the classic text from Exodus, but according to the Vulgate version. In his commentary on the text, however, he refers to Gratian's distinction between the formed and unformed fetus.[20] He continues to comment that several possibilities must be considered, the death of both mother and child, the death of one or the other, and the death of neither. Thus there may be a double homicide, a single homicide, or no homicide at all. It also makes a difference in assigning the penance whether the person caused the abortion deliberately or accidentally. He states finally, that according to the law of the Church even if the fetus was not formed, the penance for homicide should be imposed. For this he refers the reader to the *Si aliquis*, which he cites under canon 13. He sees a contradiction between this position and that of Exodus, at least as the law is stated in Gratian, but he explains this away by saying that the one norm belongs to the Old Testament, the *Si aliquis* to the New Testament, that is, the law of the Church.

It was not long, however, before the highest ecclesiastical authority for the distinction between the animated and unanimated fetus was provided. Innocent III made use of the distinction in a response to a Carthusian prior regarding one of his monks. The monk, indulging in some kind of levity with a woman (whom he had made pregnant) caused an abortion, and the question was whether he would have to give up his ministry. According to canon law he would have to do so if he was guilty of homicide. Innocent's response to the prior, the *Sicut ex litterarum*, stated that if the conceptus was not yet *vivificatus*, he could continue his ministry; otherwise, not.[21] This was an implicit recognition by the highest ecclesiastical authority of the distinction between the formed and unformed (animated and unanimated) fetus, and the classification of only the former as homicide. To be precise, however, it should be observed that the explicit reference is only to the clerical status of the monk. Nothing is said about the validity of the distinction in other contexts. But the response made its way to Bernard's *Compilatio IV*,[22] and from there into the *Decretals* of Gregory IX, where it would give rise to considerable controversy.

During the century that followed the appearance of the *Decretum* legislative activity continued with such vigor that in less than a hundred years the situation of confusion that existed before the *Decretum*, and which it was intended to remedy, recurred. During that period five new compilations of legislation appeared. These collections not only contained the new legislation that was enacted since the *Decretum* but also some previous legislation which Gratian for one reason or another had bypassed. Moreover, the work of Gratian was the work of a jurist and had only the authority of the school behind it. What was needed now was not only a new concordance, but a work that would have behind it both the authority of the school and that of the Holy See, that is, legislative authority. It was with this in mind that Gregory IX engaged the services of Raymond of Pennaforte (d. 1275), a Dominican canonist who studied at Bologna, to publish a new collection.

This new collection, the *Decretales* (1234), has both the authority of Gregory IX and the learning of Raymond of Pennaforte behind it. More than Gratian, Raymond depended on previous canonical legislation for his *Decretales*. Significant in this respect is his selection of the *Si aliquis* rather than passages from the Fathers in dealing with the question of sterilization and abortion.[23] It appears under the general heading *De homicidio*. Like his predecessor, Burchard, Raymond also traces this canon to a Council of Worms, although it more likely has its origin in

Regino of Prum who claims to have taken it from Iulius
Paulus.[24] Raymond revises the wording of the canon
somewhat but does not seem to change the meaning of it
significantly. It clearly goes counter to the Gratian thesis
which saw only the abortion of the formed fetus as
homicide.[25] The *Si aliquis* in the *Decretals* classifies as
homicide all efforts to prevent conception or offspring, and
hence sterilization and abortion of the unformed as well as
the formed fetus.

But the position of the *Decretals* on this question is not
unambiguous. Another canon on abortion contains the response *Sicut ex litterarum* of Innocent III to the Carthusian
prior regarding the possible irregularity of one of his
monks.[26] It will be remembered that the monk engaging in
some kind of levity with a pregnant woman caused her to
miscarry. The *Decretals* list this canon under the heading:
One who causes an abortion is guilty of homicide if the
conceptus is animated with a rational soul; otherwise not.
There is at least a superficial contradiction between this
canon and its heading, and the *Si aliquis* mentioned above.
In choosing the *Si aliquis* Raymond seemed to be opting
against the Gratian thesis that only the abortion of the
formed fetus would be classified as homicide. Is he now
reverting to the position he seemed to be taking a stand
against? The work of reconciling these two positions,
which antedated the *Decretals*, will continue to occupy the
attention of Raymond's successors and commentators.

As for Raymond himself, an attempt to reconcile the
two canons is given in his *Summa de penitentia*.[27] There he
asks whether one who strikes a woman or gives her a drug
(or whether a woman who takes a drug) to cause an abortion
or prevent conception should be considered a murderer or
incur an irregularity. His response is that the one who does
this will not be considered a murderer as far as the irregularity is concerned unless an animated fetus is aborted. But
he will be considered a murderer in regard to sacramental
penance. And so will the one who gives or takes a drug to
prevent conception. What Raymond is saying here is that

although all abortion, and even sterilization, must be classified as homicide, the irregularity will be incurred only for
aborting an animated fetus. The person who does these
other things is committing the sin of murder and must
approach the sacrament of penance for forgiveness and
sacramental penance, but he does not incur the irregularity. Raymond seems to be willing here to accept two different concepts of homicide, a broad one that would apply to
the sacrament of penance, and a strict one that would be
used in dealing with irregularities.

Others in trying to reconcile these two approaches to
abortion (and sterilization) look to the civil law to explain it.
Goffredus de Trano (d. 1245), for instance, argues that
abortion is considered homicide in civil penal law and
appeals to the *Qui abortionis* to support this point.[28] He
agrees with Raymond that it must also be considered
homicide as far as spiritual penances are concerned, point-
ing to the *Si aliquis* as proof. But the canonical irregularity
attached to corporal homicide will not be incurred unless
one kills a person already born or a formed fetus. A similar
position is taken by Innocent IV (d. 1254),[29] Bernard of
Parma (d. 1263),[30] and Bernard of Montemirato.[31]

Not all interpreters of the law agreed with this solution.
Henricus de Segusio (d. 1271) in his *Summa* does not want
to admit any discrepancy between the civil law and canon
law.[32] He argues that since homicide involves killing a
homo, it is impossible to commit real homicide before the
soul is infused into the body. He admits that the *Si aliquis*
seems to imply a more inclusive definition of homicide.
Some want to say that this is more in accord with civil law,
since even one who gives another a love potion is considered a homicide in civil law. Henricus says that one has to
distinguish between interpretive and real homicide. The
distinction is clear, according to him, in civil law. If the
fetus is unformed, one who strikes a woman and causes an
abortion is charged according to the *Lex Aquilia* (not the
Lex Cornelia de sicariis) with causing damage, not with
homicide. Similarly, a woman who causes an abortion before the fetus is formed is not put to death but sent into

exile *(Si mulierem)*. The death penalty is imposed only if the fetus is formed. Here he cites the *Qui abortionis* stating that the death penalty will be imposed only if a *homo* perishes. The civil law imposing penalties for abortion as homicide is in accord with the canon law regarding irregularities. Both consider only the abortion of the formed fetus homicide. To the extent that the *Si aliquis* is more inclusive, it must be understood to be speaking of interpretive rather than real homicide.

Other authors come up with other, although similar, distinctions in trying to explain the discrepancy between Gratian and the *Decretals*, or perhaps more pointedly the discrepancy between canons 5 and 20 of the *Decretals*. Guido de Baysio (d. 1313), known as the Archdeacon, distinguishes between homicide in act and homicide in will.[33] Actual homicide involves the killing of a man (already born) or a formed fetus. Homicide in will or virtual homicide occurs when one does something to prevent a human being from coming into existence. What all these authors may be groping for is a distinction between sin and crime. This became explicit in William Durand (d. 1296), who simply bypassed the whole question of homicide and asked when abortion is a sin and when it is a crime.[34] He responds that it is always a mortal sin but becomes a crime (and therefore subject to ecclesiastical penalty) only when a formed fetus is aborted. Although he does not deal explicitly with the issue of homicide, his response is moving in the direction of Gratian's thesis, which eventually won general acceptance.

Commentators on the *Decretum* and the *Decretales* have often appealed to Roman law regarding abortion. This was done, for instance, by Ioannes Teutonicus in his gloss on the *Decretum*. He was making the point that even when an abortion (of an unformed fetus) was not considered homicide in the Mosaic law it was still punished by the civil law. He mentioned explicitly the *Si mulierem* of the *Lex Cornelia de sicariis* and added the *Lex Aquilia* as well. What is surprising, however, is his attribution of the distinction between the animated and unanimated fetus to the civil law, and without any attempt to justify it. Goffredus de Trano, in commenting on the *Decretals* even went so far as to say that in the civil law (as in the *Si aliquis*) all abortion was considered homicide, citing the *Qui abortionis* of Iulius Paulus as his source. Henricus de Segusio, like Ioannes Teutonicus, found the distinction between the formed and unformed fetus in the civil law. He adds that the law regarding a woman who causes an abortion on herself must be understood in this sense also. If the fetus is not formed, she will be exiled. The death penalty will be meted out only if the fetus is formed. He establishes this interpretation by an appeal to the *Qui abortionis* of Paulus, arguing that this is what is meant when it says that if a *homo* dies, the death penalty will be imposed. Otherwise a lesser penalty will be imposed according to the social status of the culprit. He is interpreting the *homo* in the law to include a formed fetus.

It is not easy to reconcile these interpretations of Roman law with the picture of Roman law presented in an earlier chapter. There is no evidence to indicate that it classified all abortion as homicide. The *Qui abortionis* may be open to the interpretation offered by Henricus, but such an interpretation might have surprised Paulus himself. In Roman times the fetus was considered part of the mother until it was born. One who accepted this position could hardly classify the abortion of the formed fetus as homicide. The interpretations of the canonists mentioned above seem to spring from efforts which were being made at the time to bring about a reconciliation between Roman law and canon law, and vice versa. These commentators were all canonists, but they were not alone in their efforts. Accursius, a thirteenth-century civil jurist and glossator of Justinian's *Digest*, introduced the distinction between the formed and unformed fetus into his gloss on the *Divus*.[35] He comments that the punishment of exile for the woman who causes an abortion on herself holds for the first forty days, because at this time the fetus is not yet a *homo*. After forty days the woman would be charged with homicide not only according to the law of Moses but also according to the *Lex Pompeia de parricidiis*. The latter legislation dealt with the murder of children by parents. Bartolus, a later commentator, accepted this distinction but added that if the abortion was done for money, the death penalty would be imposed without distinction.[36] He explicitly traces the distinction between the animated and unaimated fetus to the *Sicut ex litteris* in the *Decretals*. It should be remarked at this time that this response in the *Decretals* represents a movement in the direction of leniency whereas the introduction of the distinction into Roman law involved a tightening of the law.

Not all the commentators on the civil law accepted the canonical distinction. Baldus de Ubaldis, for instance, held on to the old Roman concept of the fetus.[37] It was not to be considered a *homo* as long as it was in the womb, and even after it was animated. From later authors, however, it seems clear that the abortion of the formed fetus was generally considered homicide in the civil law, at least from the time of Accursius. And the same was true of English civil law. Sir Henry Bracton in his *De legibus* says explicitly that if anyone strikes a pregnant woman or gives her an abortifacient, he is guilty of homicide if the fetus is formed or animated, and especially if it is animated.[38] A recent author traces this statement to Raymond of Pennaforte, but it has already been seen that the distinction between the formed (or animated) and unformed (or unanimated) fetus had a much earlier origin in the English penitentials, so it was not unknown to the English before the time of Sir Henry.[39] To what extent, if any, Bracton would want to distinguish between a formed and animated fetus is not clear. Certainly, it is not the formation as such that is of primary importance in this matter, but the infusion of the human soul, and it may be that this is what Bracton wanted to emphasize. If he wanted to allow for a time distinction between formation and animation, he was certainly going beyond Raymond. Precedent for this distinction was seen only rarely in the past, that is, in the *Old*

Irish Penitential, but since no criterion for animation (other than formation) was set down, it was impossible to understand this distinction. Conceivably, Bracton wanted to exclude from the charge of homicide the abortion of a formed fetus that was already dead, but this would have been a clear departure not only from Raymond but from the whole tradition. The issue had always been whether the human soul was already infused when the fetus was aborted, not whether the fetus was dead. The latter would have been a rather curious distinction, especially since more than likely the abortion itself caused the death of the fetus.

The period from Gratian to the end of the thirteenth century was marked by considerable controversy regarding the classification of abortion (and even sterilization) as homicide. The confusion was dispelled by general acceptance of the distinction between intentional (interpretative, spiritual) homicide and real or actual homicide. It was only to the latter that the Church attached an irregularity. Also, even though abortion of the unformed fetus and sterilization were considered homicide in some sense, a lesser sacramental penance was imposed for them than for abortion of the formed fetus. Later authors, bypassing to some extent the dispute about homicide, would distinguish between abortion as a sin and abortion as a crime. Irregularities (and ecclesiastical penalties) would be attached only to the latter, and only the abortion of the formed fetus would be classified as a crime.

At the same time interest in the Roman law was growing among ecclesiastical jurists. The period saw the application of the canonical distinction between the formed and unformed fetus also to the Roman law, and hence to civil penalties. There is no clear evidence that prior to this time abortion was ever classified in the Roman law as homicide.

The period also saw considerable discussion of the question of responsibility, particularly in cases where the abortion was accidental. This discussion brought out different points of view, but for purposes of the present work it is perhaps of less interest than that mentioned above. It will, however, provide a background for a controversy of later origin over the distinction between direct and indirect abortion. Although the distinction between accidental and deliberate or intentional abortion may not coincide perfectly with the above, it is clearly related.

CHAPTER SEVEN

Beginnings of
Theological Discussion
(1200-1500)

Before taking up the scholastic theologians of the period, it would be profitable to review briefly the development of thought regarding abortion that has already occurred. Abortion was condemned in the Church right from apostolic times. The early Fathers often condemned it as homicide, and if a parent was involved, parricide. Early penitential legislation made no distinction between the formed and unformed fetus; the penance was the same for any abortion, and it was quite severe. It was gradually lessened in the course of time, but the mitigation was not the result of any reclassification of the crime. It reflected rather a general tendency to temper penances imposed for sin. The distinction between the formed and unformed fetus was introduced by the Fathers from the Septuagint, but was not immediately accepted in the law. In fact conciliar legislation, rather than limit the classification of homicide to the formed fetus, tended to extend it to include even sterilization. This trend was epitomized in the canon *Si aliquis* of Regino of Prum. But the distinction between the formed and unformed fetus did make its way into the penitential books, and consequently into the practice of private penance. Many of these books classified only the abortion of the formed fetus as homicide. The abortion of the unformed fetus, while still a serious sin, did not merit as severe a penance. The distinction gradually made its way into ecclesiastical legislation, first on the local level, and eventually, through the *Sicut ex litterarum* of Innocent III, into the legislation of the whole Church. It might have been established without further questioning, had not Raymond of Pennafort chósen the *Si aliquis* as his basic canon on abortion. This involved the Decretists and the Decretalists who followed in attempts at reconciling these two positions. But it was clear from the beginning that even though sterilization and the abortion of the unformed fetus might be classified as homicide in some sense, the law did not attach an irregularity to them. The irregularity was attached only to the abortion of the formed fetus. Only this was considered homicide in the legal sense.

The contribution of the early scholastic theologians will be disappointing to anyone who expects from them a thorough theological discussion of abortion. For the most part they were content to accept the conclusions of their canonical predecessors. Attention has already been called to the fact that besides the strictly legal collections there began to appear broader based works called *Sententiae*. These *Sententiae*, besides legislation, also made use of scripture and the Fathers as theological sources. The most important of these *Sententiae* was easily that of Peter Lombard (1095-1160). In dealing with abortion it was not necessary for Lombard to do original work either in the Fathers or the Old Testament. That work, as pointed out, was already done by Ivo of Chartres, and made use of by Gratian. It is not certain whether Lombard was dependent on Ivo or Gratian, but he did nothing more than repeat the one or the other, using exactly the same texts from Augustine and Jerome, and adopting the same theses.[1] Husbands and wives who take sterilizing drugs and procure abortions are not acting like husbands and wives, but fornicators.

Yet they are not guilty of homicide unless the fetus is already formed and animated. Peter's second thesis is more explicit than the statement in Gratian, but it is not certain that he is saying any more. It does, however, clearly demand formation as well as animation for a homicidal charge, whatever one may want to hold about the possibility of prior animation.

Nor do the major commentaries on the *Sentences* go much more deeply into the question. The first important commentary was undoubtedly that of Albert the Great (1206-1280), a Dominican theologian. Albert's thesis is the same as that of Peter Lombard, but he presents it as a response to objections.[2] This method, used exclusively by St. Thomas in his *Summa*, became known as the scholastic method. One of the objections contends that parents who sterilize themselves should be called parricides, since in so doing they occasion homicide. Albert says that this is doubtful, since it is not certain that conception would take place anyhow, or if it did take place, that the fetus would be animated and eventually born. Another objection argues that sterilization is worse than abortion, since it is worse to destroy a whole field than to destroy a single crop. Similarly, it is worse to make a woman incapable of bearing any children than to destroy one or two. Albert admits that sterilization is probably more damaging, but denies that there is greater deformity in this sin than in abortion, and it is according to the amount of deformity that the gravity of a sin is assessed, not precisely the amount of damage.

Although he does not advance the theological discussion of abortion to any great extent, Albert is the first theologian to treat embryological development with any depth. In this as in other areas, he follows Aristotle, whom he was the first to rediscover for the Western World, although he also shows his independence. In dealing with the all-important question of the time of formation he gives three estimates. One estimate follows the Augustinian computation allowing forty-five days for formation. He puts it in meter as follows:

Semen conceptum sex primis rite diebus
Fit quasi lac, reliquisque movem fit sanguis; at illud
Consolidat duodena dies, bis nona deinceps
Effigiat, tempus sequens producit ad ortum.[3]

One will recognize the Augustinian time division here, six days as a milklike substance, nine days as blood, twelve days to coagulate into flesh, and eighteen days for figuration. The rest of the time is given over to quantitative growth. The second computation is similar to the above except that only nine days are allowed for configuration, making the total period of formation thirty-six instead of forty-five days.[4] The third estimate is strictly that of Aristotle.[5] It will be remembered that Aristotle's computation was supposedly based on experience with aborted fetuses. He called anything that came from the uterus during the first week an effluxion; after that it was an abortion.[6] He added that if a male embryo is aborted on the fortieth day and placed in water it holds together in a sort of membrane, but if it is placed in any other fluid it dissolves and disappears. If the membrane is ruptured, an embryo will be revealed, as big as one of the large kinds of ants, and all of the members will be plain to see. But the female embryo, if aborted during the first three months, is as a rule found to be undifferentiated. In the fourth month however it will be differentiated quickly.

Albert referred to the so-called "effluxions" as *corruptiones*, since they are nothing more than corrupt semen which has not been converted into blood or flesh.[7] As he says, following Augustine, the semen remains a milklike substance for the first six days. In speaking of the abortion of the male fetus on the fortieth day, he follows Aristotle quite closely, but adds that if it is recent the aborted conceptus will contract and expand when pricked with a needle, a clear sign that it is already animated.[8] Although it is not explicit in Aristotle, Albert's explanation of the time difference between male and female formation is undoubtedly Aristotelian in origin. He attributes the faster formation of the male to the greater physical heat in the male.[9] And there is greater physical heat in the male because the male is less humid. This will have to be judged a rather primitive explanation, but it represents the thinking that prevailed for many centuries. It can hardly have any more claim to validity than the evidence for the time differentiation it is meant to explain.

Bonaventure (1221-74), a Franciscan theologian, comments on the same distinction in the *Sentences* and responds to an objection against the seriousness of aborting an unanimated fetus.[10] It was objected that this could not be considered serious sin because it was not homicide, and therefore was not punished with death. Bonaventure admits that the abortion of the unanimated fetus does not constitute real homicide, but says that it points to a homicidal will. It is also definitely a *maleficium*. In response to the assertion that it is not a mortal sin because it is not punished by death he simply says that there are many mortal sins that are not punished by death.

There is no way of knowing whether anyone took the position that the abortion of the unaminated fetus was not a serious sin. And the same question would have to be raised about Albert's objection concerning the greater malice of sterilization. All that can be concluded from this study is that these questions were never raised before, and there is no evidence that they were raised later. They may have been nothing more than a scholastic device to introduce a thesis. What is more noteworthy is that all these scholastics accept the Gratian distinction. But it should be acknowledged that they were writing before the *Decretals* of Gregory IX, or at least too close to them to be influenced by them.

Implicit acceptance of the Gratian thesis may also be found in St. Thomas' (1227-74) commentary on the *Sentences*, although he is discussing sterilization rather than abortion.[11] He says that although taking sterilizing drugs is a serious sin and classified as a *maleficium* (since even brute beasts accept their offspring), it is less than homicide because something else might have prevented conception. The influence of Albert the Great will be seen in this response, not to mention the pagan writer, Ovid, but the treatment adds nothing new to the discussion.

Much more important for the future discussion of abortion is another part of St. Thomas' commentary on the *Sentences*, where he takes up the question of the time of animation of the fetus.[12] Here he clearly accepts the theory of delayed animation and the Aristotelian distinction regarding the time of male and female animation. But besides the Aristotelian computation (40 and 90 days), he also gives that of Augustine for the male fetus. He describes this development in dactyllic hexameters, as follows:

Sex in lacte dies, ter sunt in sanguine terni
Bis seni carnes, ter seni membra figurant.

The time division here, like that of Albert, is Augustinian (although Augustine added a day to make the computation fit in with the prophetic text in St. John). It is obviously impossible to pinpoint the end of formation, since it must vary from individual to individual, as Aristotle himself admitted. Also, much would depend on how complete a formation is understood. Certainly the formation would be more complete according to the Augustinian computation, but this would not necessarily rule out the Artistotelian figure (for male formation) as representing some lesser degree of completion. Modern authors will say that by the end of the seventh or eighth week the fetus will have all the internal organs of the adult and the familiar external features, although not fully developed.[13]

Following Aristotle, St. Thomas holds that the dynamic power of procreation is the male semen. The woman provides the matter, which both considered to be the menstrual blood. On this basis St. Thomas was able to say, for instance, that the body of Christ was formed from the blood of his mother.[14] He was also able to maintain that ordinarily the product of conception should be a male, since every agent tends to produce its like. According to St. Thomas a female will be the product of conception only when there is some defect in the semen or in the matter, although he grants that extrinsic forces may also be influential, for example, the southwind.[15] He does not explain, as does Albert, the reason for the slower formation of the female, but neither does he question it. Legislation on abortion after Albert and St. Thomas will no longer be satisfied to mention a forty-day dividing line between the formed and unformed fetus, but will speak explicitly of the time of female formation.

In his *Summa Theologiae* St. Thomas takes up questions pertinent to abortion only twice, and then only in dealing with objections. The first reference occurs in the question on homicide. He is discussing the issue of responsibility for accidental death, a question already familiar to the jurists.[16] St. Thomas argues that purely chance or accidental killing is unintentional; it is therefore not sinful. But it is possible for an act which is not willed *per se* to be willed *per accidens*, and this can happen in two ways. If one is doing something illicit and a death follows, the death is willed *per accidens*. Similarly, if one does not use the necessary caution and a death follows, it is also willed accidentally. In both of these cases the agent will not escape responsibility for the deaths that occur.

It is in response to an objection that he refers to abortion.[17] The objection is that one who strikes a pregnant woman (and causes an abortion) is charged with homicide even though the agent may not have intended to cause an abortion. Although it is not the primary issue, St. Thomas, accepting the Gratian distinction, states explicitly that the person will be charged with homicide only if the fetus is formed. He goes on to say that the person's basic responsibility will derive from the fact that in striking a pregnant woman he is doing something illicit, especially since such a blow is likely to cause an abortion. One might want to question the accidental nature of the abortion if it resulted from a blow likely to cause it, but it could still be that the one responsible did not know the woman was pregnant, or even if he did, that the blow as an expression of anger rather than an intention to cause an abortion. In either case the abortion would still be accidental, at least in the sense that it was unintentional. But it is not clear that St. Thomas has solved the problem of responsibility in either of these cases.

Another reference not dealing with abortion as such but pertinent to the discussion is found in the third part of the *Summa* where St. Thomas is discussing baptism.[18] He asks whether it is permissible to section the uterus of a pregnant woman if this is the only way to baptize the fetus. The argument in favor of doing this is that the eternal life of the fetus is more important than the temporal life of the mother, so that sacrificing the latter would be the lesser of two evils. St. Thomas refuses to allow this and quotes St. Paul (Rom 3:8) that evil may not be done in order to accomplish some good purpose. One may not, therefore, kill the mother to baptize the fetus. The assumption, which was certainly true in those days, was that a caesarean section on a live woman would have been a lethal procedure. The same would not be true today, so a negative response would no longer be called for. But it is clear in St. Thomas that killing the mother for the benefit of the fetus is not acceptable, even if a greater good is at stake.

Although the initial discussions of abortion by the theologians were not particularly impressive, they did constitute the beginnings of a tradition that would develop side by side with legal tradition, and gradually surpass it in importance. But in the fourteenth century the discussion of abortion was still carried on chiefly by the jurists, and ordinarily in connection with commentaries either on Gratian or the *Decretals* of Gregory IX. The whole issue of abortion as homicide would still be the subject of lively discussion. The only new question that was raised in this connection was that of the doubtfully animated fetus. Ioannes Andrea argued that in such cases animation was to be presumed and the person considered guilty of homicide.[19] He seems to be speaking in terms of the law, as well as the conscience of the guilty party. A distinction in this regard will be made only by later authors.

Also of interest to fourteenth century jurists was the question of responsibility for accidental abortion and that relating to the motivation behind abortions. The question of motivation, for instance, is taken up by Peter of Anchara (1330-1416)[20] and Ioannes Andrea (d. 1348).[21] Both are interpreting the expressions *causa libidinis* and *odii meditatione* as used in the *Si aliquis*. According to Andrea a lustful motive would pertain to those who wanted to have intercourse but because of poverty or embarrasment did not want to have children. The motive of hatred might have as its object either the husband or the child. The child might be unwanted because of the danger of diverting some inheritance. But what if the motive is not lust or hatred but love for the woman? What Andrea is referring to here is not altogether clear, but it may be that he is thinking of a love potion which causes an abortion or sterilization.[22] At any rate, his response is that he would still consider the act homicidal.

Andrea deals more directly with accidental abortion in commenting on the case of the Carthusian monk referred to in the *Sicut ex* of Innocent III. He remarks that although monks are supposed to be dead to the world they do not lose their power to procreate.[23] In discussing the imputability of the abortion to the monk he relies on the principle that it is imputable if it results from some illicit act, although he interprets this principle in a more inclusive way than some of his predecessors. He argues that the monk is responsible because monks should not be indulging in levity with women. The monk was therefore doing something illicit. The same could not be said if the person involved were the husband or brother of the woman, provided the game was otherwise harmless. Other commentators take a less rigid view of the imputability of effects following from illicit actions, and while they do not condone what the monk had done, will not impute the abortion to him unless there is some causal connection between what he has done and this unfortunate effect.[24] In other words, if the abortion was spontaneous, he would be no more responsible for it than a husband or a brother. The fact that he was a monk and should not have been indulging in levity with a woman would not of itself make him responsible for the abortion.

The commentators of the fifteenth century do not advance the legal discussion in any notable way. Such commentators as Dominicus de S. Geminiani (d. before 1436),[25] Nicholas of Tudeschi (1386-1435), commonly known as *Abbas Panormitanus*,[26] and Ioannes Turrecremata (1388-1466)[27] do little more than repeat what their predecessors have said. But it was at this time that considerable impetus was given to the theological discussion in the work of Antoninus (1389-1459), archbishop of Florence. Antoninus, who was also a Dominican, was obviously dependent in his *Summa* on the moral theology of St. Thomas, although he builds the section in which he treats homicide around the capital sins rather than the virtues. In this respect he is following more in the footsteps of the penitentials and the collections. He also gives much more attention to the question of abortion than does St. Thomas, but he is quite dependent on an unpublished work of another Dominican, John of Naples, also a follower of St. Thomas, who died around the middle of the first half of the fourteenth century.

Antoninus' first treatment of the moral aspect of abortion is found in his general discussion of homicide.[28] There he deals with it under the question whether homicide can be justified when necessary to avoid some evil. By way of example he speaks of women who have committed fornication, adultery, or incest and try to hide their crime by abortion or infanticide. They do this to preserve their reputation, or even their lives. Antoninus says that none of these reasons excuses them from a very serious sin. And if the child is not baptized, the sin is even more serious. He admits, however, that there will be no question of homicide in causing an abortion unless the fetus is already formed. He says that this occurs after forty days in the male fetus, eighty days in the female fetus, thus following in general the Aristotelian time distinction between male and female formation.[29] He goes on to say that it is not permissible for a woman, who is going to die anyhow, to shorten her life to save the fetus, nor on the contrary is it permittted to take the life of the fetus to save the mother. Anyone who does this, and all who cooperate with such a person, will be guilty of homicide. Although a little more detailed than the treatment of St. Thomas, it is clear that Antoninus is not making any significant addition to it.

Far more vital to the future discussion of abortion are his comments when he is speaking of the duties of physicians.[30] There he says that any physician who gives a woman medicine for an abortion to cover up some sin is guilty of mortal sin. But if he gives her such medicine to save her life, Antoninus says that a distinction must be made. For this distinction he cites the *Quodlibeta* of John of Naples, the fourteenth-century theologian already mentioned.[31] In dealing with this question John had distinguished between the animated and unanimated fetus. Following this distinction Antoninus says, quoting his source, that if the fetus is already animated, the doctor who gives the mother such a medicine is guilty of mortal sin. The reason is that it would cause both the physical and spiritual death of the fetus (who would die without baptism). Nor can the doctor be faulted for allowing the mother to die in these circumstances. By not giving the mother the medicine the doctor is neither directly nor indirectly responsible for her death. There is no direct responsibility because it is the disease that is causing the mother's death, not the lack of medicine as such. Nor is there any indirect responsibility, since there is no neglect present. There would be neglect only if the doctor failed to give the mother medicine which he could have and should have given her. In this case, although the medicine might have been available, the doctor could not legitimately give it to her because of the danger to the fetus.

Antoninus and his Dominican predecessor are the first authors to consider specifically the question of abortion to save the life of the mother. But in regard to the animated fetus they do no more than explicate the traditional teaching, which condemned abortion without exception. In dealing with the unanimated fetus, however, they depart from this teaching. For several centuries the distinction between the animated and unanimated fetus has been accepted by jurists and theologians. But it was used only for purposes of classification and distinguishing penalties. It was never used as a dividing line between moral and immoral abortion. Now Antoninus, relying on John of Naples, makes use of it in a limited way to allow for the abortion of the unanimated fetus to save the life of the mother. With John of Naples he says that the doctor may and should give the mother a medicine that would cause an abortion if necessary to save her life. Although this would prevent the animation of the fetus, it would not cause the death of a human being. On the other hand, it would save the life of a human being, the mother. But the doctor must be sure that the fetus is not animated. If he is not sure, it would not be permissible to cause the abortion.

Since Antoninus was one of the great moral theologians of all times, acceptance by him of this opinion undoubtedly assured it a hearing. In fact, it is only through him that we know of this exception since the *Quodlibeta* of John of Naples were never published. Discussion of the exception will occupy the attention of moral theologians for the next three or four centuries, that is, until theories of delayed animation on which it was based begin to give way. Although Antoninus and John of Naples will have a respectable following, there will not be unanimous agreement with their opinion about this case.

The question of therapeutic abortion was also taken up by a close contemporary of Antoninus, but more from the standpoint of law than morality. He is also dealing with the animated rather than the unanimated fetus. The jurist under discussion was Marianus Socinus (d. 1467), and the question was raised in his commentary on the *Si aliquis*.[32] After making what had by his time become standard comments on this legislation, he presents a case in which a doctor, unable to do anything else to save the life of a pregnant woman, urges her to abort an already animated fetus. Marianus asks whether the doctor or the mother will be held responsible in this case. This is the first time the question of therapeutic abortion of an animated fetus has been raised in a published work, but Marianus claims that Simon of Brescia, another jurist, raised the question in his commentary on the Clementine decretals; he responded that both the doctor and the mother would be held.[33] Socinus says that there are many reasons for thinking that the mother should be excused and then goes on to enumerate these reasons. First, she is acting on the authority of the doctor, not on her own authority. Second, the likelihood is that both mother and child will die without the abortion. Third, the mother is permitted to mutilate herself if necessary to save her life. He also argues that she is injuring no one, that abortion is the lesser evil in the case, and that in homicide one must consider not only the fact but the intention behind it and the circumstances surrounding it.

Whatever one may think of these reasons, it seems obvious that although Marianus' original doubt concerned only the liability of the mother, some of his reasons would apply equally to the doctor. Also, although his original interest may have been legal rather than moral, some of them would affect the morality of the act as well as its legality. In the end Socinus does not really answer his own question. He simply says that it is a question which deserves attention but one which he does not wish to decide. And he never does return to the question of the mother's guilt. Later, in commenting on the *Sicut ex*, he simply states without qualification that if the fetus is animated, abortion constitutes homicide.[34]

Shortly after Socinus raised the question of therapeutic abortion of the animated fetus, another jurist, Felinus Sandaeus of Ferrara (d. 1503) also discussed it in his commentary on the *Decretals*, more precisely in his commentary on canons 5 and 20 of the treatise *De homicidio*.[35] He asks whether a woman can be excused who has an abortion on the advice of a doctor who claims that she will not be able to escape death unless she destroys the fetal life within her. In responding to the question he claims that Marianus said she would be excused and alleged that Simon of Brescia was also of this opinion. This seems an obvious misinterpretation of both of these authors. According to the quotation cited above Socinus claimed that according to Simon both the doctor and the mother would be liable to a penalty in this case. Although Socinus himself admitted that there were reasons for excusing the mother, he said explicitly that he did not want to decide the issue at that time. It is hard to understand how Sandaeus could have so misread these statements. Curiously, when it comes to giving his own opinion, like Socinus he backs away and merely recommends the case for thoughtful consideration.

Sandaeus was also confused regarding the time of animation, calculating eighty days for the male fetus and forty days for the female, just the opposite of the common estimate of the time. The same judgment would have to be made of his interpretation of the jurist, Baldus. It will be remembered that Baldus, following the judgment of Roman law, did not consider the fetus a human being the whole time it was in the uterus. He did not think therefore that abortion should be punished as homicide. Sandaeus says that Baldus was speaking only of accidental abortion, not deliberate abortion. This may or may not be true, but if the fetus is not a human being the whole time it is in the womb, there is no reason why even deliberate abortion should be considered homicide.

Sandaeus will be remembered more for his inaccurate interpretation of the opinions of Simon and Socinus than for his other inaccuracies. Later authors, such as Thomas Sanchez, who apparently had no first-hand contact with the works of these two jurists, saw them only through the eyes of Sandaeus. They would go down in history as holding an opinion which they never really held, and would be exploited in the nineteenth century by those advocating therapeutic abortion of the animated fetus.

It was at about this time, the last half of the fifteenth century, that handbooks for confessors began to multiply. These were neither legal commentaries nor theological treatises, but strictly practical presentations of information whether theological or legal, that would be useful for a confessor engaged in administering the sacrament of penance. Unlike earlier *Summae* for confessors, these were arranged in alphabetical order. Although this might have provided the opportunity of presenting all the useful information on the subject under the heading *abortion*, even those who have such an entry continue to deal with many aspects of the problem under the more standard general headings of the past. Many of them presented most of what they had to say about abortion under the general treatment of *homicide*. This was true, for instance, of one of the earliest *Summae* of the period, the *Summa Rosella*, or *Baptistana*, the work of an Italian Franciscan named Trovamala (d. 1495).[36] He presents norms both for accidental and deliberate abortion, at least in reference to incurring an irregularity. The case of accidental abortion (the Carthusian monk case) he solves according to the three rules he has set down for accidental homicide. Since the monk was doing something illicit, he would incur an irregularity for the accidental abortion. This was according to the third rule Trovamala had laid down. According to the first rule an irregularity would not be incurred for an accidental abortion if the cleric was doing something licit and had taken the necessary precautions. According to the second rule, he would incur the irregularity, even if he was doing something licit, if the homicide resulted from some neglect. Although they summarize very neatly what has been said about this subject by many previous authors, these rules contain nothing new, and need some further precision. The underlying presumption in the above rules is that the irregularity will not be incurred if the fetus is not formed.[37] If the fetus is probably formed, however, the guilty monk should not advance in orders or engage in the ministry.

Another summist of the period, Angelus de Clavasio (d. 1495), in his *Summa Angelica* devotes a special heading to abortion, although most of what he has to say on the subject is under the word *homicidium*.[38] It goes beyond the *Rosella* by including the civil penalty for abortion. The source given for the civil penalty is the familiar *Qui abortionis*, which, according to Clavasio, imposes a capital sentence on the abortion of the animated fetus. Punishment for the abortion of the unanimated fetus differs, as has already been seen, according to the social status of the one responsible.

Under the heading *homicide* Clavasio makes the usual distinction between deliberate and accidental abortion and gives a fuller treatment of the latter than Trovamala. Among other cases he discusses the familiar *poculum amatorium*. If a death follows, even though unintended, since what the agent did was illicit, he would be guilty of homicide and irregular. But if death did not follow, that is, because the fetus was not yet formed, although he would be guilty of mortal sin, he would not be irregular.

In connection with the above two *Summae* mention must be made of a third, commonly known as the *Summa Tabiena*, the work of Ioannes Cognazzo de Tabia (d. 1531).[39] Since he was a Dominican, the references to St. Thomas are to be expected, but his treatment of abortion is quite similar to that of Clavasio, so there is no reason for going into further detail. The same cannot be said, however, for the work of another Dominican, Sylvester Prierias (d. 1523). In his *Summa* he is the first to take up the question of abortion of the unanimated fetus to save the life of the mother, the exception to the general prohibition against abortion presented with approval by Antoninus. He treats it under the word of *Medicus*.[40] There he says first that it is a mortal sin to give a pregnant woman something to cause an abortion in order to hide a past sin on her part. But if the medicine is given to preserve her life he says that one should distinguish with John of Naples. He then goes on to give the distinction between the animated fetus and the unanimated fetus. If the fetus is unanimated, the doctor may and should give the medicine. But if the fetus is formed, it would be a mortal sin to give the mother medicine to cause an abortion, since it would involve both the physical and the spiritual death of the fetus. In case of doubt about animation, the medicine should not be given since the one giving medicine in these circumstances would be exposing himself to the danger of committing homicide. This section in Sylvester is almost verbally the same as that in Antoninus, and both give John of Naples as the source.

Sylvester also takes up the question of abortion under the words *Aborsus* and *Homicidium*, following very closely the treatment in the *Angelica*. Unlike previous authors, however, he does not speak of a fetus not yet animated by a rational soul, but rather a fetus animated only by a sensitive or vegetative soul, thus accepting an Aristotelian or Thomistic succession of souls. In setting a norm for doubtful cases (where there is doubt about the presence of a human soul), he seems to be the first to distinguish between the judicial forum and the forum of conscience. When there is question of a penalty, a doubt is solved in favor of the defendant. But in the forum of conscience, where there is doubt, the safer course must be followed. The one who does not follow the safer course is guilty of homicide. His treatise on homicide is the most thorough of all the summists, but he does not say anything essentially different in regard to abortion. There is the same condemnation of deliberate abortion, the same rules for determining the morality of accidental abortion, the same distinction between the formed fetus and the unformed fetus in determining penalties and irregularities. He also follows the Thomistic distinction and estimate regarding the time of infusion of the rational soul in the male and female fetus.

Exception is made for the abortion of the unanimated fetus to save the mother in two other *Summae*. The *Summa aurea armilla* of Bartholomaeus Fumus, after classifying abortion as a *maleficium* and *contra naturam* (since even

wild beasts accept their offspring) takes up the case and
simply follows the opinion of John of Naples.[41] This is true
also of the *Manuale confessariorum* of Martin of Azpilcueta
(1493-1586), commonly known as *Doctor Navarrus*.[42] This
work was in the tradition of the summists, although it
departed from the alphabetical order of treatment which
they followed. Martin opted for the order of the Decalogue.
He takes up abortion under the fifth precept. *Non occides*
(Thou shalt not kill!), but deals with abortion to save the life
of the mother in his treatment of the duties of physicians
and surgeons. There he says that a physician who gives a
woman something to cause an abortion, even if he does so
to save her life, does wrong if he thinks the fetus has a
rational soul, or even is not sure. But if he thinks that it
probably has not yet been animated, he may give her such
medicine if necessary to save her life. He is able to say that
this opinion which originated with John of Naples and was
approved by Antoninus is commonly held.

———————◆———————

The initial discussions of abortion by the scholastic
theologians did not advance the subject significantly, but
the rediscovery of Aristotle by Albert the Great brought
with it a renewed interest in the underlying embryology of
the problem. For the first time explicit reference is made to
the time difference between male and female formation.
There seems to be general acceptance by the scholastics of
delayed animation and identification with the time of formation, but somewhat less uniformity about the time of
formation. The most significant development during the
period was the introduction to and acceptance of the opinion of John of Naples regarding therapeutic abortion by
Antoninus. This exception to the prohibition against abortion was accepted by a sufficient number of the followers of
these theologians to be considered safe in practice. The
same could not be said for the abortion of the animated

fetus to save the mother's life. Although this question was raised by a few jurists of the period, and more in reference to penal law than morality, it received no clear affirmative response from any of them. The jurists of the period continued to be preoccupied with the question of motivation for abortion as well as that of responsibility for accidental abortion, but largely in reference to the question of irregularity.

124

CHAPTER EIGHT

Discussion of
Therapeutic Abortion
(1500-1600)

From the time the case was introduced by John of Naples in the early fourteenth century, abortion of the unanimated fetus to save the life of the mother won considerable support from theologians. It was accepted first by Antoninus and then by several summists, namely, Sylvester, Fumus, and Navarrus. Its inclusion by the summists in their manuals is an indication that it was considered safe to be used in confessional practice. The question of aborting an animated fetus to save the life of the mother was raised by a few jurists, but although one of them, Socinus, offered reasons that might justify such a procedure even from a moral standpoint, there was no clear evidence that any of them really accepted it. Also, the question was raised only about the liability of the mother, which seemed to indicate that there was no question of exonerating the doctor. At about this time, the middle of the sixteenth century, a Franciscan theologian, Antonius de Corduba (1485-1578), introduced a distinction into the discussion of abortion to save the life of the mother that would take on great importance during the next several centuries.

Corduba introduced his distinction in responding to the following question: May a pregnant woman in danger of death take some medicine, or do something (or have someone else do it for her) that would result in an abortion and the death of an animated fetus? May a doctor or obstetrician (midwife) do the same? He responds that according to Sylvester this may not be done. Others, he says without naming them, hold that the woman herself may do this, but the doctor may not. Corduba himself says that a distinction must be made. If the medicine, or whatever procedure is used, is of itself immediately, directly, and principally conducive to the health of the mother, as, for instance, bleeding, bathing, a cathartic, or a pain-killer, it is permissible both for the mother and the doctor to (obtain and) use it. The doctor and midwife may even be bound professionally to give this help to the mother, just as one is bound to help a neighbor in extreme danger, or may at least licitly do so, when what he does is otherwise licit.

Corduba argues that this is permissible since the medicine (or other procedure) is *de se salutifera* (naturally therapeutic), even though it accidentally and indirectly causes death, and the death of the fetus (or some innocent person) follows. He draws an analogy between this case and a case of defense against unjust aggression in which an innocent bystander is accidentally killed. He seems to think that taking the medicine is even more justifiable since the mother has a *prior right (ius potius)* to life. The fetus depends on the mother, not vice versa.

But if the medicine or other measures causing the abortion are immediately, directly, and principally conducive to the death of the fetus *(de se mortifera)*, such as poisonous drugs, beating, *dilaceratio*, [2] striking the woman, knocking her down, or trampling on her, neither the woman herself nor the doctor (nor anyone else) may resort to them even to save her life. Taking the life of another in this way is not allowed any private person except in just self-defense. Corduba says that if Sylvester's condemnation of aborting an animated fetus to save the mother is understood in this sense, he would agree with it.

Corduba then contrasts this case with another mentioned by Sylvester.[3] Sylvester, in dealing with accidental homicide, had stated that if a person who was struck by another or was trying to escape such a blow knocked someone else down and killed him, it would not be considered homicide (and the person would not be irregular), at least unless he could have foreseen this consequence and avoided it. Corduba speaks more concretely of a man on horseback fleeing an unjust aggressor who unavoidably tramples a child in the path of his escape. Corduba would not allow this, and precisely because he considers the act of the horseman *de se mortifera* (in itself lethal). It is not the flight itself he considers *de se mortifera* but the *proculcatio*, that is, the trampling of the child. It falls into the same category, then, as beating a pregnant woman or giving her a poisonous drug to cause an abortion. Corduba would allow the horseman to continue his escape only if he tried to sidestep or jump over the child, even without success. As long as he does what he can to avoid direct killing of the child, even if he does not succeed, the death of the child will be unintentional and his act will be licit.

Corduba raises these questions at the end of his treatise on self-defense against unjust aggression but they involve an innocent third party (non-aggressor) rather than the aggressor himself. In the one case it was an innocent child in the path of a horseman escaping an unjust aggressor. In the second it was an innocent fetus whose life was being threatened as the mother defended herself, as it were, against some disease. St. Thomas, dealing with unjust aggression, maintained that killing the aggressor would be permitted as long as it was not intended but only an effect *praeter intentionem* (unintentional).[4] The intention had to be the self-defense itself. Different authors have offered different explanations of this difficult thesis in St. Thomas, and Corduba discussed these various opinions thoroughly. But what is quite clear in his treatment of the above cases is that he would not allow actions that might be admissible against an unjust aggressor when the victim was an innocent non-aggressor. In the case of the pregnant woman he would not allow actions aimed principally at aborting the fetus, even with the intention of saving her life. As he says, such actions would be allowed only in self-defense. Besides postulating the intention to save the life of the mother, he demanded that the action itself be aimed principally at this goal. In dealing with innocent victims of attacks on combatants in wartime, Vittoria was willing to allow means which seemed just as effective in killing the innocent as in killing the combatant, as long as the intention was limited to the latter.[5] Later authors would also extend Corduba's opinion to include means which were only *equally* salutary by nature, even though lethal to the fetus to the same degree. But Corduba himself demanded that the means used to save the mother's life be of their nature *principally* salutary.

How does Corduba's opinion relate to previous discussions about accidental or unintended abortion? The general norm set down by St. Thomas and others was that if what a person was doing was licit and there was no neglect, an abortion that might result would not be imputed to him. The reader will remember in this connection the cases of the Carthusian monk and Placidus. The supposition was that the abortion was not intentional, and perhaps not even foreseen, except in a confused sort of way. Some authors held that if the act was illicit for any reason the subsequent abortion should be imputed. A more sophisticated approach demanded that there be some connection between the illicit act and the abortion. In the case Corduba is dealing with there seems to be clear foreknowledge of the danger of abortion. Could this problem still be solved simply by appealing to the traditional rules for accidental abortion?

Corduba's first concern seemed to be to establish the fact that the abortion was accidental, that is, unintentional. He would not allow the *proculcatio* in the case of the horseman escaping the unjust aggressor but was satisfied that the death of the child was beyond his intention if he did his best to sidestep, even without success. In the abortion case the requirement regarding intention seemed to be satisfied by the nature of the medicine itself. The fact that it was aimed by nature at curing the mother rather than the abortion was sufficient to keep the abortion unintentional or accidental. Once the abortion was established as clearly accidental, he did not seem too concerned about the question of imputability. He simply argued from analogy with the case of self-defense in which an innocent bystander was killed. Since the person attacked was doing what was licit in defending himself, the death of the bystander was not imputed to him. He seemed to think that the mother was more justified in the abortion case since she had a prior right to life. This could not have been claimed for the person defending himself in reference to the innocent third party, so the presence of a prior right was not essential to his argument.

Corduba's distinction met almost immediately with basic acceptance by those who came after him. One of the first of these authors was Peter of Navarre (d. 1594). In his work *De ablatorum restitutione* he takes up abortion to save the mother and summarizes succinctly the opinions which were current in his time.[5] He says that some hold that abortion either before or after animation is a mortal sin and intrinsically evil, even to save the life of the mother, just as it is wrong to expel semen outside of intercourse even to save one's life. A second opinion (he names Sylvester, John of Naples, and Antoninus) holds that it is permissible before animation to give a mother a drug, from which an abortion may follow, to save her life, but not after animation. A variation of this opinion would allow the woman to take the drug but would not allow the doctor to give it. The third opinion allows a woman to take a drug which is *directe sanativa* either before or after animation, even though an abortion may result. But she may not take a medicine which is *directe causativa mortis* (directly lethal) either before or after the animation of the fetus. All of these opinions have already been encountered, and the last one particularly will be identified as that of Corduba. Navarre illustrates Corduba's view with the example of a pregnant women fleeing a wild bull. She has a right to protect her life even at the cost of causing an abortion. Thus if she needs bleeding to save her life, this would be permitted even if it caused an abortion. He appeals to the *ius potius* of the mother to justify this, although it is not clear that this was the basic reason offered by Corduba.

In giving his own opinion Navarre distinguishes between a case that involves a fetus before animation and one that deals with an animated fetus. Before animation he accepts Corduba's opinion without qualification. The means used are not illicit, but indifferent or, more accurately, by nature aimed at preserving life. The accidental result, the abortion, is therefore not imputed to the woman. But he contends that it would be a mortal sin to use a means aimed directly at abortion. Navarre says that everyone holds this latter position, a statement that will be challenged later by Thomas Sanchez. Navarre can make this statement only if he can interpret what John of Naples and his followers said about aborting an unanimated fetus to save the mother in the sense of the Corduban distinction. In other words he would have to maintain that they were speaking of using medicine aimed principally at curing the mother, not medicine aimed at abortion. There is no clear evidence for this claim.

After animation Navarre holds that it would be permissible to give the mother a medicine that is directly *sanativa* if there is question only of the physical welfare of the child. If, however, there is a chance that the fetus will otherwise survive and be baptized the mother may not take the medicine. The spiritual good of the child must be preferred to the temporal or material welfare of the mother. But if the doctor judges that the child will die with the mother if he does not give the medicine, it is permissible for him to give it. In thus introducing a consideration of the spiritual welfare of the fetus into the discussion Navarre is qualifying Corduba's opinion.

Corduba's distinction also attracted the attention of a Jesuit theologian of the period, Gabriel Vasquez (1551-1604), sometimes referred to as a Spanish Augustine. Like his contemporaries Vasquez was preoccupied with the question of abortion to save the life of the mother, although he treats it under the more generic question: Is it ever permitted to kill an innocent person in self-defense?[6] He is not referring to the aggressor in this question, but, like Corduba, to an innocent third party, that is, one who is not the aggressor. He considers two cases of this kind: killing an innocent person when fleeing an aggressor and aborting an animated fetus to save the life of the mother. He challenges Corduba's response regarding the first case, as well as his interpretation of Sylvester, and then discusses the second case. He cites with approval the opinion of Sylvester that it is wrong to give a pregnant woman a drug to cause an abortion even if it is certain that she will otherwise die. This is true because it is wrong to intend or accelerate the death of one person to save another. The means here are intrinsically wrong and cannot be justified by a good end. He then proceeds to point out the distinction between *medicina mortifera* and *sanativa* which Corduba introduced into the solution or response to this question, allowing the use of *medicina sanativa*.

Vasquez says that on first consideration this opinion seems to be false. The fact that the death of the fetus is not intended is not really relevant, since it follows necessarily from depriving the fetus of his necessary sustenance. It would be just as wrong to do this as it would be to take food from another in extreme need to save one's own life. He then takes up the illustrative analogy offered by Navarre in support of Corduba's opinion, the example of a pregnant woman fleeing a wild animal. Everyone agrees that the woman has a right to do this, even though it would involve the danger of abortion. Vasquez denies the validity of the analogy. The woman in fleeing the wild animal is trying to save the life of the fetus as well as her own life. In the present case the woman is trying to save her own life at the expense of the fetus. Later authors will see more of an analogy between these two cases, but Vasquez himself did not analyze them that thoroughly, perhaps because he was in basic agreement with Corduba.

Before discussing Corduba's opinion further he states his opposition to Sylvester's opinion that it is licit to abort an unanimated fetus to save the life of the mother. Vasquez maintains that this is contrary to the nature of generation, and even more wrong than deliberately expelling semen. But he does allow the use of *medicina sanativa* to save the mother, and by way of proof he draws an analogy with indirect explusion of semen (which all permit). His reaction to Corduba's opinion that it is permissible to use such medicine even when the fetus is animated is that it is *probabilior* (a more probable opinion). He argues in terms of the concrete example of bloodletting. The mother has a *jus potius* (prior right) to her own blood; her obligation to supply the fetus is *ex solo superfluo* (from what is superfluous). The case therefore differs from that of taking food from a starving man. There the presumption is that the food belongs to the man, and to him alone, and it is wrong to take it from him. In the present case the blood belongs to the mother rather than to the child. So there is really no analogy between the two cases. Vasquez dismisses Navarre's concern for the spiritual welfare of the fetus with the statement that the mother is not obliged to sacrifice her life when her own spiritual welfare is in doubt. Some of Vasquez' successors will question this facile dismissal of the problem.

Although in basic agreement with Corduba's distinction, Vasquez is not altogether satisfied with it. He is willing to go along with it in regard to such procedures as bloodletting and bathing. But he does not allow the use of a medicine that would cause some positive alteration (*alteratio positiva*) in the condition of the fetus. He says that it would be wrong, therefore, for the mother to take a potion that would have some positive effect on the fetus. Corduba had already ruled out the use of poisonous drugs as *princi-paliter mortifera*, but he seemed to imply in making his distinction that even if the remedies were *mortifera* to some degree, as long as they were *principaliter salutifera*, they could be used. Although he is not entirely clear on the point, Vasquez seems to be ruling out a remedy that would be *mortifera* in any positive way, even if not *principaliter mortifera*. Unfortunately, he does not get specific about the type of medicine he would outlaw for this reason, but he may have been thinking of something like a cathartic (which Corduba allowed), which would positively disturb the pregnancy. He argues that one does not have a right to take another's life by a positive act unless the other party is an unjust aggressor.

To establish his point he has to deny any analogy with a drug taken for health reasons which would positively stimulate an expulsion of semen or, as it is called, a pollution, which he himself and his contemporaries allow. He argues against the analogy by denying any comparison between a pollution and homicide or killing. According to Vasquez the evil of pollution is in the intention; the evil of homicide is in the external act. He concludes from this that it is never permissible to place an external act which positively causes the death of an innocent person. Even if the killing is not intended, it is still imputed to the person placing the act. To the objection that this is exactly what happens in war when innocent people are killed accidentally he responds that this is justified by the common good. But in this case only the good of another person is at stake. In another section dealing explicitly with the morality of expelling semen he sheds a little more light on the distinction between this and killing.[7] There he says that a pollution can be procured either immediately or through an act having no other effect; in either case it is intended. But it can also happen as the result of a natural dynamic force which operates within us without our intention, and even against our will. It is for this reason that a direct intention is required for wrongful pollution. In homicide the situation is entirely different. There is no natural force impelling us toward killing independently of an act of our wills. So a direct intention of homicide is not necessary. To be culpable it is enough to place an external act that positively causes it. Whatever merit this distinction may have, there is no evidence that it won many adherents.

Another Spanish Jesuit of that time, Ioannes Azor (d. 1603), also accepted Corduba's distinction, and it would seem, without qualification. He asks specifically whether a pregnant woman may undergo bloodletting, take baths, cathartics, or pain-killers if necessary to save her life, even though they may cause an abortion.[8] He cites John of Naples, Antoninus, and their followers as authors who do not consider this licit if the fetus is already animated. Another opinion (that of Corduba) holds that if the mother intends to protect her own life and uses a means which is not naturally and directly aimed at the destruction of the fetus (as the above means), it would be permissible By way of illustration he uses the example of a pregnant woman fleeing, not a wild animal, but a fire or a flood. If, however, the means are aimed by nature at abortion, the mother would not be permitted to use them. To the objection that it is permissible to kill the innocent along with combatants in warfare he answers that this is justified by the common good. To the objection that it is licit to kill an unjust aggressor to save one's life he responds simply that the fetus is not an unjust aggressor. It is the disease that is threatening the mother's life; the fetus is using no threatening force. Azor concludes the section with the statement that the authors cited for the first opinion above would have no difficulty about allowing the use of such procedures if the fetus was not animated and they were necessary to save the life of the mother. Finally, in the next section Azor makes it clear that the use of procedures or medicines aimed directly at abortion would be wrong even if the intention were not to kill the fetus, but to save the mother.[9]

Corduba's opinion was also accepted by an English Benedictine theologian. In his *Clavis regia* Gregory Sayrus (1570-1602) accepts the distinction of Corduba but with the qualification that even *medicina salutifera* may not be used if the spiritual welfare of the fetus is at stake.[10] Sayrus also raises a further question about possible remedies in cases of this kind. Corduba had demanded that the medicine (or other procedure) be principally *causativa sanitatis* (principally curative). What if the medicine is by nature as destructive as it is therapeutic? He is supposing the same situation, namely, that both the mother and fetus will otherwise die. If she takes the medicine, however, it is not certain whether the fetus or mother will be saved. Some authors have denied that it is licit to give the mother medicine in this situation, since in doing so one is exposing her or the fetus or both to danger of death. Other authors allow this, arguing that in extreme cases of this type where there is no other remedy, it is permissible to experiment. It is better than certainly losing two lives. The opponents would accept this opinion if there were question only of the mother but do not feel that it can be followed when the life of the fetus is also at stake.

Sayrus argues that since in this case there is no hope for either without the remedy, he does not see how any injury will be done to the fetus if the experiment is used on the mother. But if the case were doubtful, that is, if it were doubtful whether the fetus would otherwise die or survive, he would allow the experiment only if the fetus was not formed. If the fetus were already formed, he would not permit it. Sayrus' discussion of this case is not as clear as one would like; he seems to be dealing simultaneously with two distinct questions, namely, the use of means equally *salutifera* and *mortifera*, and the use of doubtful means. The next author to be discussed will bring greater clarity to these questions by treating them separately.

Thomas Sanchez, (1550-1610), a Spanish Jesuit, offers what is perhaps the most thorough treatment of abortion to save the life of the mother that had appeared up to his time.[11] He is the first author, also, who explicitly accepts the opinion of John of Naples and his followers regarding the abortion of the unanimated fetus to save the mother as well as Corduba's distinction regarding the animated fetus. He goes beyond those immediate predecessors of his, such as Corduba, who oppose the opinion of John of Naples and allow only the use of *medicina sanativa*, even when the fetus is unformed. Sanchez introduces the subject with the question whether it is permissible to procure an abortion if this is the only way of saving a mother's life.

He begins his response by making the traditional distinction between the animated and unanimated fetus. If the fetus is animated, even doubtfully so, all agree that it would be wrong to procure an abortion, since taking the life of an innocent person is an intrinsically evil thing. He advises that Simon of Brescia and Marianus (Socinus) should not be listened to in this regard. As already mentioned, he was under a misapprehension regarding the opinion of these two jurists due to Felinus' misreading of them. Neither actually subscribed to the opinion that abortion was permissible in these circumstances. Sanchez says that one might want to prove that it was licit by arguing that the fetus is part of the mother as long as it is in the uterus, and that it is permissible to sacrifice a part of one's body for the good of the whole. This would be true if the fetus were a real part of the mother and not endowed with a distinct soul of its own. But it is clear that the animated fetus does not fit this description, so this argument cannot be valid.

He pursues that same question regarding the fetus before it is animated with a rational soul and quotes Peter of Navarre's statement that it is the opinion of everyone that it is not licit to procure an abortion of a fetus even before animation to save the life of the mother. In addition to naming the authorities Navarre quotes in behalf of this opinion, Sanchez also presents arguments for it from reason. The first is the familiar *a fortiori* argument drawn from an analogy with procuring a seminal pollution. Since this is intrinsically evil and never permitted, although more remote from the goal of generation than even the unformed fetus, aborting an unformed fetus would likewise, and for a stronger reason, be illicit. Also, if abortion of the unanimated fetus were permitted to save the life of the mother, it would have to be allowed even to prevent a danger that might come only at the time of delivery. And why would it not be allowed also to protect the reputation of a woman who had sinned, or even her life when threatened by an angry husband or father? It makes no difference whether the danger is present, or in the future, whether it comes from inside or from some outside source, with or without fault. It is just as permissible for one to cut off his foot to escape death when he is being held by an enemy (even through his own fault) as it is to amputate it when diseased.

Sanchez simply denies Navarre's statement that all are in agreement that it is wrong to abort an unanimated fetus to save the life of the mother. His own experience is that no one disagrees with the opinion that is is permissible. This statement of Sanchez seems as questionable as Navarre's original claim. Besides Navarre himself both Corduba and Vasquez have challenged the abortion of the unanimated fetus to save the mother. The facts seem to indicate that the opinion of John of Naples had its followers, but it also met with opposition. The opposition would grow as the Corduban distinction took hold, providing a different, and more acceptable, solution for problems that would arise both before and after animation.

To Sanchez the opinion that allows the abortion of an unanimated fetus to save the life of the mother is the more probable opinion. The reason he gives is that abortion in this case does not involve homicide. Also, since the fetus is part of the mother, not yet endowed with a rational soul, there is no reason why the mother should be obliged to continue to protect it when it is the source of imminent danger to her life, especially since there is little or no chance that it will ever be animated with a soul of its own if the mother dies. But Sanchez is not willing to allow abortion in the cases presented above as analogous. He would not allow it to avoid a difficult delivery because in this case the danger is not present and the problem can be solved by other means. As for the other cases, the fetus cannot be considered an aggressor in any sense in these cases. In the present case, however, the fetus is a quasi-aggressor and the cause of the mother's death, and the danger is present and cannot be removed by other means. Although Sanchez speaks of the unanimated fetus as a quasi-aggressor (like a diseased member) rather than an aggressor in the strict sense, this statement will become an issue among later authors. Later authors will also continue to push the analogy between this case and those where the danger comes from an outside source.

Another point should be mentioned in connection with Sanchez' refutation of the arguments against the position he has taken. It will be remembered that one argument used by previous authors was drawn from an analogy with the morality of procuring an emission of semen. The prohibition here was considered absolute, and it was argued that for an even stronger reason the prohibition of abortion of the unanimated fetus should be absolute. Sanchez sees an important difference here.[12] The reason why any kind of administrative decision allowing the expulsion of semen is denied to man is the intense pleasure associated with it. The implication is that if this decision were ever left to man, it could not be controlled. Since there is no such pleasure associated with abortion, there would not be the same danger. There is not the same reason, therefore, for an absolute prohibition. So this analogy cannot be used to outlaw abortion to save the life of the mother.

After his discussion of abortion of the unanimated fetus to save the life of the mother, he raises the more difficult question of aborting an animated fetus in the same circumstances. He asks whether when the fetus is probably animated a pregnant woman or a doctor may, if her life is in danger, use medicines necessary to save her life but carrying with them the danger of abortion. He adds that it is commonly stated that John of Naples and his followers respond negatively to this question. Sanchez comments that they were speaking rather of the use of genuine abortifacients. Rather than say they gave a negative response to the above question, it might be better to say that they did not even consider it. Sanchez quotes Corduba to the effect that according to some it is permissible for a woman to use such medicines, but not for a doctor or midwife to give them. Sanchez is mystified by this distinction.

Sanchez makes use of Corduba's distinction between lethal potions and medicines or procedures of a predominantly salutary nature, condemning the use of the former, but allowing the latter. He gives his reasons for allowing the use of *medicina salutifera*, many of which have already been seen. But he does add a new dimension to the discussion by appealing to St. Thomas' article on self-defense. Up to the present the whole discussion of unintentional abortion has been related to the question of killing an innocent nonaggressor. Relating it here to the discussion of self-defense against an unjust aggressor will be a source of confusion in some later authors, but certainly in the mind of Sanchez the animated fetus was not an unjust aggressor. In the case in question St. Thomas' requirement regarding the intention of the agent is undoubtedly fulfilled. It is aimed at saving the mother rather than the death of the fetus. But it is aimed in this direction precisely because the means themselves are by their very nature aimed at this goal.

St. Thomas' concern in dealing with self-defense was chiefly with the intention of the agent. He says that the moral species of an act is determined by its intention, not by accidental effects resulting from it. This statement presents its difficulties even in reference to self-defense, but the intention of the agent is clearly not the primary concern in the Corduban distinction. The emphasis there is more on the nature of the means. Certainly, limiting one's options to means that were therapeutic by nature would be indicative of a good intention, but the good intention was not enough. If the means were by nature destructive rather than therapeutic, the fact that they were used ultimately to save the mother's life was not enough to justify them. Corduba has already pointed out this significant difference between taking the life of an unjust aggressor and taking the life of an innocent nonaggressor. Destructive action against the unjust aggressor was justifiable as long as the intention of the agent was good, that is, to save his own life. But saving the life of the mother would not justify destructive action against a fetus, at least if it was principally destructive.

Sanchez draws another argument from an analogy with killing innocent people during wartime. As in a just war it is permissible to bombard or set fire to legitimate military targets even though innocent people may perish in the attack, as all agree, it is permissible to attack lethal "humors" in a pregnant woman with medical weapons, even though the death of an innocent fetus may result accidentally. Whether Corduba would have accepted this analogy is not certain, since the common good is not involved in the abortion case, but it is not without merit. The other arguments Sanchez brings to bear have all been presented by previous authors.

If one agrees that it is permissible for the mother to use such medicines to save her life, Sanchez sees no reason why a doctor may not do the same. This curious distinction may have had its origin in the original query of Socinus about the possibility of excusing a woman who would cause an abortion to save her life, but on the advice of the doctor. Socinus said nothing about exonerating the doctor who gave the advice, or perhaps even the medicine. It will be remembered that Socinus was commenting on the *Si aliquis*. Since this legislation deals explicitly with drugs, or other remedies, given a woman by someone else, he may have felt that there was no way in which the doctor could be considered immune. But since Sanchez was approaching the question more from the standpoint of reason than the letter of the law, he could not understand the distinction. As a matter of fact, he felt that the doctor might even be obliged to give a pregnant woman some such drug, if she asked for it. The woman herself, of course, has no obligation to take such a drug; if she wishes she may sacrifice her life for the good of the fetus. Even one attacked by an unjust aggressor may do this if he wishes.

Sanchez agrees that there is only one case in which it would be wrong for a mother to take a *medicina salutifera*, namely, if the fetus might otherwise survive and be baptized. Charity demands that the spiritual good of the fetus be preferred to the temporal welfare of the mother. In practice, however, he feels that the case would be very rare when the fetus would survive the mother. If the mother herself is the victim of some fatal disease, the fetus itself will be affected and it will be miraculous for it to survive. So, although there may be a theoretical obligation, in practice it will rarely be present.

Up to this point Sanchez has been dealing with the type of medicine or remedy of which Corduba spoke, one that was *principaliter sanativa*. He now moves the discussion into a more difficult area. What if the medicine is not *more* conducive to the health of the mother, but only *equally* conducive to her health and to the abortion of the fetus? He cites some authors who will not allow this, but says he sees no reason for this. In arguing he seems to rely heavily on the *ius potius* of the mother, although he qualifies this somewhat when he adds that from a practical standpoint it would be miraculous for the fetus to survive the mother whereas with the use of the medicine both might survive. He also argues that in this situation the intention of the agent can determine the morality of the act. Since it is aimed at the health of the mother, it supports as it were the healthgiving qualities of the medicine, rather than its destructive qualities.

A final question is rasied regarding a drug whose effects are doubtful, that is, it is not known whether it will be helpful or harmful. If some more certain drug were available, it would not be permissible to use such a drug. But suppose mother and child will die otherwise, and no other remedy is available? In this situation Sanchez feels that it would be permissible to use the drug. Since both mother and child would die anyhow without the medicine, the damage it would do is minimal. On the other hand, if it works, it offers great benefits. He appeals to the example of a person who can escape a wild beast only by jumping off a precipice, preferring a doubtful death to a certain one. Sanchez feels that no one would deny the liceity of this choice.

Briefly, then, Sanchez allows the abortion of an unanimated fetus to save the life of the mother when threatened by disease, but will not allow it for other reasons. His basic argument is that of John of Naples, as already seen, but some of the supportive statements he made, that is, the unanimated fetus is *pars viscerum mulieris* and a quasi-aggressor, as well as his explanation of the malice of pollution, would eventually raise as many difficulties with his position as he was attempting to solve. The position itself will be challenged by several of his successors. The distinction between *medicina sanativa* and *medicina mortifera* in reference to the abortion of the animated fetus to save the life of the mother will continue to be generally received, although with some qualifications by a few authors. Vasquez already ruled out the use of remedies that would cause an *alteratio positiva* in the fetus, even though it was *principaliter sanativa*. Sanchez, however, went even farther than Corduba, allowing the use of remedies that were only equally *sanativa*. He also allows the use of doubtful remedies if the death of both mother and child is otherwise certain, and no more sure remedy is available.

CHAPTER NINE

Further
Legal and Theological
Developments

Before continuing with the theological debate, it will be helpful to turn attention to the development that took place on the juridical level, both civil and canonical, during the sixteenth century. Although these represent different approaches to the problem, they have been frequently and intimately related to the theological dimension in the past. For instance, the distinction between the animated and unanimated fetus was introduced from the Fathers through the penitential books into canonical legislation. In the thirteenth century it was introduced even into the civil law. From that time on it was generally accepted by civil jurists and was the basis for penalizing later abortions (after animation) with the death sentence.

In the second half of the sixteenth century a civil jurist, Iacobus Menochius (d. 1583) questioned the whole idea of legislating the death penalty for abortion, even abortion of the animated fetus.[1] Menochius wanted only a *poena extraordinaria* for abortion. In other words the penalty should be a fine, exile, or work in the mines, but not the death sentence. He admits that the opposite opinion is commonly held, but argues that since the law itself does not distinguish between abortions before and after animation, no distinction should be made. He is speaking here of the *Lex Cornelia de sicariis* which was applied to abortion by Iulius Paulus. All the law says is that if a *mulier* or *homo* dies from the drug potion, the death penalty should be invoked. Menochius does not think that the fetus can be considered a *homo*. He can fall back on the Roman concept of the fetus as part of the mother to establish this point. Nor does he admit a contrary argument from the Septuagint text of Exodus. Old Testament laws are not observed in the New Testament unless approved by one who has legislative power. He also observes, calling attention to the difference between the Hebrew and Greek texts of the Exodus statute, that the status of the fetus is not clear even in the Old Testament. Although he would want to see abortion punished, he does not think it should be the punishment for homicide.

Menochius also has something to say about punishment for an abortion to save the life of the mother.[2] He alludes to the question raised by Socinus and Felinus regarding the imposition of canonical penalties, at least on the mother herself. He adds that there are some who think that in this case the punishment of the doctor should be at least mitigated, if not removed. He himself is doubtful. It can be argued in favor of no penalty at all that the doctor is doing what is licit, since it is better for one to perish than two. But it can also be argued that decisions of this kind should be left in the hands of almighty God who can in his providence protect the mother, if he wishes. Finally, it often happens that the child survives the mother and can be extracted alive, so one cannot be sure that two will otherwise perish. After debating this issue briefly, Menochius concludes that in the forum of conscience the doctor and the mother will not be excused from sin, but as far as temporal punishment is concerned, some penalty should be imposed on the doctor who performs an abortion, even to save the mother's life, if he does this without consulting the magistrate.

Another jurist of the time, Antonius Tessaurus (d. 1590) also takes issue with imposing the death penalty on abortion of the animated fetus.[3] Although he considers several cases, most of his discussion of the issue is centered around a case of deliberate abortion. For the punishment he cites the *Qui abortionis*, but since the type of penalty it prescribes is no longer in use, he suggests that criminals of the lower class be condemned permanently to the triremes, that those of the upper classes be permanently exiled. The woman herself should be whipped and then put to work in a hospital for the rest of her life. He admits that while the *Qui abortionis* makes no distinction, jurists in his time usually apply the distinction between the animated and unanimated fetus to the law. He traces the practice back to Accursius, as well as canonical sources, and says that it is common practice. These jurists, of course, impose capital punishment on aborting an animated fetus. Tessaurus says that this has always seemed *nimis dura* (too harsh) to him, although he admits that jurists did not simply get this distinction out of their heads.

He traces the canonical origin of the distinction to the *Moyses* of the *Decretum*[4] and the *Sicut ex* of Innocent III. The civil origins go back to the *Divus* of the emperors and the *Si mulierem* of Ulpian. Appeal is also made to the rule of law according to which a fetus should be considered just like a child already born whenever it was to his advantage. But whatever these authorities may say, Tessaurus feels that the death penalty is too severe for the abortion of an animated fetus, and although he would admit the distinction between the animated and unanimated fetus, he thinks that some lesser penalty should be imposed even on the abortion of the animated fetus. He then tries to prove his position by attacking the basis for the contrary opinion.

He challenges, first, the scriptural origin of the *Moyses* text. The text in Exodus (undoubtedly the Hebrew text) says nothing about an animated or unanimated fetus. The death penalty is imposed only if the mother dies. And this fits in perfectly with such Roman laws as the *Qui abortionis*. Augustine himself, whose text this is, says nothing about an animated or unanimated fetus but only about a formed and unformed fetus. Tessaurus says that according to Hippocrates the fetus is perfectly formed only after eight months. For all practical purposes, then, Augustine is distinguishing between a fetus almost ready to be born and one who is not. Tessaurus has no objection to the canonical use of the distinction between the animated and unanimated fetus in the *Sicut ex*, but he objects to its use as a basis for inflicting a death sentence. His reason is that he does not consider abortion even of the animated fetus true homicide. The law of the gospel tends to look upon some things as homicide which are not homicide in the true sense. Tessaurus gives the impression that he associates manhood with a completely developed fetus. Since this can be verified only after eight months, or when a fetus is ready to be born, only an eight–month fetus would be a *homo*. Practically speaking, this means that one becomes a man only when he is ready to be born. This is certainly a unique, and it seems, quite unfounded interpretation of Augustine who allowed only forty-five or forty-six days for the basic formation of the fetus. Tessaurus is willing to admit that the penalty for abortion should be greater if the fetus is animated. What he objects to is the death sentence.

Tessaurus finds no basis in the *Digest* for imposing a death sentence on abortion of the animated fetus. There is no distinction there at all between the animated and unanimated fetus. The only instance of a death sentence for abortion is in the law *Cicero*, but the reason for it there is that the abortion was done for money.[5] He does not accept the application to abortion of the rule of law that a fetus is to be compared to a child already born whenever it is to its advantage. How will it help the fetus to punish the delinquent with the death sentence? One should be slow to sacrifice the life of a *homo* for an immature fetus. One becomes a man in the true sense only after he is born. While the fetus is in the womb it is being formed, but even though it has a soul, it is not completely formed until after the eighth month, and ordinarily will not survive if born before that time. He appeals finally to the Stoic position that the fetus is part of the mother until birth, and hence is not considered a *homo* in the Roman law until that time. For all these reasons he is opposed to the death sentence for abortion.

Tessaurus then considers the question of therapeutic abortion and argues that especially in this case the death sentence seems too severe. Although some hold that even in this case a capital sentence should be imposed if the fetus is animated, he thinks that the opinion of Socinus and Felinus is the truer one. According to Tessaurus these two jurists said that a *poculum abortionis* could be given with impunity in this case as long as it was done with the consent of doctors. He adds that since Antoninus classifies such an abortion as a mortal sin, some salutary penalty also (presumably a spiritual penalty) should be imposed on the sinner. He agrees that if the potion is given without the consent of doctors, some civil penalty should be given, but something less than that called for by the *Lex Cornelia*. Temporary exile, or the equivalent, would perhaps be a sufficient penalty.

The same trend toward mitigating the civil penalty attached to abortion is found in English civil law. It will be remembered that Bracton charged with homicide one who struck a woman or gave her a poisonous drug to cause an abortion, if the fetus was formed, and especially if it was animated.[6] In the fourteenth century Fleta (a pseudonym for an English jurist) made the same charge against anyone who by a potion destroyed an animated fetus in the womb or who gave someone something to prevent conception, reflecting in this respect the *Si aliquis*.[7] By the second half of the sixteenth century, however, Sir Edward Coke, a contemporary of Menochius and Tessaurus, can say that if a woman is *quick* with child and by a potion or otherwise kills it, or if a man beats her whereby the child within her dies, and she is delivered of a dead child, this is "a great misprision and not homicide."[8] But if it is born alive and then dies of the potion, it is murder, for in the law it is accounted a reasonable creature when it is born alive. In making this distinction Coke is not departing as much from the tradition as Menochius and Tessaurus would like, but he is clearly less demanding than Bracton or Fleta, neither of whom clearly require that the child be born alive before a homicide charge may be made. But while Coke considers abortion as such less a crime than murder, like his contemporaries he feels that so horrible an offense should not go unpunished.

It is interesting to note that in the twelfth century when canonists and civil jurists came back into contact with Roman law, the effort was in the direction of adjusting it to canon law.[9] It was in this spirit that the distinction between the animated and unanimated fetus was introduced into the Roman law. But the spirit of the Renaissance moved in the opposite direction, and the trend among jurists under this influence was toward a return to the original Roman law. Ultimately, this spirit would win out and over the next few centuries the death penalty would disappear from penal legislation regarding abortion. In one sense this trend toward mitigated penalties corresponded with what took place in the early Church regarding penitential discipline. Although abortion was frequently classified as homicide, the full penance for homicide was rarely imposed. There was also a gradual mitigation of all penances in the history of the early Church, reflecting a more understanding and humane attitude toward the weakness of man. Although still severe by modern standards, penances for sin were less severe at the end of the first millenium than at the beginning of the fourth century.

The Renaissance brought with it not only an appreciation of the accomplishments of the Roman and Greek world, but also, and unfortunately, a reappearance of some of the vices that plagued that society. The practice of abortion, according to Sixtus V, became such a problem to the Church at the time that it was necessary for Church authority to legislate special penalties against it. Historically, excommunication was really a part of the penitential discipline of the early Church. But as the practice of granting reconciliation immediately after confession took over, the separation from the Church which serious sin carried with it lost most of its meaning. But excommunication was gradually reintroduced into the Church as a special penalty for more serious sins and one which called for a special absolution. In the fourteenth and fifteenth centuries some local synods attached an excommunication to the sin of abortion.[10] But it was not until the end of the sixteenth century that the penalty was legislated for the universal Church. In 1588 Sixtus V in an apostolic constitution commonly known by its introductory word, *Effraenatam*, attached an excommunication to the crime of abortion.[11] The excommunication would be incurred not only by the pregnant woman but also by anyone who would give advice, assistance, a potion, or other kind of medicine for the commission of this crime. What is of special interest, however, is that the constitution, instead of accepting the distinction made in the *Sicut ex litterarum* in reference to irregularities, followed the model of the *Si aliquis* and attached the penalty not only to all abortion but even to sterilization.[12] Absolution from the penalty was also reserved to the supreme pontiff, except when the one who had incurred it was in danger of death.

The departure from the ecclesiastical precedent of distinguishing between the animated and unanimated fetus, as well as the rigid control placed on absolution from the penalty, must have come as a shock. And perhaps it was meant to be just that, since shock can sometimes have a salutary effect. But the legislation was found to be too harsh, particularly in the two respects mentioned above. As a result, in 1591 it was modified by the new pontiff, Gregory XIV. In the new constitution, *Sedes apostolica*, the excommunication for the abortion of the unanimated fetus and for sterilization was withdrawn; it was limited to the abortion of the animated fetus.[13] Also, absolution from the excommunication was no longer reserved to the supreme pontiff but could be given by the local bishop or anyone delegated by him. This constitution remained in effect for almost three centuries, being revised only in 1869 by Pius IX.

The Church did not enter the abortion debate again until toward the end of the 17th century. In the meanwhile the theological discussion centered largely around the question of abortion to save the life of the mother. The opinion of John of Naples continued to win supporters, some even attempting to extend it to include other cases, but it also met with considerable opposition. Corduba's distinction will fare better. However qualified it may be, it will receive general support, and unlike the opinion of John of Naples, will encounter almost no opposition.

An Italian contemporary of Sanchez, a Jesuit named Comitolus (1545-1626), vigorously opposed the abortion of an unanimated fetus to save the mother.[14] After stating the opinion of John of Naples, he says simply that this is never permitted. His argument is that of Vasquez and derived from an analogy with pollution.[15] He denies what seemed to have been a supporting argument of Sanchez, namely that the fetus is an unjust aggressor. If one wishes to use this kind of terminology, he would have to say more accurately that it is the disease (presumably of the mother) that is the aggressor, not the fetus.

Comitolus presents his opinion on the abortion of the unanimated fetus to save the mother in his first *effatum*. In his next statement he adopts the Corduban distinction and says that it is permissible to give the mother salutary medicine to save her life, even if it involves the danger of abortion. He tells his readers that all hold this regarding the unanimated fetus, and that many admit it even if the fetus is animated. Comitolus himself makes no distinction, but argues to the permissibility of such a procedure on the basis that a disease is similar to an unjust aggressor. The mother may defend herself against unjust aggression of this kind, even if it means the death of the fetus. He compares the situation to a just war where innocent people are killed in an attack on the aggressor. In this case the fetus is the innocent victim of an attack on an aggressor, the disease. He even implies in his argument that defense of the mother is defense of the fetus as well, since the fetus would also succumb if the attack on the mother was successful.

Comitolus seems to argue that the mother is really obliged to take such medicine. A pregnant woman must take food, even if it means the death of the fetus; the same is true of medicine. If she refuses, she is implicitly willing her own death. There is no difference to Comitolus between dying this way and dying by one's own sword. In imposing such an obligation Comitolus is clearly going beyond his predecessors, none of whom argued that the mother would be obliged to take the medicine. But Comitolus does introduce a refinement not explicitly mentioned, although probably understood, by previous authors. It must be a matter of life and death. If there were a question only of her health, he would not allow the mother to take medicine that carried with it the danger of abortion.

Comitolus also takes up the question of positive action against the mother to save the life of the fetus—just the opposite of the above question. St. Thomas argued that it would not be permissible to kill the mother (presumably by a caesarean section) to make baptism possible for the fetus. Antoninus had stated that it would be wrong to shorten the life of the mother to save the fetus, just as wrong as it would be to shorten the life of the fetus to save the mother. Comitolus also refuses to allow an attack on the mother to save the fetus. He lashes out against those doctors (he calls them butchers) who do caesarean sections on live women to save viable fetuses. Such surgery is tantamount to killing the mother, and one is never allowed to kill innocent persons even if it means saving many lives.

Although he condemned the opinion allowing the abortion of the animated fetus to save the mother, Comitolus was probably too close in time to Sanchez to take an explicit stand aginst him. But this was not true of Leonard Lessius (1554-1623), a Belgian Jesuit. In his *De iustitia et iure* he explicitly opposed Sanchez and his opinion on this question.[16] After stating the opinion and the reasons given for it, he observes that although he would not condemn it, he does not see how it can be true if it involves the direct expulsion of the fetus. Lessius does not think that it is permissible to give a woman a drug precisely to cause an abortion either before or after animation. After animation it would involve killing an innocent person. To prove that it would be wrong before animation, besides appealing to authority, he has recourse to the familiar argument from analogy with direct pollution. It will be remembered that Sanchez denied the parallel with direct expulsion of semen. He claimed that this was absolutely condemned because of the intense pleasure attached to it. Since this would not be present in expelling a fetus, there would not be the same reason for an absolute condemnation. Lessius refuses to accept this argument. The expulsion of semen (even for health's sake) is not wrong because of the pleasure involved. The morality of pleasure depends on the morality of the act to which it is attached. It is because the expulsion of semen takes place apart from its procreative purpose that it is wrong, not because it is pleasurable. If the use of sex was wrong because of the pleasure attached to it, it would be wrong for married people as well.

In justice to Sanchez it should be pointed out here that he was not arguing that direct pollution was wrong because of the pleasure attached to it. His argument was rather that the pleasure attached to the use of sex was a factor that had to be taken into consideration in estimating the danger of abuse. He did not say that it constituted the abuse. There is, of course, the implication that in a lifesaving situation the absence of a procreative goal is not the decisive moral factor in judging the morality of direct expulsion of semen; it is rather the danger of abuse. It may be that Lessiu intended no more than to express his disagreement with this position. But his charge against Sanchez appeared much more general.

Lessius also addressed himself to the supportive argument Sanchez uses; namely, that the unanimated fetus is a quasi-aggressor. He says that semen can also be considered an unjust aggressor in a situation where *ex abundantia* it is undermining a man's health. But direct expulsion of semen is not allowed even for health purposes, and no one questions this. There is even less reason for questioning the prohibition of direct expulsion of a fetus for health purposes. Also, if the unanimated fetus can be considered an unjust aggressor, the animated fetus will be even more so, since as it grows it makes greater demands on the life and health of the mother. To be consistent, Sanchez would have to allow abortion of an animated fetus, but this he does not do.

Lessius also offers a second reason against aborting an unanimated fetus to save the mother, namely, that it is not a means *per se* necessary to restore the health of the mother. Since he does not elucidate any further, one cannot be entirely sure of the meaning of this reason. The implication seems to be that the basic cause of the mother's problem is some disease from which she is suffering, not precisely the pregnancy. If this is so, the remedy would be some medicine or treatment aimed at curing the disease, not an abortion. But whatever the meaning underlying this reason, Lessius does not think abortion is either a licit or a necessary means to restore the health of the mother.

He tries to explain away authors such as Antoninus who held the position Sanchez was trying to defend. He admits that they do not speak too clearly but insists that they really mean to say no more than that it is permissible to give the mother medicine which causes an abortion, but not with this purpose in mind. He espouses this latter opinion as his own, allowing a mother to be given a drug directly conducive to her health, even though it carries with it danger of abortion, as long as the fetus is not animated. If the fetus is animated there must be concern for the spiritual welfare of the child. But if it is very probable that without the medicine both the mother and the fetus will die, it will be permissible to take it. To justify this position he appeals to the basic right of the mother to take medicine for her health. This right is not compromised by the fact that she is pregnant. She may take the medicine, then, even if it involves risk for the fetus.

There seems to be quite a bit of confusion regarding the opinion of Antoninus and his predecessor, John of Naples, about aborting an unanimated fetus to save the life of the mother. Peter of Navarre denied that anyone ever held this opinion. Sanchez, however, said that he has found no one who disagrees with it. Now Lessius, while admitting that Antoninus does not speak too clearly, says that he and his followers really meant to say no more than that it is permissible to give the mother medicine which causes an abortion, but not with this purpose in mind. Understandably, an author would like to put a benign interpretation on the opinion of his predecessors, especially if they seem to be defending something which he thinks wrong. Authors also like to list as much support for their opinions among their predecessors as possible. But is there any validity, for instance, to Lessius' assessment of Antoninus' opinion? Perhaps some explanation will be found in an examination of the distinction Corduba makes regarding *medicinae*. If one looks closely at these medicines, he will discover that only those which Corduba classifies as *de se salutifera* can be considered medicines in any strict sense, for example, baths, bloodletting, cathartics. Those which he called *de se mortifera*, such as beating a pregnant woman, knocking her down, trampling on her, giving her a poisonous potion, would hardly be considered medicines in any sense of the term. It seems inconceivable that John of Naples, Antoninus, or anyone else, would allow the use of such measures, especially on a dying woman. How could anyone reasonably think that such measures would help a dying woman? They would more likely bring on death. There is reason to think then that John of Naples and his followers were thinking in terms of medicines which Corduba considered *de se salutifera*, even though they carried with them a danger of abortion. One of the Hippocratic aphorisms actually stated that a pregnant woman will miscarry if bled. Another aphorism associated the danger of abortion with the use of purgatives.[17] Finally, Soranus, a Roman physician of the early second century, recommended protracted baths in his instruction on inducing abortion.[18] But all of these *medicinae* were considered general remedies, and in the days when little was known about specific diseases, and much less about specific remedies, they were prescribed very commonly for physical ailments.

The key question is whether John of Naples and his followers considered the pregnancy itself the source of danger to the mother, and therefore prescribed these remedies to remove the pregnancy. In one place, at least, Antoninus, citing John of Naples, says that the mother is in danger of death from the pregnancy. In another, however, (where he is speaking of an animated fetus) he assures the doctor that if he does not give the mother the medicine, he will not be the cause of her death, but the *morbus* (disease) will be. This seems to imply that it is some disease in the mother that calls for the medicine. Lessius obviously assumes that the source of the danger is some disease in the mother and that this is what the treatment is aimed at. The abortion then will be incidental. But if Antoninus really did consider the pregnancy the source of the danger, even though the recommended treatment might be bloodletting, it would be aimed at causing an abortion. Whatever may be said for the unclarity of Antoninus and John of Naples, Lessius has no doubt that Sanchez considered the fetus itself the source of danger to the mother. Lessius seems unwilling to admit this, and hence unwilling to consider abortion a necessary solution.

Lessius is also the first author to discuss in any critical way the time of animation since St. Thomas introduced the Aristotelian calculation regarding the time difference between the male and female fetus. He does not understand why there should be such a difference between the time of male and female animation. It seems more reasonable to him that both should be animated when they are formed. In support of this he cites the Septuagint version of Exodus, which seems to intimate that the fetus is animated as soon as it is formed. It is not clear here just what he had in mind, since it will be recalled that Aristotle and his followers seemed to hold a time difference in formation itself. At any rate Lessius goes on to cite the physician, Lemnius, who claimed that Hippocrates taught that the male fetus was formed from thirty to forty-five days after conception, and the femal fetus, thirty-five to fifty days. Lessius denies correctly that this is the opinion of Hippocrates and ascribes to him a thirty to forty-two day calculation for male and female formation.[19] Lessius' concern seemed to be only with the degree of difference; he did not question the difference itself. This would be left to later authors. Lessius never says which opinion he prefers.

Vincent Filliucius, another Italian Jesuit of the same period, also opposes direct abortion of the unanimated fetus even to save the mother. In his treatment of abortion he adopts the distinction Azor had already made between three kinds of abortion.[20] The first kind, which would ordinarily be classified as contraception today, consisted in taking a sterilizing potion, getting up immediately after intercourse to remove semen, or attempting to remove it in some other way. The other two types have as their object the unanimated and the animated fetus. All of these kinds of abortion involve mortal sin, although with a different degree of gravity. In speaking of abortion proper he makes use of a distinction introduced by Cajetan between perfect and imperfect killing. The mentality behind the distinction, which sought to extend the notion of homicide beyond the destruction of an animated fetus, was not new. Only the terminology was new. To Filliucius, imperfect killing, the destruction of the unanimated fetus, is not the killing of what is presently a man but of something that will be a man.

Filliucius argues against the direct expulsion of the unanimated fetus to save the life of the mother because it goes against the nature of generation and is intrinsically evil. He also agrees with Lessius that it is not a means *per se* necessary to save the life of the mother.[21] He even cites Sanchez in favor of this same position, commenting that what he says about procuring an abortion in this case must be understood in terms of an indirect abortion. He tries to argue this point by calling attention to Sanchez' opinion regarding a woman taking a sterilizing potion. In no case does Sanchez allow this. If he is to be consistent, he cannot then allow direct expulsion of the unanimated fetus. Filliucius has a point here, but even though there may be reason for challenging Sanchez' consistency, anyone who reads his text can hardly doubt that he is speaking of what later authors will call direct abortion. And this is the way he has been understood generally by his successors, even those who disagree with him.

As already hinted, Filliucius will allow the indirect abortion of the unanimated fetus to save the life of the mother. Surprisingly enough, he uses an argument which Sanchez used to justify direct abortion. The fetus is considered a quasi-aggressor, which gives the mother a right to defend herself. The argument from analogy with indirect pollution he uses only as confirmatory. He rules out abortion to save the reputation of the mother, or even her life from an outside threat, just as he does to remove the danger that might eventually come from a difficult parturition. As other authors already treated, he uses the Corduban distinction in dealing with abortion of the animated fetus, but with the restriction Sanchez set down regarding the spiritual welfare of the fetus.

More opposition to the opinion that it was permissible to abort an unanimated fetus to save the life of the mother came from Basilio Ponce (Pontius) (1569-1629), a Spanish Augustinian from Leon.[22] He sides with those who hold that it is never permitted to procure an abortion directly, even if the fetus is not animated. This seems truer to him than the opinion which Sanchez says is common, namely that if the fetus is unanimated it may be aborted to save the mother. He refuses to accept any of Sanchez' arguments. While he admits that it does not constitute homicide, he says that it is against nature and is as evil as direct pollution. He affirms against Sanchez the analogy between pollution and abortion. Semen and the unanimated fetus both have to do with human generation, and have no other purpose. They are not aimed at the health of the man or the mother. Nor is the unanimated fetus

part of the mother. So there is no analogy with the removal of a diseased organ or member. Or if it can be
considered a part of the mother, he would agree with
Peter of Navarre that it should also be permissible to
abort an unanimated fetus to save the mother from some
extrinsic threat either to her life or reputation. These
reasons can be just as urgent as saving her life from some
intrinsic threat, and it is just as possible that there would
be no other means available. Lessius had already turned
one of Sanchez' arguments against him, namely that the
fetus in this situation is a quasi-aggressor, arguing that
this would force him to justify not only direct expulsion of
semen but also the abortion of the animated fetus. Both
could be just as much aggressors. Now Ponce does the
same with his argument that the unanimated fetus is part
of the mother. He shows that this would also justify the
removal of the fetus to protect the mother from some
extrinsic threat to her life or reputation. Sanchez had argued explicitly against abortion in these cases. It should
be kept in mind that he used these arguments only as
supports to his main argument (that the unanimated fetus
was not yet a human being), but if they confirmed his
position regarding the exception he wanted to make, they
weakened it against the exceptions he opposed.

When the fetus is animated, Ponce says that authors
commonly do not allow direct abortion to save the life of
the mother. All allow the use of drugs or treatments aimed
directly at the mother's health, but many set down limitations. Some allow the mother to take such treatments, but
will not allow the doctor to give them. Others demand that
the treatment be more conducive to the health of the
mother than to the expulsion of the fetus. Still others do
not allow the use of such treatments if there is good
reason to expect that the fetus will survive the mother and
be able to be baptized. Ponce then presents briefly the
arguments used to justify the basic position taken here.
They are the arguments already used by Sanchez. Ponce
considers all of them probable, but makes some qualifications of his own.

He sees no difficulty with the use of such treatments as bloodletting. In this type of treatment one is merely depriving the child of nourishment which belongs by right more to the mother than to the child. But he agrees with Vasquez that if the treatment involves some *alteratio positiva* in regard to the fetus, it would be sinful homicide. He does not consider the spiritual condition of the child a decisive factor. The spiritual condition of the mother is doubtful also, and she has no duty *ex officio* to feed the child. It is no clearer here than it is in Vasquez what is meant by calling the spiritual condition of the mother doubtful. But when he says that the mother has no duty *ex officio* to feed the child, he is probably speaking of an obligation in justice, such as a pastor might have to minister to his parishioners in extreme spiritual need even at the risk of his life.

Generally speaking, Ponce is allying himself with Vasquez in the position he takes. Nor does he feel that the arguments given to support the general position taken by other authors really justify any more than he is willing to allow. The argument from St. Thomas is not convincing to him, since it is not clear. St. Thomas says that an act gets its moral species from the intention of the agent.[23] Ponce says that an act can also get its species from what is only indirectly willed. He offers the example of the hunter who shoots intending to hit some game, but actually kills a man standing close to the game. As long as he foresees the danger and places the cause from which it will probably result, the hunter will be responsible, even if he does not directly intend the death of the man. The same would be true of an act that would positively induce an abortion. He argues, as Vasquez did, against the analogy with indirect expulsion of semen. He refuses also to accept the analogy with killing an innocent person in a just war. This is justified by the common good. There is no common good here, but only the good of an individual, the mother. He would admit the analogy with the horseman fleeing an unjust aggressor who runs over a child in the road, but since he denies that this is permissible, the analogy is in his favor. No one has a right to protect his own life by some act that would positively imperil some innocent person. He may protect himself only if his act provides protection without positively contributing to the death of an innocent person.

At about the same time a German Jesuit, Paul Laymann (1574-1635), in a brief statement on abortion to save the mother follows in the footsteps of Sanchez.[24] He allows the abortion of the unanimated fetus to save the life of the mother because the fetus in these circumstances is in some sense an unjust aggressor. This gives the mother the right to defend herself. If the fetus is animated he will allow only the use of treatments aimed at restoring the mother's health. This is no more than the position of Corduba and his followers, but Laymann gives a more positive slant to the reason behind this allowance. Previous authors had seen this as more of a conflict situation, or at least as a legitimate option in favor of the mother. Laymann sees these treatments as basically conducive to the health of both mother and fetus. Since it is extremely rare that the fetus will survive the mother in these cases, whatever is conducive to the health of the mother will be conducive also, even if secondarily, to the health of the fetus. If the abortion occurs, it will only be *per accidens*. Laymann's predecessors had frequently observed that it is rare that the fetus survives the death of the mother, but did not regard the treatment, at least explicitly, as contributing in any way to the welfare of the child. Their attention was fixed more on the danger to the child.

Perhaps the most extensive study on the mother or child dilemma at that time was the work of a French Jesuit, Theophile Raynaud (1582-1663). A very prolific writer in many fields, he wrote a monograph *De ortu infantium* which dealt in a tangential way with the problem of therapeutic abortion.[25] The author was really more concerned with the problem of caesarean section, but in Chapter IX he deals with the case where this means death to the fetus, either because of the immaturity of the fetus or lack of skill in the surgeon. There is reason to believe that in the early seventeenth century a caesarean section may have been as lethal an attack on the mother as on the child. Otherwise, it would be hard to understand the harsh language Paul Comitolus used in discussing it. But however impractical the question may have been at the time, Raynaud devotes considerable space to it, and in so doing gives a comprehensive treatment of what his predecessors have said about aborting an animated fetus to save the life of the mother.

In introducing the question he first considers the norm which according to Antoninus was used by John of Naples to condemn the abortion of the animated fetus to save the life of the mother.[26] The norm is that of St. Ambrose, that if you cannot help one person without harming another, it is better not to help him. Raynaud shows by examples that this would lead to absurdities if considered a universal principle. So he rejects it as such, and more in particular as applying to the present case. He then presents the reasons why some authors give preference to the mother in this case. She has the stronger right, since she is the cause of the child. It is not right to destroy a cause in order to preserve an effect. From another viewpoint it is not right for a person conferring a benefit on another to suffer injury or harm at that person's hands. Finally, if the fetus could express his own mind on the subject, he certainly would not want to bring about his mother's death in order to survive. A person with the use of reason would consider this the worst kind of ingratitude. For these reasons some authors, unnamed, allow a caesarean section that will bring death to the fetus but save the mother's life.

Raynaud then goes on to point out that those doctors who allow the destruction of the fetus when it cannot be delivered otherwise to save the life of the mother would agree with his solution. He also claims the support of Tertullian, as well as Simon of Brescia and Socinus. From the discussion of these authors already seen, this claim would have to be questioned, if not denied.

He admits that most authors do not allow the use of means aimed directly at the death of the fetus even to save the life of the mother, and that these authors will not allow a caesarean section in this case, since it seems to be aimed directly at the death of the fetus rather than the life of the mother. This is true even of authors who allow the use of treatments aimed at restoring the health of the mother. There would be even less chance of approval by an author like Vasquez who would not approve even of treatments aimed at the health of the mother if they positively affect the fetus. These authors allow only such treatment as phlebotomy. Raynaud mentions finally the opposition that would come from those who allow the mother to use means directed at the death of the fetus but do not permit anyone else to do so. Since a caesarean section would have to be done by a doctor, they could not allow it.

In introducing his own position Raynaud says that in this type of case a distinction should be made between the demands of justice and those of charity.[27] This is because there are many things that can be done without violating justice but which do violate charity. His initial stand is that if one is considering only the demands of justice it would be permissible to perform a caesarean section to save the life of the mother even though this would bring death to the fetus. In judging what is permissible when the life of the mother is at stake, he is not concerned either with the nature of the means used or the intention of the agent. Even if the means tend directly to the death of the fetus and the intention of the agent is to kill the fetus, it makes no difference. The reason he can take this position is that he considers the fetus an unjust aggressor. To the objection that it is the disease that is the aggressor, not the fetus, he responds that this is like saying that the murderer is not the unjust aggressor, but the weapon in his hand. It is not clear whether he is speaking of a disease in the fetus or a disease in the mother caused by the pregnancy, but in either case he considered the fetus an unjust aggressor. And if the fetus is an unjust aggressor, it makes no difference to Raynaud whether the mother or doctor causes its death.

Raynaud does not consider the fetus a formal aggressor, that is, one responsible for his act, but he argues correctly that one may defend himself even against a material aggressor. He then goes on to compare this case with that of the child playing on a narrow bridge in the path of a horseman who is fleeing an unjust aggressor. Even though the child is not an unjust aggressor in this case, serious authors allow the horseman to continue in his flight even if it means the death of the child. The fetus in the case he is considering is at least an obstacle (as the child on the bridge) to the safety of the mother. It should be permissible then to sacrifice the fetus to save the mother's life.

When the death of the fetus is involved in saving the mother's life, Raynaud argues that it does not make any difference what means are used. The fact that the child is innocent, that is, not a formal aggressor, makes no difference. Neither is the insane person a formal aggressor, yet one can take positive measures against him. There are even authors who allow the horseman to take the life of the child on the bridge by positive action, that is by trampling. If you are taking the life of another person, it makes no difference whether it is by the sword, by starvation, or by poisoning. So Raynaud has no sympathy for the distinction made by Vasquez or Pontius. One gets the impression also that he would not even make the Corduban distinction regarding means, but he never mentions this explicitly. If one tries to follow the tenor of his argument, what is not clear is the reason behind his unconcern about means. If this is because he considers the fetus an unjust aggressor, although this would be questioned, his conclusion about means would have validity. But if he compares the fetus to the child on the bridge, who is not even a material aggressor, however he might feel about Vasquez' distinction, he cannot ignore that made by Corduba without parting company with all his contemporaries. This seems to be precisely what he did.

Raynaud also denies the pertinence of the distinction between direct and indirect intention. One cannot say that an indirect intention in this case would be licit, while a direct intention illicit. It is generally accepted that an indirect intention is sufficient for most sins. For an act to be sinful, therefore, it is sufficient that the intention be indirect. On the other hand, if one admits that an act would not be sinful with an indirect intention, it is a sign that it would not be sinful with a direct intention.[28] If what a person is doing is just, he can directly intend it and all its adjuncts. He illustrates again with the case of self-defense. In so doing, however, he aligns himself with those authors who go counter to St. Thomas and those followers of his who would not allow a direct intention even in self-defense. With Lessius and others he holds that when the death of an aggressor is necessary in self-defense, it can be directly intended as a necessary means to a good end. Again, Raynaud puts his case in a context of self-defense against unjust aggression. In this context there is clearly a difference of opinion among the moralists of his time regarding the morality of the intention behind the act. In allowing a direct intention Raynaud is still in good company. Outside of this context, however, he would stand alone. Where there is no question of unjust aggression, no other author would allow a direct intention of killing. So the strength of Raynaud's position depends on whether the fetus can be considered an unjust aggressor. No other author of his time or previous periods has suggested this, at least regarding the animated fetus.

Having solved the case to his own satisfaction on the level of justice, Raynaud proceeds to a consideration of the demands of charity. His fundamental principle here does not differ from that of his predecessors.[29] If the procedure would deprive the child or fetus of a baptism it might otherwise receive, it would be wrong, since the spiritual good of the child must be preferred to the physical welfare of the mother. But he makes it clear that he is not basing his conclusions on any general obligation not to take the life of an unjust aggressor because it would jeopardize his eternal salvation. Raynaud would deny, and correctly, that the adult aggressor is in a state of what moralists call extreme spiritual need. This is the state of a person who cannot escape eternal damnation without the help of someone else. The adult aggressor could solve his problem without help, that is, simply by stopping his aggression. So there is no question in this case of spiritual need that cannot be relieved in any other way. Also, if one were inhibited in this way, a tremendous advantage would be given to evil persons, and the incentive to observe justice would be taken away. But the situation of the fetus is different. There is no other known way his salvation can be achieved but by baptism, so his spiritual welfare is really in the hands of the doctor and mother.

Raynaud then turns to Vasquez' statement that this obligation in charity would ordinarily not be present because of the doubt about the spiritual state of the mother herself. She certainly does not have to prefer the eternal salvation of the child to her own eternal salvation, and since no one is ever sure of his or her salvation, an obligation in charity could hardly be present. Raynaud argues correctly that all that is required is moral certitude regarding one's own spiritual state. If more were required, it would never be permissible to forego self-defense to save an aggressor from eternal damnation. Yet all authors permit this. One does not need the kind of certitude in this matter that removes all doubt. It is enough that the person be at peace and have the freedom from doubt of the ordinary conscientious person. In the last analysis, of course, Raynaud admits with his predecessors that if there is no chance the fetus will survive anyhow, there would be no obligation in charity.

Raynaud dealt only with abortion (caesarean section) to save the mother from an intrinsic threat to her life and argued that there was no injustice, whatever the means and whatever the intention, without distinguishing in any way between the animated and unanimated fetus. At about the same time a Spanish jurist, Francis Torreblanca

(d. 1645) in his *Epitome delictorum* extended the exception of John of Naples to include cases where the threat to life was not immediate or came from an extrinsic source or even where only the mother's reputation was at stake.[30] As sources for this broader view he mentions Antoninus, Sylvester, Covaruvvias, Navarrus, Corduba, and Thomas Sanchez, none of whom really endorsed it. In fact, Corduba does not even allow the original case of John of Naples. Torreblanca himself must be credited with whatever distinction is deserved for being the first one to hold this opinion.

At about the same time another Spaniard, Ioannes Aegidius Trullench (d. 1644), took up the same issue, that is, whether and under what circumstances it would be permissible to abort an unanimated fetus.[31] He accepts the abortion of the fetus to save the life of the mother, arguing that this is not so intrinsically evil that it cannot be allowed for some justifying reason. He denies the analogy with direct pollution for the reason given by Sanchez, namely, that there is no pleasure involved in abortion. He continues, however, with the statement that an abortion would not be permissible just to hide a sin, or even a threat to life or reputation that would result if the pregnancy became public. His reason is that already given by Sanchez, namely, that the fetus is not an aggressor in this case, and the danger can be avoided in other ways. He does not find the opposite opinion acceptable, although he says that it may not be altogether improbable. But his own opinion is more probable and closer to the truth.

Trullench holds that the fetus is animated after forty and ninety days. Although he mentions the opinion ascribed to Hippocrates and accepted by others, he says his own opinion should be followed both because it is more common and also because it lends itself less to causing scruples. In a case of doubt the presumption is that the fetus is animated after forty days; before that time the presumption would be, at least in regard to penalties, that it was not animated.

After accepting the basic Corduban distinction regarding the abortion of the animated fetus to save the life of the mother, he takes up the further questions raised by Sanchez in this regard. The first has to do with medicine which is not principally but only equally *sanativa*, being also equally *mortifera*. Trullench gives no opinion of his own, but merely says that while some allow this, others claim that it is wrong, even when it is certain that both mother and fetus will otherwise die. The next question deals with medicine or treatment which is uncertain; that is, it is not known whether it will be beneficial or harmful. Truellench does not consider the opinion which allows the use of such medicine improbable, but he feels that the opposite opinion is more probable and safer in practice, at least in so far as the former would *oblige* a doctor to use a doubtful treatment. Trullench will allow the use of a doubtful medicine, when no more certain remedy is available, but only where the doubt is whether the medicine will be beneficial or not, not where the doubt is whether it will be beneficial or harmful.

———————◆———————

The legal developments of the period seem to be related largely to the Renaissance atmosphere of the time. Renewed contact with the Roman law raised questions in the minds of civil jurists about the death penalty for abortion, even of the formed or animated fetus. Contact with the culture of Rome and Greece also brought with it an increase in vice. This prompted a counterattack by the Church. In the area of procreation this took the form of an excommunication attached to any attempt to interfere with it either by sterilization or abortion. Within a short time this penalty was limited to abortion of the formed fetus, and it remained such for the next three centuries. In the theological debate the exception made by John of Naples for aborting an unanimated fetus to save the mother's life met with considerable opposition, although it would continue to claim followers. The opposition centered largely around the consistency of making this exception without allowing other exceptions which the same arguments would seem to justify.

The Corduban distinction would continue to be accepted but with some modification by authors like Pontius. Laymann took a more positive view of medicine or treatment aimed at saving the mother's life than previous authors. He saw such medicine as benefiting not only the mother but the fetus as well, although only secondarily. Previous authors saw more of a conflict here. Raynaud was the first author to argue in favor of taking the life even of an animated fetus to save the mother's life. He would not have any followers for the next several centuries.

More of a following could be claimed for the opinion which wanted to extend the exception of John of Naples to cases where the life or reputation of the mother was threatened by some extrinsic source. But even this exception met with general opposition by the moral theologians of the time. It was condemned toward the end of the century by Innocent XI.

CHAPTER TEN

———————◆———————

Discussion Continued
(1600-1679)

The time of infusion of the human soul has been under discussion during the whole Christian era. For many centuries, however, the opinion that the soul was infused at the time of formation was generally accepted. Generally, also, the Aristotelian estimate of forty and ninety (80) days was accepted as the time of formation, although after Lessius some theologians showed a preference for the Hippocratic computation, or that of Lemnius. Aristotle himself held a succession of souls, postulating first a vegetative soul and then an animal soul before the infusion of the rational soul, and in this he was followed by St. Thomas and many scholastic theologians. Theologians like Sanchez, however, considered the fetus a part of the mother until the rational soul was infused, and so would not have to postulate a prior vegetative or animal soul for it. In 1620, Thomas Fienus (De Feynes) (1567-1631), a Belgian physician and professor at the University of Louvain, wrote a book entitled *De formatrice fetus liber* in which he challenged the idea of delaying the infusion of the rational soul until the fetus was formed.[1] Fienus held that the soul is infused on or about the third day after conception.[2] After ruling out other causes of formation, that is, the uterus itself, the semen, the generative faculties of the parents, he concludes that it must result from a soul introduced into the conceptus about the third day. He deduces this from the fact that the *membranum,* which covers the semen and which is completed by the fifth day, begins to form at this time.[3] Thus far his opinion would not depart from that of Aristotle. Where he differs is in postulating a rational soul right from the beginning. He argues that the same soul that is ultimately responsible for the formation of the fetus must be responsible for the formation of this membrane, and this must be the rational soul.[4] A succession of souls makes no sense to Fienus, and he presents several strong arguments against it. The rational soul, then, which all agree is the ultimate soul present in the fetus, according to Fienus, must be there from the beginning.

Fienus realizes that in taking this position he is opposing what is practically a universal tradition, namely, that the human soul is infused only after the fetus is formed. So he devotes considerable time to refuting the authority behind this tradition.[5] The authority is both sacred and profane. The sacred authority behind the tradition is that of scripture, the Fathers, and the canons; the profane authority, Hippocrates, Galenus, and Aristotle. To the familiar objection from the Septuagint he responds that the Latin (Vulgate) text, which is authoritative in the Church, makes no distinction between the formed and unformed fetus. Morever, even the Greek text does not say that the fetus which is not formed does not yet have a human soul. All it says is that a fetus that does not yet have *motum et sensum* (movement and senses) is not a perfect man, but only imperfect.[6] Therefore, one who destroys such a fetus should not be given the death penalty, as though he had destroyed a perfect man. The death penalty should be imposed only for the destruction of a perfect man, that is, one who has *motum et sensum.* As for the argument from Genesis, that God did not breathe a soul into Adam until he was formed, one cannot argue that because God created Adam this way, everybody else is produced in the same way. He argues correctly also that Augustine cannot be cited as an authority for this position, since he was not at all clear in this own mind that animation did not occur until the fetus was formed. And the same indecision will be found in Jerome. Fienus adds that not too much confidence can be put in the opinions of profane authorities, since they have such a variety of opinions. Strangely enough, he has no response to the authority of the sacred canons.

After Fienus, another physician, Paolo Zacchia (1584-1659), physician general of the Vatican State, also argued against delaying the infusion of the rational soul until the time of formation. In the first book of his *Quaestionum medicolegalium* he discusses the various opinions that have been proposed in this regard.[7] At that time, after considering the various estimates that have been made ranging from three days to ninety, he opts for the thirty- to forty-two-day estimate since this is based both on reason and experimentation. Either that, or settle for an estimate of sixty days for both male and female fetus. But when he returns to the question at the end of his work, he argues in favor of immediate animation, that is, that animation takes place at the time of conception.[8] He comes to this conclusion after a lengthy argument against a succession of souls. Like Fienus he holds that there can be only one soul from the beginning and that is the human soul. In defending this position he knows that he has to respond to all the arguments for the traditional position. But before doing so, he shows that although Hippocrates said that formation took place after thirty and forty-two days, he said nothing about delayed animation. According to Zacchia, Hippocrates was actually a traducianist as far as the origin of the soul was concerned. The theory that the human soul was infused at the time of formation was really that of Aristotle.

The main objection to immediate animation came from the Septuagint text of Exodus. Zacchia's response to this is that the Septuagint is really not a translation but a commentary *proprio marte factum*.[9] The Vulgate makes no distinction between the formed and unformed fetus. As for the *Qui abortionis*, he maintains that the *mulier* in the law refers to the *poculum abortionis*, the *homo* to the *poculum amatorium*.[10] The word *homo* does not include an animated fetus. He admits that the canonists and the laws themselves have made the distinction between the animated and unanimated fetus, but adds that in matters of this kind they depend on the opinions of philosophers. Also, they were more interested in varying the penalty for abortion than they were in the distinction. Even if one accepts immediate animation, there are many reasons for imposing a heavier penalty on a later abortion. Greater damage is done in the abortion of a fetus after forty days than of a younger fetus, just as it is more damaging to cut down an older tree than a young one. Also, abortions after forty days are more difficult and more dangerous for the mother. Then too one can be more certain of the pregnancy after forty days than before because of the movement of the fetus.[11] Zacchia says finally that the distinction may merely represent the limitations of our knowledge. It is linked to the presence of observable movement in the fetus. But one cannot rule out the presence of the soul even before this occurs, although it cannot be established with clear evidence.

From another viewpoint, however, Zacchia has often wondered why philosophers use the criterion of motion to determine the presence of the rational soul.[12] Motion is no more a sign of the presence of a rational soul than nourishment, growth, or sensation. If one is going to argue to the presence of a rational soul from some functional sign, it would have to be from some function peculiar to the rational soul. Some may want to argue that the presence of motion indicates that the fetus is perfectly formed. This may be, but the perfection of the fetus at this stage makes it in no way suitable for rational operation. It can hardly be said then that the fetus is disposed at this stage for the reception of the rational soul.

Another argument against immediate animation is drawn from the fact that fetuses aborted before forty days are not baptized. Zacchia admits this practice but explains that they are so fragile at this stage that they die immediately. If there were any signs of movement even at this stage, the fetus would be baptized.

Before leaving Zacchia, it might be well to call attention to another minority position he defended, namely, that the female as well as the male contributed semen to human procreation.[13] The common opinion, reflected in St. Thomas, but stemming originally from Aristotle, was that only the male provides the semen, that is, the active agent, in generation. The woman provides the matter, *viz*, the blood. It made no sense to Aristotle to say that generation resulted from two seeds. The so-called *lympha* produced by the woman in intercourse was not seed in any real sense, and not necessary for generation. Women could become pregnant without producing this substance at all. On the other hand, if a woman produced seed, since she also provided the matter of generation, there would be no need for contact with the male at all. Hippocrates, however, held that this female secretion was semen in the strict sense and as such was needed for conception. But neither Aristotle nor Hippocrates had any concept of the female ovum or the function it performed in conception. They were aware of the existence of ovaries. To Hippocrates they served the same function as the testicles in the male. The difference between the male and the female was that in the male the semen was ejaculated outside the body; in the female it was ejaculated into the uterus. But to some the female ovaries did no more than provide a certain symmetry with the male physiology, in much the same way as the male breast.

The opinion of Aristotle was generally accepted, but Hippocrates was followed by one of the greatest physicians of the Roman world, Galenus, during the second century of the Christian era. It was this opinion also that Zacchia was now defending. His basic argument was that nature does nothing in vain. Since the female has all the equipment the male has for producing semen, the female must produce such semen. His argument was, of course, valid. What he was not aware of, however, was the fact that the function of the ovaries was to produce *ova* rather than *semen*. But this knowledge came only gradually and the ovum itself was not discovered until the early nineteenth century. The question regarding female semen is treated briefly here because a few later moralists seemed to accept the theory and reflected it in their condemnation of abortion of the unanimated fetus as the destruction of *duplex semen* (double semen).

The discussion regarding the kind of treatment permitted a pregnant woman to save her life was continued by Antonius Diana (1585-1663), a Clerk Regular from Palermo, in his *Resolutiones*.[14] In accepting the Corduban distinction, he does not argue in terms of the *ius potius* of the mother but rather in terms of the more positive approach taken by Laymann. The fetus is so dependent on the mother that anything that contributes to her health contributes secondarily to its health. If it causes the death of the fetus, this will be accidental. Diana sides with Sanchez regarding medicine that is equally conducive to abortion, as well as medicine that is doubtful. The presumption in all these cases is that the mother and the fetus will both die otherwise. If there is reason to believe that the fetus will survive the death of the mother, the spiritual welfare of the fetus must be taken into consideration.

Diana knows of two cases where the fetus survived the death of the mother and was removed alive after her death. He is not pleased with the opinion of such authors as Vasquez and Pontus, who would allow the mother to take the medicine even in these cases if she is doubtful about her own salvation. If she is in a state of doubt, her duty is to get back into the state of grace. But even if she is in the state of grace, he says, some authors will allow her to take the medicine, since she is not bound *ex officio* to take care of the spiritual needs of the child. This would apply, for instance, to a pastor who by reason of the office he holds would be obliged in justice to take care of the spiritual need of his parishioners. Others, according to these authors, are not bound to risk their lives to relieve even extreme spiritual need.

If the fetus is unanimated, Diana thinks it probable that one may use means directly tending to abortion if necessary to save the life of the mother. But he does this only after citing the objections of a theologian by the name of Mazuchellus to the supporting arguments made by Sanchez. Mazuchellus would not admit, because of arguments already seen, that the unanimated fetus is either a part of the mother or an aggressor. Diana himself will not allow any other exceptions to the prohibition against abortion. He will not allow an abortion to protect the reputation, or even the life, of a woman who became pregnant as the result of adultery or fornication. Neither will he allow it where there are prospects of a dangerous delivery because of a narrow pelvis or some other reason. As already noted, Sanchez did not admit the analogy between these cases and that which he allowed. Ponce, on the other hand, did admit the analogy and felt that one would either have to allow abortion in all of these cases or none of them. Ponce chose the latter. Diana names Torreblanca as an author who is willing to allow all of them. In this first resolution Diana says that he will leave the discussion of Torreblanca's opinion to more learned men, but he admits that he does not like it.[15]

In the following resolution, which was written some time later, Diana says that he did not think Torreblanca would have any followers but to his surprise he finds that he does.[16] He mentions Zambelli, Bordone, Lezana, and Trullench. He also mentions a most learned member of the Society of Jesus whom he does not name, but whom he consulted. But Diana himself is not moved. In another resolution he says that it would be no more licit to destroy a child at this time than it would be to suffocate it after birth. Also, the fetus is not the unjust aggressor. The cause of the mother's trouble is her own sin, and the aggressor is some third party, the husband or the father.

Diana also took up the controversy that was developing over the time of animation of the fetus. Lessius had cast doubt on the Aristotelian computation by questioning the time difference between male and female animation. He opted in favor of animation taking place at the same time as formation, implying that there would be no such difference if this norm were followed. He mentioned explicitly Lemnius' and Hippocrates' computations of the time of formation, but did not really go beyond expressing his dissatisfaction with the traditional reckoning of the time of animation. Diana mentions for the first time the opinion of Thomas Fienus that the fetus is animated with a rational soul about the third day after conception at the latest. In spite of this he says that he still prefers the forty and eighty day estimate and supports this preference with the statement that the Sacred Penitentiary follows this estimate. He thinks that to avoid causing scruples it is important not to depart from it.

The question of abortion to save the mother was taken up at this time by one of the most illustrious theologians of the period, Ioannes de Lugo (1583-1660), a Spanish Jesuit born in Madrid.[17] He taught for twenty years at the Roman College of the Jesuits and was later considered by Alphonsus Liguori *facile princeps* among theologians since Thomas Aquinas. After posing the question about abortion to save the life of the mother Lugo says that a distinction must be made. If the drug is taken directly to cause the abortion, it would be wrong both before and after the animation for a woman to take it. In putting his response in these terms Lugo is departing somewhat from the distinction made by Corduba. Corduba's distinction was based largely on the nature of medicine or treatment used. Lugo approaches the issue more from the viewpoint of the intention. If one intends the abortion, even bloodletting would be wrong. It will be remembered that this was one of the medicines which Corduba considered *principaliter sanativa*, and therefore permissible. It may be that Corduba would have agreed with Lugo, but he never really considered the possibility of using such a treatment with the intention of abortion.

Lugo says he knows that some allow direct abortion before animation to prevent the danger to a mother's life that might come from a future delivery, or to prevent the danger to her life or reputation that might come from some extrinsic source. Others, such as Sanchez, will allow an abortion only when the mother is immediately threatened by some disease. Lugo himself is not satisfied with the reasons Sanchez gave for the limitation he set, but he merely repeats objections already seen. Because of these objections he concludes that it is better to deny with Vasquez that direct abortion is ever licit, arguing from an analogy with the obligation never directly to expel semen.

It may be recalled that Sanchez opposed this analogy.[18] As Lugo says, Sanchez argued that nature does not permit man to expel semen outside of intercourse under any circumstances, not precisely because it is an antigenerative act, but because of the danger arising from the intense pleasure associated with it. If seminal emission were ever permitted outside of intercourse, it would not be possible to control abuse. The same danger would not arise from abortion, since there is no such pleasure attached to it. Lugo does not challenge Sanchez, as Lessius did, arguing that the pleasure attached to the expulsion of semen is not the basic reason for the malice of the act. He points out rather that if one examines the question carefully, he will find that there is a clear analogy between the two cases. If abortion were ever allowed, it would also give rise to the danger of abuse. It is precisely the fear of pregnancy that serves as a brake to passion and often prevents fornication and adultery. The allowance of abortion for any reason would tend to encourage fornication and adultery, just as the allowance of the expulsion of semen outside of intercourse would tend to encourage this practice (or other violations of sex morality). To prevent such abuses of the generative function nature has denied to man any authority to expel either semen or the fetus independently of the goal of generation.

Having disposed of the question of direct expulsion of a fetus to save the life of the mother, Lugo asks whether it is permissible for a pregnant woman to take some drug not to cause an abortion but rather to protect her life. In response he states that one must still make a distinction. If the drug promotes the health of the mother only by causing an abortion, the abortion is still directly intended, although to achieve another purpose. But if the drug is useful for preserving the life of the mother, even though it consequently and unintentionally causes an abortion, it is permissible to use the drug if the fetus is not yet animated. He argued this thesis on the basis of the familiar analogy with indirect pollution.

Lugo is having recourse here to a distinction made previously in relation to the general question of killing an innocent person.[19] He says that this is permitted if it is not intended. The meaning of this statement is not simply that it is permissible if it is not intended as an end, so that if it were just a means to an end, it would be permissible. It is rather that if killing an innocent person is either intended as an end or chosen as a means (to some other end) even though it is not the ultimate goal, *directe tamen eligitur et amatur* (it is directly chosen and embraced.) It is in some sense intended, that is, in so far as it is conducive to the goal ultimately intended. Lugo illustrated this with the example of the unjust aggressor who protects himself with an innocent child. Self-defense is permissible even though it means the death of the innocent child as long as the act terminates in the death of the aggressor, which is directly willed. But it would not be permissible, for instance, in time of war to shoot innocent children to get their parents to surrender. In this case the death of the children would be a means to the end sought, and therefore willed directly. Similarly if a drug achieves its goal of saving the life of the mother only by causing an abortion, it is willed or intended as a means to an end, and therefore directly.

So Lugo adds a new dimension to the whole discussion of abortion to save the life of the mother. Corduba responded to this problem with a distinction based on the nature of the treatment used to achieve this purpose. Lugo apparently did not feel that the problem of direct intention could be solved merely by an appeal to the nature of the treatment used. It would be possible to have a direct intention of abortion even with the use of a strictly therapeutic means such as bloodletting. By putting the emphasis on the intention he could guarantee against this. But in shifting the emphasis he had to make it clear that a direct intention covered the means as well as the end. So even if the abortion was a means to save the life of the mother, the intention would have to be considered direct.

In the discussion thus far Lugo had in mind the unanimated fetus. He now brings up the problem of the animated fetus. As for the time of animation he prefers what he thinks is the estimate of Hippocrates, thirty to forty-five days for the male fetus, thirty-five to fifty days for the female. Curiously enough, in treating the abortion of the animated fetus, he shifts his attention to the nature of the means again. He says that he is in agreement with Vasquez that the drug or treatment used should not bring about the death of the fetus in some positive way. He would allow such things as bloodletting or baths, which tend only negatively to the death of the fetus, namely by taking away what would be necessary for the sustenance of the child. But he does not allow anything that would be positively conducive to the death of the fetus. This would be tantamount to giving a poisonous drug to an innocent person to save one's own life. The conclusion seems to be that if the drug contributed in any positive way to the death of the fetus, the abortion must be judged a means to the desired end.

It is hard to see how this requirement can be reconciled with what Lugo said previously about a direct intention. There he seemed to be satisfied that if an action did not enter into the intention either as a means or an end, it was not directly intended, and therefore could be permitted. Is he backing away from this position when he demands that the medicine or treatment cause no positive change in the status of the fetus? It will be remembered that Vasquez, who originally made this qualification in the Corduban distinction, demanded more than just the absence of a direct intention.[20] One who placed a positive cause of death would be responsible even without a direct intention. Vasquez made a distinction in this respect between placing a positive cause of death and placing a positive cause of expelling semen. The difference between the two was a dynamic force behind the expulsion of semen which was not present in killing. The existence of such a force was sufficient to excuse one from the consequences of placing a positive cause of seminal expulsion unintentionally. The consequent expulsion would be traceable to this force rather than the act placed. In the absence of such a force in killing the consequences would be traceable to the positive cause itself. The one who placed the cause would be accountable even if he did not intend the consequences.

What makes Lugo's appeal to Vasquez' norm surprising is that he has just said that killing an innocent (nonaggressor) person in self-defense could be justified as long as it was not intended as a means or an end. And in the cases of which he was speaking (the child on the road, the child used as a shield) there is no doubt that the act of self-defense was positively conducive to the death of the innocent party. Even in dealing with the unanimated fetus his whole concern was with the intention. It is only in reference to the animated fetus that he adds the Vasquez requirement. Since there is no indication that he accepts Vasquez' ideas about the sufficiency of an indirect intention in any of the above cases, it seems quite inconsistent to impose the added requirement here.

When the fetus is animated Lugo also demands that the order of grace be considered as well as the order of nature. If the spiritual good of the child is considered, the mother may have to abstain from the use of medicine that would save her life but only with a resulting abortion. Here Lugo cites the opinion of Turrianus who held that in practice such an obligation would rarely be present. The mother would have to be certain of her own spiritual condition and certain also that the eternal welfare of the child would be thereby secured. But it rarely happens that both of these conditions are verified. Lugo does not react favorably to this opinion. As for the spiritual state of the mother, if she thinks that she is probably in the state of mortal sin, she has an obligation to get back into the state of grace, for which she can prepare herself by prayer and the sacraments. Otherwise even a pastor or other person bound *ex officio* to relieve the extreme spiritual need of a parishioner would not be obliged to do so if he thought he himself was probably in the state of mortal sin. Also, if one demands certainty not only about one's own salvation but also that of the other party, the precept to lay down one's life for his neighbor would be purely speculative.

Lugo prefers the opinion of Sanchez, namely that the obligation to abstain would rarely be present in this case because it would be almost miraculous if the fetus survived the mother anyhow. It would have to be very probable that the fetus would survive long enough to be baptized before an obligation could be present.

A German contemporary of the authors recently seen, a Jesuit named Herman Busenbaum (1609-68), wrote a very influential handbook of moral theology. It became the basis of three important commentaries (by LaCroix, Alphonsus Liguori, and Ballerini) which spanned the next two centuries. Busenbaum is important chiefly because he presents a convenient summary of the opinions of his predecessors, but on the question of abortion he also contributes some interesting interpretations of his own. He first states the common opinion regarding abortion, namely that it may never be committed maliciously, since it involves homicide or at least tends toward killing and is against the nature of generation.[21] He then presents the divided opinion of his predecessors regarding abortion of the unanimated fetus to save the life of the mother, but adds his own opinion that in practice Lessius and his followers must be followed. He gives no reason for this, but simply asks why anyone would want to cause an abortion directly when an indirect abortion would solve the problem.[22] He seems to be dealing with the case where the mother in danger of death from some disease needs some kind of medicine or treatment that might also cause an abortion. A resulting abortion in this case would only be indirect. The problem is solved by taking the medicine, not by the abortion. St. Alphonsus will say later in commenting on this passage that a direct abortion would be needed only in two cases: where the danger to the mother comes from some extrinsic threat to life or reputation, and where the danger would come from a future delivery problem. Only the removal of the fetus will solve these problems. But Busenbaum does not even mention these cases. Certainly, if he feels that the opinion allowing only indirect abortion must be followed in practice, it can be presumed that he would reject abortion in these cases. But Alphonsus' examples throw some light on the meaning of Busenbaum's query regarding the need for direct abortion.

In dealing with abortion of the animated fetus to save the mother, he presents without objection or comment the common opinion allowing indirect abortion, but then gives a new turn to the reason behind it. He says that where there is equal need the mother may look to her own good rather than that of the fetus. He is appealing here to the principle of charity which does not demand that one love another more than he loves himself. So when the goods at stake are equal, one is not obliged to forego his own good for that of the neighbor. Previous authors had appealed to charity only in reference to the spiritual good of the fetus. Since this was a greater good than the material or physical welfare of the mother, charity would demand that it be given precedence. Busenbaum is using the same principle to show that when the physical welfare of the fetus is compared to the physical welfare of the mother, charity does not demand that preference be given to the fetus, since the goods at stake are equal.

It may be interesting to compare here the various reasons given by different authors to justify taking medicine that would carry with it the danger of abortion. Corduba's basic argument seemed to be from analogy with the case where an innocent third party was killed in self-defense against an unjust aggressor. But he went on to say that the mother had more justification since she had a *ius potius* to life. The implication in the argument from analogy would seem to be that the *ius potius* would not be demanded. Certainly one cannot claim an *ius potius* on the part of the person being attacked in reference to an innocent third party. Peter of Navarre, however, simply made use of the *ius potius* argument. Vasquez also used an *ius potius* argument but he was not comparing the mother's right to life with that of the fetus. He was speaking rather of the right to the blood that would be removed (in bloodletting) to save the mother's life. It was the mother's blood, so she had the greater claim. It is not clear whether Vasquez thought the fetus had a right to the mother's blood, but there is no doubt that he felt the mother was obliged to provide it, even if *ex solo superfluo*.

Lessius and his followers simply argued from the mother's right to take medicine to restore her health. Pregnancy would not compromise this right. Other authors such as Laymann elaborated this argument somewhat urging that the medicine would help not only the mother, but also the fetus, although secondarily, since anything that would prolong the mother's life would *per se* prolong that of the fetus as well. Busenbaum makes the obligation of the mother to feed the child one of charity, and argues that where the need is equal the obligation ceases. Those authors who argue from the stronger right of the mother to life are open to the charge or claim that it would also justify direct abortion. They themselves never allowed this. The basic requirement was always that the abortion be accidental. Actually, only one author (Apicella) in the nineteenth century attempted to justify direct abortion on this score. Others who tried to justify therapeutic abortion or craniotomy did not argue from a comparison of rights but rather (when they argued this way) from a violation of the mother's right to life by the fetus who was in these circumstances considered an unjust aggressor.

So, although Corduba's followers accepted his distinction as a basic guarantee that the subsequent abortion would be accidental, they demanded assurance that the act from which the abortion resulted was licit. Lessius seemed satisfied that taking such medicine was licit in itself, and offered no further reason to justify it. The same seems to be true of those who put the emphasis on the mother's stronger right to life. Laymann would need no further reason, since he considered taking the medicine beneficial to the fetus as well as the mother. Busenbaum felt that taking the medicine would be wrong only if the mother had an obligation in charity to the fetus not to do so. Satisfied that such an obligation was not present, he considered taking the medicine licit. And if it was licit, presuming that there was no negligence, the accidental abortion would not be imputed.

If there is hope that the child can be baptized after the death of the mother, Busenbaum says that many authors do not allow the mother to take the medicine, since the spiritual need of the child would take precedence. But he adds that some consider it probable that even in this case the mother may take the medicine. These authors hold that one does not have to risk his life even to relieve extreme spiritual need. He does not mention the obligation of one who by reason of office must minister to the spiritual needs of others, perhaps because it would not be pertinent in this case (since the mother does not have an obligation in justice).

Busenbaum says very little about the time of animation of the fetus. He gives the common estimate, but adds that it is very uncertain. Lessius was the first theologian to raise the question about this estimate. Further doubt was thrown on it by the publications of Thomas Fienus and Paulus Zacchia. The question was now taken up by Ioannes Caramuel Lobkowicz (1606-82), a theologian from Prague. He was called by St. Alphonsus the *prince of laxists*, and he was the author of a number of opinions later condemned by Alexander VII and Innocent XI. Caramuel puts boldly the question which previous authors adverted to somewhat in passing.[23] He asks bluntly whether the distinction between the animated and unanimated fetus is still pertinent. The reason behind his questioning is the recent appearance of two opinions challenging this distinction, although for opposite reasons. The first opinion has already been seen; it is that of Thomas Fienus who held that the rational soul was infused into the embryo on the third day at the latest after conception. Since an abortion would hardly be performed before the third day, any abortion that might be committed would involve an animated fetus. It would not be pertinent or practical then to speak of the abortion of an unanimated fetus.

To the objection that this is an improbable opinion Caramuel responds that a man as intelligent and respected as Thomas Fienus would hardly be swayed to adopt an opinion by frivolous reasons. Moreover, a man of great learning (unnamed) had attacked the book but did not succeed in refuting Fienus' opinion. Finally, the great University of Louvain permitted him to teach this opinion and allowed the publication of the book. Caramuel presents all these reasons as part of a defense that followers of Fienus might make in his behalf. He himself will ultimately opt against Fienus' opinion.

The opinion of Fienus was not the only challenge raised to the traditional position regarding delayed animation. John Marcus, a doctor of philosophy and medicine, as well as the physician general of the Kingdom of Bohemia, who was also a close and respected friend of Caramuel, wrote a book defending the opinion that the fetus does not have a rational soul distinct from that of the mother the whole time it is in the womb. This will be recognized as similar to the opinion of the Palestinian school, as well as that underlying Roman law. But Caramuel does not make it clear whether Marcus has any new reasons for reviving this opinion.

Caramuel is not entirely satisfied with the traditional position, especially if it involves a succession of souls. Must one confess the sin of abortion according to the stage of development of the fetus. For example abortion of a fetus with a vegetative soul? Can one really know with any degree of accuracy at what stage the fetus is when an abortion is contemplated? Caramuel is rather sceptical about this possibility, since women can be mistaken, sometimes by a whole month, about the time of conception.

But he does not want to depart from the traditional forty- and eighty-day estimate in spite of such difficulties. Against the opinion of Fienus he objects that many hold a succession of souls. Also, what about the Scotist opinion regarding a *forma corporeitatis* (bodily form)? Even if one did not want to hold a succession of souls, given a *forma corporeitatis*, there would be no need for an immediate infusion of a rational soul. Against the opinion of Marcus he raises mostly scriptural difficulties from passages which seem to presume a living fetus in the womb. Caramuel says that all of these passages call for the presence of a human soul in the fetus before birth. In the end he finds both the opinion of Fienus and Marcus improbable, but he adds that the opinion of Marcus is also intolerable.

Caramuel returns to the abortion issue in another section of his *Theologia fundamentalis.*[24] There he is concerned initially with abortion to save the mother's life. He says that married women frequently have *fetus morbidos*, or they can anticipate difficult deliveries because they have small pelvises. Theologians in the past have allowed abortion in these cases if the fetus was unanimated because it constituted a threat to the mother. Caramuel confesses to a certain ignorance here and for this reason does not want to lure anyone away from the common opinion, but he would like to offer something to sharpen their thinking on the subject. In this kind of abortion two things happen: the destruction of the fetus and the preservation of the mother's life. If the mother intends her own safety, the death of the fetus is *per accidens* and not imputable, whether the fetus is animated or not. If she intends the destruction of the fetus, what she does is wrong, again, whether the fetus is animated or not. Caramuel seems clearly to regard the fetus as an unjust aggressor in this case and solves the problem according to the Thomistic principle of self-defense; the fetus may be aborted as long as the intention is not to destroy the fetus but to save the mother. In dealing with the case where the source of the difficulty is not a *fetus morbidus* but some disease in the mother he has recourse to the Corduban distinction. The mother may use only those medicines, such as bloodletting, baths, and cathartics, which are helpful to her.

Caramuel makes a distinction here which was never explicitated before, that is, between a case where the pregnancy is the cause of the mother's problem and one where the cause is rather some disease in her. This may have been implicit in earlier authors, but was never clearly expressed. Caramuel also seems dependent on St. Thomas' treatment of self-defense in his solution of the case where the fetus itself is the origin of the mother's problem, although he gives no reference. In his solution of the case where the origin of the problem is some disease in the mother, he is obviously dependent on the Corduban distinction.

Juan Cardenas (1613-84), a Spanish Jesuit and a severe critic of Caramuel, is the first moral theologian to draw practical conclusions from the challenge offered the traditional computation of the time of animation by Thomas Fienus. He discusses the subject under the general heading of probabilism.[25] His general thesis is that an opinion may be speculatively probable without being practically so. He is willing to grant speculative probability to the opinion which allows the abortion of the unanimated fetus to save the life of the mother when threatened by disease. He says that this opinion is extrinsically probable, which means that it is accepted by several respected theologians. But he does not think it is practically probable, that is, he does not think that it can be put into practice or acted upon. He argues from the statement of these authors themselves. All admit that if there is any reason to suspect the presence of a rational soul, it would not be permissible to cause an abortion even to save the life of the mother. Cardenas maintains that this suspicion is always present.

Cardenas says that it is really uncertain when animation takes place. He refers to the work of a certain Francis Verde listing estimates of various authors that run from the third day after conception to the eightieth. Of special significance is the evidence offered by Harvey. He claims that from the third day the fetus shows signs of movement and sensitivity. He also cites Hippocrates and eight other authors who offer similar evidence. He then argues with Thomas Fienus that since a succession of souls presents great difficulties, the presence of such signs of life lead to the conclusion that a rational soul is present right from the beginning. At least this is quite probable. On the basis of this opinion a certain Maximilian Deza held that a fetus aborted at any stage should be conditionally baptized if it shows signs of life or movement. All this points to the conclusion that whatever one might say speculatively about aborting an unanimated fetus to save the mother, it would be wrong to cause such an abortion since it is highly doubtful that there is such a thing as an unanimated fetus.

The seventeenth century witnessed a challenge to the Aristotelian theory of delayed animation. The theory of early or even immediate animation, first advanced by Fienus and Zacchia, will eventually supplant the Aristotelian theory. According to these authors the developments that take place right from the time of conception call for the presence of a soul. Since the Aristotelian succession of souls made no sense to either of them, that soul had to be human. This theory met with considerable opposition from the beginning because it was contrary to the common opinion of theologians (and everybody else), the practice of the Church, and the common interpretation of the Exodus (Septuagint) passage in scripture. With such overwhelming opposition its acceptance would be slow, but by the end of the seventeenth century authors such as Caramuel and Cardenas felt that the distinction between the animated and unanimated fetus was no longer of practical significance. It would take another century, however, before it was generally accepted.

Corduba introduced the distinction between means aimed principally at abortion and those aimed principally at saving the mother when discussing abortion to save the mother's life. In other words he was putting the emphasis on the nature of the means used. He was undoubtedly presuming that the intention of the person using these means would be reflected in the direction of the means themselves. Lugo approaches the whole question from the viewpoint of the intention of the agent, but without prescinding from the means. Abortion could not be intended either as an end in itself or as a means to some other end. Apparently, however, he did not think that there was perfect correspondence between his approach and that of Corduba. When discussing the latter's opinion, he opted for the modification made by Vasquez. In other words, even though the abortion was not a means to saving the mother's life, if the procedure used was positively conducive to it (causing an *alteratio positiva* in the fetus), it would not be permissible. This qualification is not easy to understand, especially in the light of other examples which he allowed, for example, killing the innocent child used as a shield. It could hardly be said that the sword or javelin used did not positively cause the death of the child. But when he was solving this case, Lugo seemed satisfied that the intention was correct. He argued that as long as killing the child was not a means to the defendant's safety, it was not necessarily included in his intention. It is not at all clear why he makes an additional requirement in the abortion case.

CHAPTER ELEVEN

Theological Debate
(1679-1869)

Diana mentioned he had heard that the opinion allowing the abortion of the unanimated fetus to save the life of the mother from some extrinsic threat, or even to save her reputation, was condemned by the Congregation of the Holy Office.[1] There is no other indication of such a condemnation at that time. But in 1679, not too long after the death of Diana, the Holy Office under Innocent XI did condemn this proposition and with it the opinion of Ioannes Marcus.[2] Both of these opinions, as well as the sixty-three others listed, were condemned as at least scandalous and harmful. The proposition containing the opinion of Ioannes Marcus was stated as follows: It seems probable that no fetus, as long as it is in the womb, has a human soul, and that it begins to have such a soul only when it is born. Consequently, it must be said that abortion never involves homicide. Before taking up the discussion of these opinions by Dominic Viva, S.J., it should be pointed out that the condemnations do not touch the opinion that animation does not take place for forty or eighty (ninety) days after conception. Neither do they touch the opinion that allows abortion during this period to save the life of the mother when threatened by the pregnancy itself. These opinions would eventually lose their following, but they were never the subject of official condemnation.

Dominic Viva (1648-1726), a Jesuit theologian from Naples, devoted a special treatise to the propositions condemned under Alexander VII and Innocent XI.[3] He comments at some length on the two propositions mentioned above, presenting first the arguments given in their defense and then refuting them. In discussing abortion of the unanimated fetus to save the mother from some extrinsic threat to her life, or even to save her reputation, he relates three arguments used by its proponents. The first is based on an analogy with abortion to save the mother from an intrinsic threat. If this is allowed, it should also be allowed when the threat to the mother's life is from the outside. And it should be permissible as well when the threat is to the mother's reputation, since losing one's reputation can be worse than losing one's life. The basic proof for these conclusions is that a mother has a right to defend her life whether the threat is from the fetus itself or extrinsic, but because of the fetus. The only reason abortion would not be permissible if the fetus was animated is that it would die without baptism. All that is permissible in this case is to give the mother some remedy for her ailment she may not have recourse to abortion.

The second argument does not differ much from the first. It is based on the principle, which its proponents maintain is universal, that whatever is permissible to prevent death from an intrinsic threat is permissible when the threat is intrinsic. For example, it is permissible to amputate a diseased arm when it poses a threat to life. It is likewise permissible for one to cut off his arm when, for instance, a tyrant would threaten him with death if he refused. The same should hold for the unanimated fetus. The third argument is that an abortion would not be permitted in these circumstances only if it would prejudice the future animation of the fetus. If this was the case, even though it would not be homicide in the strict sense, it would be so reductively, and even more so than expelling semen, because of interference with the gift of life. But the supposition in this case is that the fetus would not survive anyhow, since the mother will be killed. This argument, obviously, would not justify abortion to save the mother's reputation, since her life, and hence that of the fetus, would not be at stake. A confirmation of this argument may be found in the norm set down for giving the mother a drug for some disease when the fetus is animated. This is allowed when both mother and fetus will otherwise die, even though there is danger of abortion. Since the supposition in this case is that the mother will be killed and the fetus never animated, it should be permissible to abort the fetus to save her.

Before responding specifically to these arguments Viva asserts that abortion in these cases must be classified as homicide in some sense. In making this claim he relies on the *Si aliquis* and the authority of Tertullian. He also argues that it would be wrong from the familiar analogy with expulsion of semen. His conclusion is that it would be licit to expel an unanimated fetus only as an aggressor. Consequently he will not allow it when the fetus is only the victim and the aggressor is some third party. So he will not allow abortion to save the life of the mother when the threat is not from the fetus but from someone else.

Viva does not permit the abortion of the animated fetus even when the fetus may be considered an aggressor, but only because of its spiritual welfare. In arguing this way he is parting company with Sanchez and his followers who, however inconsistently, refused to consider the animated fetus an unjust aggressor. Viva's thinking will be recognized as similar to that of Raynaud. The difference is that Raynaud seemed to admit the possibility that the fetus might not survive anyhow, in which case its spiritual welfare would not be an issue.[4] For Viva the possible survival of the fetus seemed to be the reason for never allowing direct expulsion of an animated fetus. It is hard to see why the spiritual welfare should be more of a deterrent in direct expulsion of an animated fetus than in indirect expulsion. As already seen, authors such as Sanchez, while respecting the priority of the spiritual welfare of the fetus, felt that practically it would not often be a deterrent in a decision regarding indirect abortion, since the fetus would rarely survive. Is there any more hope that the fetus might otherwise survive in direct abortion to save the life of the mother? The spiritual welfare of the fetus would certainly be a deterrent to abortion to save the reputation of the mother, since there is no reason to suspect that the fetus would not otherwise survive and be baptized.

One of Viva's arguments against abortion to save the mother from some extrinsic threat to her life or reputation was drawn from the analogy with expelling semen. He now takes up an objection against this argument based on Sanchez' treatment of it. Sanchez had argued that there was an important difference between expelling semen and expelling an unaminated fetus since there was no pleasure connected with the latter. Viva says that according to Sanchez the expulsion of semen could never be permitted because of the danger of consenting to the pleasure connected with it. It can be questioned whether this interpretation of Sanchez is altogether accurate, but it is certainly true that he did not accept this analogy as an argument against abortion to save the life of the mother from an intrinsic threat.[5]

Viva says that the parity between the expulsion of semen and abortion of the unanimated fetus is that both are antigenerative. It is permissible, however, to abort an unanimated fetus to save the life of the mother from an intrinsic threat because in this situation the fetus is an unjust aggressor. The expulsion of semen would not be permitted because even if it were an unjust aggressor in similar circumstances, it would be wrong because of the danger of consenting to the pleasure. So this would never be allowed. He goes on to substantiate his position by saying that whenever something is prohibited by a positive law or by natural reason because of some imminent danger, the prohibition does not cease even though the danger may not be present here and now. He gives the example of the prohibition of fornication. Even though one could guarantee in a particular case that the education of the child would be properly provided, the prohibition against fornication would still hold. Similarly, the expulsion of semen outside of legitmate intercourse is prohibited because of the danger of consenting to the pleasure involved. Hence, even though it might seem in a particular case that this danger was not present, it would still be intrinsically evil and forbidden by the natural law. One could easily persuade himself that the danger was not present in danger of death cases, and then readily give his consent.

As already indicated, the validity of Viva's interpretation of Sanchez on this point is questionable. But he is correct in insisting that the basic parity between expelling semen and expelling a fetus is that both interfere with the generative process. The presence of pleasure in expelling semen was to Sanchez an additional factor that accounted for the absoluteness of the prohibition against such expulsion. But it was not because of the danger of consenting to the pleasure that he was concerned. It was rather that the intensity of the pleasure would lead to abuse. The absence of pleasure, then, was the reason why according to Sanchez the prohibition of abortion did not have to be absolute. But it was not enough to justify abortion. Abortion to save the mother from intrinsic threat was justified because the fetus was a quasi-aggressor. But this would not be true when the aggression or threat was from extrinsic sources. So the argument from the basic parity with the expulsion of semen was quite valid against this kind of abortion.

In answering the first argument Viva admits that when the threat is from the fetus itself, it may be removed as an aggressor. He also admits that even when the threat is from some extrinsic source, it would be permissible, for example, to amputate a hand. But he denies that this can be done with an unanimated fetus. The reason is that the fetus in this situation is a person *in potentia proxima,* and it would be just as wrong to procure an abortion in this case as it would be to take the life of a nonaggressor to ward off death by an aggressor. In answer to the second argument he simply denies the universality of the principle that whatever means are permissible to ward off death from an intrinsic cause are also permissible when the cause is extrinsic. Abortion is permissible when the cause of the mother's death is intrinsic, because the fetus is an unjust aggressor in these circumstances. But when the cause is extrinsic it is not the fetus who is the unjust aggressor but the one who threatens the mother. His response to the third argument is that it proves more than anyone would want to admit. It is like saying that if one threatens me and Titius with death unless I myself kill Titius, it is permissible to do so. His basic principle is that it is better to tolerate the death of two people than to take the life of an innocent person.

Viva uses harsh language in dealing with proposition 35, calling it "madness."[6] The opinion that the fetus does not have a human soul the whole time it is in the uterus was taught by Ioannes Marcus and subscribed to without opposition by other theologians from the University of Louvain. This opinion, Viva advises, seems to be based on the judgment of certain jurists like Baldus who hold that destroying the fetus in the womb does not constitute homicide. Theological authority for this opinion is presented in a statement of St. Isidore that the fetus in the womb cannot be baptized with the mother because one cannot be reborn in Christ until he has been born in Adam. Nor can one be regenerated until he has been generated. Scripture is quoted (Sir 40) to show that original sin is contracted only from birth. Finally, it is difficult to reconcile the opinion that the fetus has a rational soul in the womb with God's salvific will. Since there is no way of baptizing these fetuses, there is no way in which they can be saved if they die *in utero.* These were the more important arguments in favor of the condemned opinion.

Viva contends in a generic response that it is completely arbitrary to hold that the rational soul is infused at birth. Either readiness for discursive reasoning is required before the fetus can be informed with a rational soul, or it is not. If it is required, the soul cannot be infused until about the seventh year of age. If it is not required, unless one wants to admit a succession of souls, the presence of a rational soul should be admitted as soon as there is vegetative growth and movement. But pregnant women generally experience the movement of the fetus within them long before birth. This is why the *Roman Ritual* prescribes that if a fetus is aborted and moves it should be baptized without condition; it supposes that the movement originates in a rational soul.

Viva also appeals to the scriptures to show the presence of life before birth, and points to premature births, as early as the seventh month, to prove that the fetus is animated before the ninth month. He mentions specifically the premature birth by caesarean section of St. Raymond Nonnatus after the death of his mother.

In response to the specific arguments he maintains first that jurists commonly teach that homicide is committed by procuring the abortion of the animated fetus. Those who teach otherwise are following the opinion of Papinian or the Stoics. Or else they must be interpreted in such a way as to refer to the abortion of the unanimated fetus. One cannot deny that, if the fetus is animated, abortion must be considered homicide.

The only conclusion that can be drawn from the statement of Isidore is that an infant should not be baptized in the womb, and that it cannot be considered baptized if the mother is baptized at that time. But it is clear from scripture that original sin is contracted from conception. If it were not, how could it be considered a special privilege for the Blessed Virgin to be immune from original sin from that moment? In response to those who have difficulty with God's salvific will if the fetus has a soul before birth he discusses various theories about the salvation of unbaptized infants. But simply, the argument is that God can save them without baptism if this is his will.

To the argument that a lesser punishment is attached to abortion than to homicide, he responds that this punishment is for the abortion of the unanimated fetus. Many jurists say explicitly that the abortion of the animated fetus should be punished as homicide. Viva would have to admit, of course, that some jurists, even those who did not question the traditional opinion regarding the time of animation, felt that capital punishment for abortion was in the words of Tessaurus "*nimis dura.*"

The second part of the condemned proposition says that since it is probable that the fetus does not have a rational soul the whole time it is in the womb, abortion can never be considered homicide. Viva simply denies this conclusion. Even if one admitted the probability of this opinion, the traditional opinion would still be probable, and abortion of the animated fetus would still have to be considered homicide. He illustrates with the familiar example of the hunter. Who would say that if a hunter saw an object that was probably a wild animal, but also probably a man, he would not be guilty of homicide if he took a shot at him? One cannot appeal to the principle of probabilism in a case like this. One may act licitly on the basis of a probable opinion only when it is practically as well as speculatively probable. But the opinion that the fetus has no rational soul the whole time it is in the womb would be at most speculatively probable. The general rule is that a speculatively probable opinion may not be used in practice if damage either to one's self or the neighbor would result if it turned out to be wrong. Thus, it is not permissible to use a probable opinion regarding the sacraments, passing up a safer one. Similarly, it would not be permissible to use a medicine only probably therapeutic, if a certain one is available. The same would apply to this opinion about the presence of a rational soul in the uterine fetus.

Viva then has to face a similar objection regarding the traditional opinion. Given the probable opinion that a rational soul is present right from the time of conception or shortly after, even the abortion of a fetus before forty or eighty days would have to be considered homicide. Unlike Cardenas, Viva does not agree that the traditional opinion is no longer practically probable. To him the new opinion carries very little weight and is therefore improbable; the traditional opinion is still morally certain. To show this he points to the practice of the Sacred Penitentiary, which still followed the traditional opinion. He also appeals to the familiar text from the Septuagint. So to Viva there is no danger of homicide in aborting an unanimated fetus.

After the condemnations of Innocent XI theologians became less and less sympathetic to direct abortion of the unanimated fetus to save the mother even from an intrinsic threat. They may have been influenced to some extent by Innocent's condemnation, but the problems raised by the opinion of John of Naples had already surfaced in the discussions of Lessius and Pontius. These problems would disturb theologians more and more, and although the condemnation of Innocent XI did not touch this opinion, it would be difficult for them to argue in its behalf without weakening the position against the condemned opinion. The Carmelite theologians of Salamanca in their monumental work on moral theology say clearly that, Sanchez to the contrary notwithstanding, the one opinion follows logically from the other.[7] They reject both, offering the usual arguments against any direct abortion of the unanimated fetus. They accept the Corduban distinction regarding abortion of the animated fetus, and do not feel that the spiritual good of the fetus will often be a deterrent. To difficulties mentioned by previous authors about the survival of the fetus they add the concern that the surgeon may not have the necessary skill to extract the fetus without causing its death.

Claudius LaCroix (1652-1714), a French Jesuit, in his commentary on Busenbaum's *Medulla*, also argues against direct abortion of the unanimated fetus for any reason.[8] He says first that abortion to prevent some extrinsic threat is not permissible even independently of the condemnation of Innocent XI, since there is always the danger of homicide. With Cardenas he bases this danger on the opinion of those authors who hold that animation takes place shortly after conception. But even if one holds later animation, it would have to be considered wrong by comparison with expelling semen. Previous authors used an *a fortiori* argument based on the more advanced stage of the fetus. LaCroix apparently holds that the woman contributes semen to conception as well as the man. This will be recognized as the Hippocratic opinion to which Zacchia subscribed.[9] The additional malice in destroying a conceptus derived, according to LaCroix, from the destruction of *duplex semen* rather than just one. Abortion to ward off death from disease he will not accept, although he admits that many consider the opinion of Sanchez probable.

A German Franciscan theologian, Patricius Sporer (d. 1714), also took a clear stand against any direct abortion of the unanimated fetus.[10] In a very orderly treatment of the question he first lines up the arguments given in support of it. Although these arguments have already been seen as presented by different authors, it will be helpful to give them all here in one place with Sporer's response. The first argument is that the fetus in this case is an aggressor, and therefore may be treated as such. The second is that the fetus is a part of the mother, and hence may be removed to save the mother's life. It is permissible to remove even a healthy member if necessary to save the life of the whole person. It is argued thirdly that aborting the fetus is a lesser evil than letting the mother die. The final argument is that there seems to be no purpose in risking the mother's life to save the fetus in a situation where if the mother dies the fetus will not be animated anyhow. It will be recognized that these arguments are more pertinent to abortion to ward off death from disease, but it is on this case that Sporer concentrated his efforts. Obviously, if this case cannot be justified, there is no hope of justifying those espoused by Torreblanca and his followers.

After giving the usual argument from analogy with the expulsion of semen, which is never permitted, he proceeds to refute Sanchez' objection to this analogy. Here he follows Lugo rather than Lessius, but he will go more into detail on this point in his response to the fourth argument given above. In answering the particular arguments he says that arguments that prove more than you want them to prove really prove nothing. If the argument that the unanimated fetus is an unjust aggressor in this case is valid, it would hold not only for semen but also for the animated fetus in a similarly threatening situation. But no one would allow expulsion in these cases. In dealing with the second argument he admits that a part may be sacrificed for the good of the whole, but simply denies that the fetus is a part of the mother or in any way subordinated to her. It has its own destiny. But even if it were a part of the mother, it would be no more a part of her than semen is a part of man. Yet no one allows the expulsion of semen for the good of the man himself. And as for the lesser of two evils, if one thinks the abortion of an unanimated fetus is a lesser evil than the death of the mother, would he not have to say the same thing about the loss of semen compared to the death of a prince or even a pope? Yet no one suggests that it is permissible to expel semen to save a man's life. He uses the same analogy in response to the fourth argument. Asked how it can be reasonable to risk the life of the mother to save the fetus when if the mother dies the fetus will die as well, he simply puts a similar question regarding expelling semen. How can it be reasonable to risk the life of a man rather than expel diseased semen when if the man dies the semen will be useless anyhow? Dead men cannot generate.

Sporer then moves into an explanation of the reason underlying the absolute prohibition of such intrinsic evils as lying, violation of the sacramental seal, as well as abortion and the expulsion of semen. The reason is not the actual damage that follows from a single performance (semel facta) of one of these actions. It is rather the repeated harm or damage that a single allowance (semel *licita)* of these actions will give rise to. If men who by nature are prone to evil know that something is licit in a particular instance, it is easy for them to fabricate other exceptions and thus do serious harm to nature and the moral order. This argument he traces correctly to Sanchez who applied it to expelling semen. Sporer, unlike Sanchez, says that it applies equally to expelling an unanimated fetus. The danger of abuse and the harm to the moral order that would result is a far greater evil than the death of a single person. He will not admit that the danger of abuse is less in connection with abortion because of the difficulty of procuring it or the perils involved. Experience shows that during the first weeks of pregnancy difficulties connected with abortion are not enough to deter a woman even if her only concern is her reputation.

Sporer agrees with Sanchez regarding the indirect abortion of the animated fetus to save the mother, accepting not only the Corduban distinction when the medicine is aimed *principaliter* at the health of the mother but even when it is aimed only *aequaliter,* or even when it is doubtful whether it is *sanativa* or *mortifera.* The spiritual welfare of the child would be a deterrent only if the fetus would most probably survive the death of the mother, and even in this case, if the mother were in a state of sin and not able to receive the sacrament of penance, first consideration could be given to her own spiritual welfare.

The opinion allowing the abortion of the unanimated fetus to save the life of the mother when threatened by disease was directly attacked by such authors as LaCroix and Sporer. It was also being attacked indirectly by the growing acceptance of immediate animation of the fetus. Cardenas accepted this opinion as probable. Now Constantinus Roncaglia (1677-1737) says that the opinion holding that the fetus is animated at the time of conception, by the third day, or at least by the seventh day, is most probable.[11] But since he held that direct abortion was never permitted anyhow, his opinion on immediate animation would only provide an additional reason for the absoluteness of this prohibition.

There were still authors, however, who continued to accept the exception introduced by John of Naples. Daniel Concina, O.P. (1687-1756), for instance, accepted it as common opinion.[12] But he was not willing to consider the animated fetus an aggressor in any sense; it was placed in the uterus by God and formed by nature. It is never licit therefore to abort an animated fetus. The exception was also allowed by Mark Struggl (d.1760), a German theologian, since the fetus in these circumstances is an unjust aggressor.[13] The spiritual welfare of the fetus is not a factor at this stage, so the order of charity does not demand that the mother sacrifice her life. One might be tempted to conclude from this that Struggl is taking a position similar to that of Raynaud, namely that this would be the only deterrent if the fetus were animated. And he does mention specifically that it would be a deterrent in this case. But he also makes the general statement that abortion of the animated fetus would involve direct killing of an innocent person, which is never permitted. Some ambiguity however, must be admitted here.

Equally ambiguous is the position of Nicholas Mazzotta (1669-1746), a Jesuit from Naples.[14] Like the theologians just mentioned, he accepts the abortion of the unanimated fetus in the usual excepted case because the fetus is an unjust aggressor. The abortion of the animated fetus in similar circumstances he will not accept, but like Struggl because the spiritual welfare of the fetus should prevail. What is unclear in both these authors, as it was in Viva, is why the spiritual welfare of the fetus should be more of a deterrent in a direct abortion than in an indirect abortion. It would seem that if in most cases the fetus would not survive the mother, it would serve as a deterrent only rarely and could hardly found an absolute prohibition.

One of the most significant and most extensive treatments of the problem of abortion in the eighteenth century was that of Francisco Emmanuele Cangiamila (1701-63), a Sicilian priest.[15] In his *Embryologia sacra* he gives a much more detailed analysis of the problem, at least from the standpoint of medicine, than previous authors.[16] He divides medicines taken to save the mother's life into three types: those helpful to the mother, but not by nature harmful to the child, although dangerous; those helpful to the mother and at the same time damaging to the fetus; and those aimed at the destruction or abortion of the fetus. Roughly speaking, this division corresponds to that made by Sanchez and other authors. According to Cangiamila, it is permissible to use drugs of the first or second type to save the mother, but not the third type. He will not allow the latter even if the fetus would die anyhow.

Cangiamila is speaking here only of what he calls corporal homicide. If there is question of spiritual homicide, the physical life of the mother must yield to the eternal welfare of the child.[17] He does not agree with Vasquez that the mother can disregard this problem since she is not certain of her own spiritual welfare. The mother can solve her doubt by having recourse to the sacraments. He does not agree either with Sanchez that, practically speaking, the mother need not be concerned because it is rare that the fetus survives the mother's death. Cangiamila admits that it is rare for the fetus to survive and grow up to be a healthy child, but he denies that it is rare for the child to survive long enough to be baptized. Also, it is very difficult to say with any kind of certainty that the mother will survive if she uses the medicine, or that she will not survive if she does not. Nature frequently saves women condemned to death by doctors. He concludes that the opinion that it is permissible to use medicines to save the mother in this situation is practically useless. It would be impossible to guarantee the fulfillment of the required conditions.

But Cangiamila still thinks it is permissible for the mother to take many of the drugs mentioned by previous authors when necessary to save her life.[18] Theologians who said that a mother would have to accept death rather than take a drug were speaking of a drug that would cause an abortion and the death of the fetus without baptism. If a case arose in which there might be the danger of abortion, but not of the death of the fetus *in utero* without baptism, it would be permissible to take such a drug. Cangiamila thinks that this is a real possibility where the fetus is more mature. Under these circumstances the woman would not have to forego the drug, since the spiritual welfare of the fetus would not be in jeopardy.

Cangiamila makes the point also that these authors were speaking of a proximate danger of abortion and death, not a remote danger. He then claims that such procedures as phlebotomy and the use of purgatives no longer cause proximate danger of abortion. He admits that Hippocrates considered these dangerous procedures, but says that the way they are administered now, this is no longer true. Less blood is removed in phlebotomy, and if more has to be taken, it is done gradually. Also, the purgatives used are much milder. As a result neither of these procedures, if they are administered properly, involve any real danger of abortion. He continues with the comment that even if a mother tries to have an abortion, she often does not succeed. How much less chance is there of an abortion when all precautions are taken against it. He even claims that the use of these procedures would ultimately benefit the fetus as well as the mother, since the poor health of the mother is bound to have an impact on the fetus.

Cangiamila concedes finally that there may be a case in which the danger of abortion (and death *in utero*) may be just as great whether the mother takes the medicine or not. In this case he would allow the mother to take the drug, since the danger to the spiritual welfare of the fetus will be no greater.

He treats at some length the question of the origin of the soul and the time of animation of the fetus.[19] He is concerned about the first question because of a resurgence of traducianism. For centuries there has been common agreement among theologians that the human soul is created when it is infused. The merit of traducianism was that it seemed to offer an explanation of the transmission of original sin. Since Adam repented and was restored to grace before he begot Seth, Cangiamila does not see why traducianism offers any explanation at all of the transmission of sin. But the new interest in traducianism was due to the discovery of sperm in the male semen.[20] With the invention of a more powerful microscope, it was now possible to detect these little *insecta* or *vermiculi* in countless numbers in semen. The discovery was made by Anthony Van Leeuwenhoek (1679) and was confirmed by Nicholas Hartsoeker. But Andry, Dalenpatius, and Gautier claimed that they saw in these little *insecta* minute forms of men. They had nothing to say about the presence of a soul in these *homunciones*, but Christopher Wolf maintained that they had souls and that all of them originated in Adam. Hence the beginnings of a new traducianism.

Cangiamila himself, on the basis of the observations of the above scientists, is willing to admit the existence of these *animalia*, but refuses to give any credence to Wolf's traducianism, and not only denies that these are minute forms of men but also that they have anything at all to do with generation. That these little animals have nothing to do with generation is clear from the fact that they are also found in the *lympha* which the ancients called female semen. They are also found in other liquid parts of the body, and even in the water and the air. Their presence in male semen is no more reason to believe that they have something to do with generation there than their presence elsewhere. Or if they do, their presence in female semen would make the cooperation of the male unnecessary for generation. Since they are present in countless numbers also, one would expect more multiple pregnancies. After giving several other reasons why these little animals cannot be generative, he also offers some theological arguments against the opinion. If *homunciones* were really present in the semen, it would not be permissible to take a vow of virginity. Also, there is no way in which such countless numbers could ever come to life, or worse, to gain salvation. All of these reasons being considered, Cangiamila rejects any connection of these little animals with generation.

Cangiamila treats at length the various opinions that have been proposed regarding the time of animation.[21] They range from those who hold that the soul is infused only at birth all the way to those that hold that animation takes place at conception. In the middle are those who claim that animation takes place when the principal organs, heart, brain, and liver, are being formed, and those who say that it takes place when the fetus is completely formed. Cangiamila objects to the opinion of Ioannes Marcus because he finds it in opposition to what scripture says about the reaction of John the Baptizer, while still in the womb, to the presence of the Blessed Virgin Mary. Also, if one is going to demand the development required for sensation and reasoning, he will have to wait until the child is seven years old. As a matter of fact, according to Plutarch and Tertullian, Heraclitus and Asclepiades along with some Stoics held that the rational soul was not present in man until the age of puberty.

He also has difficulties with the opinion of Aristotle identifying the infusion of the rational soul with the time for formation. The followers of Aristotle are not in agreement as to when formation takes place, although Aristotle says that it takes place after forty or ninety days. He judges that Aristotle is in error regarding the age of the fetus (male) he is speaking about. According to Gassendi the fetus reaches the size of a large ant long before forty days. He questions also the time difference in the formation of the male and female fetus. When twins are born (male and female) there is no time difference in birth. Why should there be in formation? He finds no confirmation of this difference in the purification regulations in Leviticus. These can have nothing to do with the time of formation.

Cangiamila also finds a serious objection to Aristotle's theory in Hippocrates' claim that movement is present in the embryo as early as the sixth day. Aristotle could explain this by postulating a sensitive soul at this time. But most modern philosophers do not go along with his succession of souls. They say that the rational soul is present in the beginning, even though it may not yet be functioning on the level of reason. Some Aristotelians would want to maintain that before the infusion of the rational soul, the embryo is maintained by the soul of the mother. This can hardly be true because in the beginning the embryo is free from the mother. Other Aristotelians postulate an embryonic form or some kind of plastic or formative force in the male semen to explain the formation that takes place before the infusion of the rational soul. Cangiamila credits these explanations with some probability.

Other estimates put the time of animation much earlier than Aristotle and his followers. [22] Some say that animation takes place a few days after conception, either when the accidental organization of the embryo has been completed, or at least when the substantial organization begins, that is, with the formation of the principle organs (heart, brain, liver). Cangiamila gives special attention to the opinion of Zacchia who held, as already seen, that the human soul is infused immediately after the male and female semen are joined. He then says that these theories of early animation are generally accepted in his day and that the medical profession considers the Artistotelian theory of delayed animation antiquated. He comments that belief in early animation was also prevalent in the early Church.

Cangiamila now faces up to the objections to early animation stemming from ecclesiastical law and practice. [23] Generally speaking, he is covering ground here already gone over by Fienus and Zacchia. He considers first the "canon" *Moyses*, but denies that it is a canon in any real sense. It is taken from Gratian who had no legislative authority at all. It may be based on scripture, but is found only in the Septuagint; it is not in the Vulgate. And even in the Septuagint the distinction is not between the animated and unanimated fetus, but rather between the formed and unformed fetus. Animated fetuses are not necessarily formed. It is true that a lesser civil penalty is imposed for the abortion of the unformed fetus, but there are many reasons for this apart from the question of animation. An early abortion can more easily be accidental; many natural or spontaneous abortions occur at this time and the fetus is already dead. For this reason many jurists do not want to attach the death penalty to an abortion before five months. Also, during the first months the pregnancy itself is doubtful, and later abortions are more dangerous to the mother. Finally, in the author's own country, Sicily, even though all abortions are classified as homicide, more severe penalties are attached to later abortions.

Cangiamila then attacks the authenticity of the *Moyses*. It is not the work of Augustine, who never clearly identified the time of animation with formation. The other text of Gratian (the *Quod vero*), which is authentically Augustinian, represents his mind more accurately. He cites Bellarmine as charging that the *Quaestiones*, from which the *Moyses* was taken, was the work of some heretic. As pointed out when discussing Augustine (Chapter 4), the *Quaestiones* were the work of some unknown author for whom Erasmus coined the name, Ambrosiaster, because of an identification with Ambrose. Presumably, the charge of being a heretic would come from an analysis of his work, at least if he was really unknown otherwise. Cangiamila does not think that the analogy with the creation of Adam is valid either. Adam was created from the mud of the earth, matter which is completely indisposed to receive a human form. It had to be preorganized before such a form could be infused. But this is not true of ordinary generation.

As for the law itself, Cangiamila says that some past laws make a distinction between the animated and unanimated fetus, and some do not. Also, when dealing with philosophical or medical matters, the law tends to follow the common opinion of the time, and at the time the present law went into effect, the Aristotelian opinion regarding the time of animation was commonly accepted. Finally, when something is doubtful, penal law tends to follow the more lenient opinion. So one can hardly argue from penal law and practice to the truth of delayed animation.

Cangiamila is careful to point out that where the question of baptism arises, ecclesiastical practice follows other presumptions.[24] The same equity which demands that in imposing penalties the fetus be presumed unanimated demands that in baptism it be presumed animated, since this would be in its favor. Aborted fetuses are to be baptized if they show signs of life. Ordinarily, any kind of movement would be interpreted as such a sign. But even though external movements may not be detectable, internal movement (diastolic and systolic) may be present, and this may happen considerably before the time of complete formation. Cangiamila then cites a recent opinion that a fetus should be baptized conditionally, even though there are no positive signs of life, as long as it is not clearly dead. The only sign of this would be the beginnings of decomposition.

Cangiamila was not at all impressed by the animalculists, or homunculists, who discovered the minute form of a man in male sperm. The same was not true of the work of the so-called ovulists.[25] Up to the eighteenth century, although science was aware of the female "testicle," it was not at all clear about its function. Some thought that it was the source of an ejaculation similar to that of the male, except that it was deposited in the uterus rather than externally. Some like Hippocrates and Galenus considered this *semen* in the strict sense. Others, like Aristotle, considered it *menstrua* and, along with menstrual blood, only the matter of generation. It was not semen in the strict sense. This came from the male and was the only active agent in generation. In the early eighteenth century such embryologists as Stenson and De Graaf discovered the follicle in the female ovary and concluded that women, just like birds and fish, generate from these "*ova.*"[26] The so-called "ovulists" thought they detected in these "ova" miniature embryos. Besides these embryos they also discovered in these "ova" what Cangiamila refers to as spirits of female semen. Of themselves these spirits were incapable of fertilizing the "ovum" or bringing about the unfolding of the parts of the embryo; male semen was required for this. The semen passes through the tubes, penetrates the pores of the ovary, and if it finds a mature egg, it fertilizes it. Once the ovum is fecondated, the ovary opens up and the fertilized ovum passes through the tubes to the uterus. The ovary itself then closes up again.

Cangiamila says that because of these discoveries the opinion of Zacchia has gained in probability. In fact, he says that some Protestants were really going back to traducianism as a result. He does not want to go into this issue. What interests him more is that many Catholic scholars are now holding that the body cannot be formed without the soul, and therefore the soul must be present from the moment of conception. Cangiamila admits that these recent discoveries do not make immediate animation absolutely certain. It is at least theoretically possible that the growth that takes place can be ascribed to a vegetative soul or an embryonal form, or even embryonal spirits. Embryonal spirits might even be able to account for the first movements of the embryo. It could be then that the rational soul is not infused until the principle organs have been formed and the systolic and diastolic movements of the heart have begun. So, although the opinion of Zacchia has gained in probability and seems far closer to the truth than all the others, the truest statement one can make is that knowledge of the time of animation is still hidden in the mind of the Creator.

It was at this time that the *Theologia moralis* of Alphonsus Liquori (1696-1787) appeared. An Italian Redemptorist, he has been recognized as one of the greatest moral theologians of recent times. His work, which was basically a commentary on Busenbaum, was really an encyclopedia of moral opinion. The general methodology he used was to cite a section of Busenbaum and then present questions he wished to discuss. In dealing with abortion he raised the questions one would have expected from the previous discussions that took place. The first question dealt with the problem of expelling an unanimated fetus to save the life of the mother.[27] After naming the authors who took one or the other side of this question, he says that both opinions are probable, but his own judgment is that the negative opinion must be followed in practice as the safer opinion. As a matter of fact, he does not see what purpose the affirmative opinion could serve and says that theologians have sweated over the whole issue needlessly. With Busenbaum he asks why one should take a drug to expel a fetus directly when a drug that would expel it only indirectly would suffice. Attention has already been called to the two cases which he says only a direct abortion would solve, but in neither case was it allowed.

Alphonsus accepts the Corduban distinction but does not agree with Sanchez, at least in theory, regarding the obligation of the mother to give priority to the spiritual welfare of the child. Sanchez said that this would exist only if it were very probable that the fetus would survive. Alphonsus holds that the obligation will cease only if the hope of survival of the fetus is only slight or very remote. In practice, however, he is not far from Sanchez, since he admits that the case will be rare, and perhaps even miraculous, where the fetus will survive the mother.

On the question of the time of animation he says that those who held immediate animation *male dixerunt* (have spoken incorrectly), since it is certain that the fetus is not animated until it is formed.[28] He presents the various estimates regarding the time of formation, but then says that in the external forum the forty- or eighty-day computation is followed and that this is the practice of the Sacred Penitentiary in dealing with penalties. But when he discusses the issue in connection with baptism, he is less categorical about the time of animation.[29] He states that any aborted fetus should be baptized conditionally if it shows signs of life. In support of this position he offers the opinion that the fetus is animated right from the moment of conception, which he says is being accepted by the experts, and not without reason.

With St. Alphonsus what might be called the classic period of moral theology came to an end. After him one would no longer see the publication of multitomed treatises of folio dimensions. Much more abbreviated works of manual size began to appear, and in fact, many of them were no more than compendia of Alphonsus' *Theologia moralis*. Generally speaking, the moral theologians of the late eighteenth and nineteenth centuries were heavily dependent upon his work and some did little more than repeat his opinions. But two significant developments did take place during this era. The first was a continuation of the move, under the leadership of medical science, away from theories of delayed animation and in the direction of immediate animation without distinction of sex. Neyraguet (d. 1845), a French theologian of the first half of the nineteenth century, in his *Compendium* presents the traditional opinion but then goes on to recognize the more recent judgment among physicians that animation takes place sooner.[30] By the time Petrus Scavini (1790-1869) wrote his compendium of St. Alphonsus he was able to say that doctors held for certain that the fetus was animated from the moment of conception.[31] Although in the matter of penalties he advised that the practice of the Sacred Penitentiary should still be followed; the moral judgment of the act should be based on the opinion of immediate animation, so that anyone expelling a fetus would be guilty of homicide. Cardinal Gousset (1792-1866) in his treatise says that no distinction should be made between the animated and unanimated fetus since it is more probable that animation takes place from the moment of conception.[32] Finally, Konings (1821-84), a Redemptorist and a native Belgian who wrote a compendium of St. Alphonsus for an American seminary course, adds a new dimension to the whole discussion, claiming that the opinion of delayed animation is without foundation since the definition of the Immaculate Conception (1854).[33]

It is safe to say that a consensus of theologians regarding immediate animation was reached in the second half of the nineteenth century. But it is doubtful that the definition of the Immaculate Conception exercised much influence in establishing this opinion. In itself, the definition said nothing about the time of animation. What was defined was the freedom of the soul of the Blessed Virgin Mary from any taint of original sin, whenever it was infused. It must be admitted, of course, that the title, Immaculate Conception, expressing this privilege, is open to overinterpretation, but what is clear is that the Church had no intention of defining the time of animation, even in the case of the Blessed Virgin Mary.

In the year 1869 the practice of the Church in attaching a penalty of excommunication to abortion underwent a change. It will be recalled that in 1591 Gregory XIV restricted the penalty to abortion of the animated fetus, thereby modifying the previous legislation of Sixtus V. This excommunication remained in Church penal legislation, and with this limitation, from that time to the pontificate of Pius IX. But when the latter issued the list of penalties which were to be in force during his pontificate no distinction was made between the animated and unanimated fetus. Henceforward, anyone causing an abortion, whatever the stage of fetal development, would be excommunicated, provided that the attempt actually succeeded.[34] This legislation continued through subsequent pontificates and was incorporated in the code of Canon Law published in 1917.[35] It still prevails in the Church today. Since 1869, therefore, the penal legislation of the Church has made no distinction between the animated and unanimated fetus. A note of caution, however, may be in place here. This is legislation, not teaching. Distinctions the Church makes, or does not make, in regard to penalties do not constitute church teaching. So while it is true that the Church today penalizes abortion at any stage, it would be wrong to conclude from this that it teaches immediate animation or infusion of a rational soul in the fetus. This it has never done.

It may be pointed out in passing that the civil law was also affected by the development of thought regarding the time of animation of the fetus. The trend away from capital punishment even for aborting an animated fetus has already been adverted to. But the distinction between the unanimated and the animated fetus was still used as a basis for grading penalties. In English law the term *animatus* was translated by the word *quickened*, and somehow became identified with the time the fetus began to stir in the womb or with the woman's first sensations of fetal movements within her.[36] This was certainly a departure from the ordinary understanding of the term *animatus*. But with the trend toward acceptance of immediate animation, the distinction based on the time of *quickening* lost its significance in the law. By 1837 it was dropped from English statutory law. The punishment for abortion was the same and without distinction of time. The same tendency was seen in American law, although some states retained the distinction right into the twentieth century.

As the controversy over the time of animation came to a conclusion, at least on the level of ecclesiastical practice and theological opinion, a new controversy was beginning to develop. With general acceptance of immediate animation, the discussion of abortion of the unanimated fetus to save the mother lost all practical meaning. But the problem of a dangerous pregnancy did not go away. If it was to be discussed now, however, it had to be in terms of the animated fetus. And this is precisely what happened. The problem of abortion of the animated fetus to save the mother, together with the related problem of craniotomy or embryotomy, would occupy moral theologians during the whole second half of the nineteenth century.

The question of abortion of the animated fetus to save the mother was raised much earlier by such canonists as Simon of Brescia, Felinus, and Socinus, but more in relation to legal penalties and only in reference to the liability of the mother. The moral issue was clearly addressed and responded to affirmatively only by Theolphile Raynaud, since he considered the fetus in this case an unjust aggressor. In the middle of the eighteenth century another Jesuit moralist, Edmund Voit, in a very brief statement said that if it was very probable that both the mother and the fetus would die, it would be permissible for a mother to take a drug that would restore her health even if it did so only by causing an abortion.[37] But Voit himself gave no reason to justify his position, and his statement remained an isolated one until the middle of the nineteenth century.

In 1852 Jean Pierre Gury (1801-66), a French Jesuit, published a *Compendium* of moral theology in which he did no more than present the common opinion that therapeutic abortion was not permissible even if otherwise both mother and fetus would die.[38] In 1857, however, the editors of the *Revue théologique* published an *Essai sur la theologie morale* which ran into several chapters, and which was basically a critique of Gury's manual. One of the issues on which they chose to depart from Gury was that of abortion to save the mother's life, at least in the case where both fetus and mother would otherwise perish.[39] They presented a case from an unnamed doctor in Antwerp. A woman pregnant four or five months was suffering from severe uterine hemorrhaging, which in spite of all the doctor's efforts could not be stopped. She was dying from the loss of blood. The doctor consulted with three or four other practitioners but their combined knowledge and expertise were not able to stop the bleeding. In a short time the woman would be dead, and a tomb for the fetus she was carrying. The four doctors all agreed that there was only one way to save the mother. They asked permission to remove the fetus from an environment where it could not continue to survive to one where it would not be able to live (since it was not viable) that is, to procure an abortion.

The doctor argued that if the fetus were not removed both mother and fetus would certainly die, and the fetus without baptism, for if there were a case in which the child could live and be baptized after the death of the mother, this was not one, since in all probability the child would die at the same time as the mother. If the fetus were removed, the mother would be saved; the fetus could not be saved since it was not viable, but at least it could be baptized.

The writer of the *Essai* thinks that the doctor not only may, but must, remove the fetus in this case. As proof he appeals to St. Alphonsus' allowance of emergency baptism with ice water even though it may shorten the life of the child. To the objection that procuring an abortion in this case is a violation of the law against killing he responds that this law is not absolute. It allows for exceptions, such as, in the case of unjust aggression. He finds a similarity between these two cases in that in both there is no intention to kill but only to defend one's self or to save the mother. In fact whatever difference there is between the two cases favors the abortion case. The surgeon does not really kill the fetus, he merely hastens its death by a few hours. Also in self-defense there is always the danger of vengeance creeping in as well as the danger of eternal damnation for the assailant. How can one who considers this permissible criticize a doctor who out of charity and compassion is trying to protect the temporal life of the mother as well as the eternal life of the fetus?

He then considers the Pauline objection that one may not do evil that good may result. He admits the principle but denies that the abortion is an evil thing in this case. It is very advantageous both to the mother and the fetus. To the reproach that he is going against theological opinion, he responds that the agreement concerns only the general principle. One will find no theologian who treats the circumstances of this case and denies the conclusion. He mentions also that he has heard from an ecclesiastic who lives in Rome that a similar case was put to the Holy Office. After a long and serious study, it judged it wiser not to give a response, but several members of the congregation expressed their preference for a conclusion similar to the one arrived at in this case. This, of course, adds to the confidence of the writer of the *Essai*.

Some time later Gury published a case book entitled *Casus conscientiae*. One of the cases he discussed was that of a certain Pelagia who was pregnant and in danger of death.[40] The name was fictitious but the parallel with the case of the Antwerp physician was too close to be coincidental. Pelagia is also four or five months pregnant and in

proximate danger of death. There is the same judgment of
the physician, the same consultation, and the same expec-
tations. But Gury's response is *no*. Although he admits that
a few *neoterici* (newcomers) allow abortion in this case, he
says that the *sententia communissima* opposes it absolutely. Direct killing is intrinsically evil, unless done by
public authority, and an abortion in this case would be
direct killing because the violent expulsion of the fetus is
intended. He will not agree that the fetus is an unjust
aggressor in this case, although he protests that even in
self-defense the killing must be indirect. To the objection
that the killing is not direct in the case of abortion, he
responds that killing is direct when the procedure is aimed
at removing the fetus and the mother is not freed from
danger except by such removal, whatever may be the
ultimate intention of the agent.

There can hardly be any question, then, that Gury's
initial stand was against therapeutic abortion, even when
the alternative was the death of both mother and fetus, and
the fetus would die without baptism. He also felt that all
but a few *neoterici* were on his side. But in the seventeenth
edition of his *Compendium* which was published in the year
of his death there seems to be a change of opinion.[41] After
making the original statement mentioned above, he says
that if death is certain or nearly certain if the medicine is
not taken, and on the contrary the life of the mother will be
certainly or probably saved if it is taken, it does not seem
illicit to take it, especially if hastening the delivery *(acceleratio partus)* of the fetus will provide an opportunity for
baptism. It is hard to reconcile this exception with the
original statement that direct abortion is not permitted.
The question will be raised later whether Gury himself
made this change, or whether it was made after his death
by Ballerini.

There is less ambiguity about the shift of opinion regarding the Pelagia case in the edition of the *Casus* published in 1867.[42] There the author clearly sides with the
neoterici. While admitting that many theologians do not
allow abortion in this case, he thinks that it should be

allowed where it involves nothing more than *acceleratio partus*. In this procedure there is no direct killing of the fetus but a mere transfer from a place where it cannot survive to a place where it cannot continue to live. The fetus is no worse off. The author says that this is permissible since the mother is not bound to continue to support the child when her own life would be endangered, just as she would not be bound to feed the child after birth, if this endangered her life. To the objection that one may not do evil to bring about good he responds that the evil in this case is not intended but only permitted. To the objection that killing is wrong he responds that only direct killing is forbidden absolutely. Gury is distinguishing here between *acceleratio partus* and direct killing. Since premature delivery of this kind does not involve an attack on the fetus itself, it is not direct killing. As will be seen, this is certainly the thinking of Ballerini. Some later authors will again ask whether it is really Gury speaking in this response, or rather Ballerini.

Whatever Gury's final opinion may have been, there is no doubt that Antonio Ballerini, S.J., his successor at the Roman College, made allowance for therapeutic abortion in the annotations which he made to the seventeenth edition of Gury's *Compendium*.[43] Before Ballerini gives his own opinion, however, he makes a few preliminary comments and distinctions. He observes first that since the opinion holding immediate animation is now more common and more consistent with both philosophical and theological principles, there is no further need to discuss the abortion of the unanimated fetus. Also, since it is now possible to baptize the fetus *in utero*, there is no need to consider cases where the mother's life would have to be sacrificed to provide for the baptism of the child. He goes on to say that there can be no question of doing anything that would involve direct injury or killing of the fetus, since a direct intention to take the life of the fetus can never be justified. So the question has to do rather with delivery of the child at a time when it cannot survive outside the womb. A premature delivery of this kind can be either direct or indirect, depending on whether the remedies used are aimed at curing some ailment the mother has or immediately at inducing delivery. And even in the case where the acceleration of delivery itself is direct by reason of the means used, it can still be direct or indirect by reason of intention. He illustrates this point from St. Thomas' article on self-defense. Just as in self-defense the death of the aggressor is unintentional, so in this case the intention is to save the life of the mother and the damage to the fetus is unintentional.

Ballerini then calls attention again but more in detail to the fact that the controversy regarding premature delivery (whether it is done by relaxing the uterine muscle or puncturing the sacs) is not whether the mother may deprive the fetus of life but rather to what extent she is obligated to preserve its life. In discerning this obligation, one must consider not only the general obligation one has in charity to help another in need, but also the special obligation the mother has by reason of the fact that nature has committed the care of the fetus to her. He then compares this obligation with that of a mother with a child in her arms who is drowning. What is the obligation of the mother to hold on to the child? If her own life is in danger, may she legitimately desert the child? He quotes Lugo to the effect that the obligation of the mother to protect the child ceases in these circumstances. In justice to Lugo it should be added that he was drawing a comparison with indirect abortion, not as Ballerini is doing, with direct abortion.

After setting up this framework Ballerini presents some norms for dealing with cases where there is conflict between the life of the mother and that of the fetus. His first norm is that where the death of mother or child is certain, but the life of the other (the mother) is certain, she is not obliged to go to death to save the temporal life of the child. This is true even if the procedure in question is a caesarean section. In presenting his second norm he appeals to the conclusion of St. Thomas and St. Alphonsus that a procedure that would bring proximate or probable danger of death to the mother would not be obligatory even to baptize the child.

His next norm deals with the controversial *acceleratio partus*. He says that if the life of the mother would be in danger if she did not expel the fetus prematurely, and if it is probable that the fetus may be delivered alive (even though it may die shortly afterwards) so that its eternal life can be assured, it not only may but should be delivered prematurely. The reason he gives is that the death of the mother would in no way benefit the fetus and would as a matter of fact jeopardize its eternal welfare. His fourth norm is that the mother may take medicine for her health if the danger of abortion is the same whether she takes it or not. In fact, if her life is at stake, she would be obliged to take it.

The fifth norm Ballerini sets down is that if there is danger of abortion, and danger also that if the abortion occurs the fetus will die *in utero*, it would be permissible to accelerate the abortion to provide more securely for its eternal welfare. The uncertain hope of its material welfare should give way to greater security regarding its eternal salvation. This situation might occur even in a case where there is no danger to the life of the mother. His final norm has to do with caesarean section. In simple language it says that if it will not endanger the mother, she would be obliged to undergo a caesarean section for the temporal or spiritual welfare of the fetus.

What is new in Ballerini's analysis is the distinction between *acceleratio partus* and causing direct injury or death to the fetus, or in more technical language, direct abortion and direct killing. Previous authors had identified the two, and considered abortion homicide for this reason. Whether Ballerini's distinction was a valid one would be a source of much controversy among his successors. It might be said in Ballerini's favor that it may have been more possible to deliver a fetus intact in his time than in previous times. Previous efforts at abortion seemed to involve direct damage to the fetus.

Another Jesuit of the period, Augustine Lehmkuhl (1834-1917), was willing to allow the abortion of the animated fetus to save the life of the mother as a probable opinion.[44] He is the first author since Caramuel to speak more precisely about the origin of such danger. He says that it can come from some disease from which the mother is suffering which could be treated more successfully if the mother were not pregnant. Sometimes, however, the danger comes from the pregnancy itself and before delivery. Sometimes, finally, it comes only at the end of term, such as, when the mother's pelvis is too small to deliver the child. In dealing with these problems, besides allowing treatment aimed at curing the mother's disease even with the danger of abortion, he says that one may deliberately induce an abortion to avert a present danger to the life of the mother. He does not think that this can be considered direct abortion in the theological sense any more than giving over a life preserver to a friend can be considered direct killing of the self. He would say the same thing if the abortion was necessary to provide for the baptism of the child. But he does not allow any procedure which destroys the fetus in the uterus, such as craniotomy or cephalotripsy, unless it is certain that the fetus is already dead.

Lehmkuhl admits that many consider it illicit to abort a fetus to save the life of the mother. There is no dispute that the mother is not obliged to preserve the life of the fetus at the risk of her own life. The problem arises, he says, from the fact that to bring about the abortion one has to puncture the amniotic sac or disturb the pregnancy in some other way. But in spite of this he thinks it can be justified. There is no doubt in his mind that the fetus has a right to uterine existence, but he thinks it is a right the fetus can renounce. In proving his point he considers the possibility that uterine existence is an extrinsic good of the fetus, as well as the possibility that it is an intrinsic good. If it is an extrinsic good, the fetus can renounce it just as one in a shipwreck can give up a lifesaver to a friend, thus endangering his own life. There is reason to believe that the fetus would do this because it cannot survive anyhow, and also because its supernatural welfare is also in danger. Even if uterine existence is an intrinsic good of the fetus, he can still renounce it. The reason Lehmkuhl gives is that it is not the fetus itself that is the immediate object of the procedure, but something which belongs with equal right to the mother. In a conflict of interests the right of the fetus is threatened, just as a person's right to air would be threatened in a situation where there was not enough air for him and a companion whom he had received into his home.

Lehmkuhl then asks whether this thinking can be applied to the case where the danger will arise only at the time of delivery. In other words, to prevent a dangerous delivery, would it be permitted antecedently to induce an abortion? Lehmkuhl responds that if the abortion can be put off until the fetus is viable (after seven months) it should be delayed until that time. But if it would be dangerous to delay it even to that time, it would be permissible to induce the abortion earlier. As soon as the fetus reaches that point in its growth that a further increase in size would make delivery dangerous, an abortion may be induced. The only qualification he would make is that the hope of validly baptizing such a fetus be equal to that of a baptism at term.

In approaching the problem of therapeutic abortion from another angle (apart from the question of rights) Lehmkuhl argues from a comparison of the effects achieved. One effect involves some evil, some acceleration of the death of the fetus. The good effect, saving the life of the mother and providing more securely for the baptism of the fetus, is equally immediate and far surpasses whatever evil is involved. In stressing the equally immediate aspect of the good effects, he seems to be implying that the evil effect is not a means to the good effect, and that the procedure does not therefore involve the direct intention of the evil effect. Ultimately, his position is that *acceleratio partus* cannot be considered direct abortion *sensu theologico*, since it is not an *occisio fetus*; the death of the fetus which follows is only permitted.

Lehmkulk does not think that any of the above can be applied to procedures, such as craniotomy, which constitute a direct attack on the fetus. Such procedures violate the first condition required for placing a cause that has both good and evil effects. This condition, already adverted to, is that the good effect be equally immediate, and not obtained through the mediation of the evil effect. He will not listen to the argument for craniotomy that the fetus is an unjust aggressor. While admitting that this whole question has been debated for a long time in connection with abortion, he finds it difficult to accept. One has far more reason to consider the mother the aggressor in these circumstances, since the obstacle to the child's birth is the narrow pelvis of the mother. He likens the case to the presence of a person with a contagious disease. One can order such a person out of his home, but he cannot take his life beforehand. Similarly, it would be permissible to remove the fetus from the uterus when it is threatening the life of the mother, but it would not be permissible to kill it.

Lehmkuhl went into greater detail than Ballerini in arguing for therapeutic abortion, although basically his argument was the same. But it did not impress Dr. Carl Capellmann (1840-98), a German physician and a contemporary of Lehmkuhl. In his *Medicina pastoralis* he first challenges Lehmkuhl's assumption that the fetus would consent to the abortion (if he could) in the case of which he was speaking.[45] Lehmkuhl seemed to emphasize as his reason for this assumption the fact that it would provide an opportunity for the child's baptism. Capellmann says that experience shows few fetuses alive after abortion, so this cannot be a valid reason. And as for saving the mother, experience also seems to show that when the mother is suffering from some other disease, the hope of saving her life through abortion is not very realistic. But his real reason for disagreeing with Lehmkuhl is that he would consider an abortion in this case direct. Since the danger to the mother's life is removed only through the abortion, it is a means to an end, and therefore directly intended.

Capellmann goes on to present two cases in which he thinks the conditions for indirect abortion would be met. The first has to do with such problems as retroversion and retroflexion. It may happen in these cases that the uterus with the fetus becomes locked in the upper abdomen. Capellmann holds that if all other means of turning or replacing the uterus fail it is permissible to solve the problem by perforating the membranes, thus allowing the amniotic fluid to escape. Since the mother's problem is not caused by the pregnancy as such but by the mechanical enlargement of the uterus, the discharge of the fluid will allow the uterus to contract and it will be possible to replace it. Even though an abortion may follow, it is not the abortion as such that solves the problem. The second case in which he feels an abortion could be considered indirect involves the removal of a cancerous uterus which is carrying a fetus. Since it is the removal of the diseased uterus rather than the removal of the fetus that restores the mother's health, he argues that the abortion is indirect, and therefore permissible to save the mother.

The opinion allowing abortion to save the life of the mother from extrinsic threat, or even to save her reputation, was condemned by Innocent XI. Also condemned was the opinion of Ioannes Marcus reviving the Roman concept of the fetus as part of the mother before it was born. Since the trend was in the opposite direction, it is doubtful that this opinion would have won much acceptance even apart from a condemnation. Although the first condemnation (proposition 34) did not touch John of Naples' original exception, this also lost ground among subsequent theologians. This may have been partially due to the condemnation of the other exceptions, but it may be more attributable to the trend toward acceptance of immediate animation with a rational soul. This tended to make the whole question somewhat speculative.

With progress in medical science, remedies for maternal ailments carried with them less danger to the fetus. Cangiamila was able to say that such remedies were no longer problematic even in reference to the spiritual welfare of the fetus. Either the danger of abortion was remote, or if it was proximate, the child might still live long enough to be baptized. Cangiamila was skeptical about the relation of the newly discovered sperm to generation, and consequently completely unsympathetic to any suggestion that it was a miniature *homo*. He was more open to the other "discovery," namely, that the "ovum" contained an embryo. He felt that this gave support to Zacchia's theory, but in no way did it make immediate animation certain. Other explanations could be offered, although not quite as plausible. By the end of this period, however, authors could point to a consensus regarding immediate animation.

The end of the period also saw the beginnings of a new controversy; abortion of the animated fetus to save the mother's life. Authors who defended this position felt that a distinction could be made between direct abortion and direct killing. If the procedure, referred to as *acceleratio partus*, did not involve a direct attack on the fetus (any more than ordinary delivery techniques) they did not consider the procedure direct killing. To them it was quite different from embryotomy, which they clearly felt was an attack on the fetus. The period ended with official removal of the distinction between the animated and unanimated fetus from the penal legislation of the Church by Pius IX. This, of course, was disciplinary and in no way involved church teaching.

CHAPTER TWELVE

---------◆---------

Craniotomy Controversy:
Craisson, Eschbach,
Avanzini, Viscosi

According to the testimony of Capellmann, up to the beginning of the nineteenth century, the fetus was never dissected in the uterus unless it was certainly dead.[1] From that time on, however, the practice of performing such procedures as craniotomy or embryotomy on live fetuses to save the life of the mother became more and more frequent.[2] Even at the time he wrote, although according to Capellmann caesarean section had become just as safe, craniotomy was still the preferred procedure.[3] To Capellmann it constituted direct killing, and therefore could never be permitted. The first mention of the procedure by a moralist came from Kenrick, Archbishop of Baltimore, in his *Theologia moralis*.[4] Although, strictly speaking, craniotomy (and similar procedures) should not be classified as abortion, it was in listing abortive procedures that Kenrick mentioned it. Kenrick quite clearly condemned the procedure, although he realized that he was going against the thinking and custom of many American physicians who considered it imperative to subordinate everything else to the safety of the mother. In this type of climate he recognizes the pastoral problem of the priest with a doctor or surgeon who sees nothing wrong with craniotomy (or abortion) when the life of the mother is at stake. Kenrick feels that it will do no good for the priest to interfere spontaneously in this case, and may even do harm. If he were to interfere and the mother died, the blame would be put on him. But what if the doctor asks the priest what he should do? According to Kenrick, he should tell him that he does not see how the life of the fetus can be destroyed without fault. If the mother asks the priest what she should do, he should advise her to tell the doctor to do everything he can to save the child.

Craniotomy and other such destructive procedures were to become a source of great controversy among moralists during the second half of the nineteenth century. It was given an impetus which it might not have had in earlier times by the first appearance of clerical and learned journals of ecclesiastical science which were published periodically. Such frequent publication allowed for a much faster exchange between proponents of different and especially opposing opinions. In fact, a large part of the debate regarding craniotomy, as well as *acceleratio partus*, was carried on in periodical publications.

The debate was initiated by a case which was presented to the Sacred Penitentiary for solution.[5] A priest, apparently from the United States, sent a practical case regarding craniotomy to this tribunal. Fictitious names are always used in these cases, so it is impossible to identify either the priest or the persons involved. The suspicion that it came from the United States is derived from a quotation from Kenrick (seen above) that many doctors resorted to this procedure in the United States. The presentation of the case is somewhat confused, but it dealt with a certain Julia who was not able to deliver her child normally and faced death unless the fetus could be dismembered even though still alive and then delivered by forceps. The question was whether this was permissible. In response (September 2, 1869) the Sacred Penitentiary merely advised the petitioner to consult the approved authors for an answer.

Whatever may have been the reason behind it, this response turned out to be quite ambiguous. M. Craisson, a canonist and theologian, discussed the case and response in a section he ran on moral problems in the *Revue des sciences ecclésiastiques.*[6] In his opinion the reason behind the rather noncommittal response was that the case was so clear it needed no further clarification. No matter how common the practice may be, it is never permitted to take the life of an innocent person, however important the person may be who is saved by it. One cannot argue in this case that the fetus is an unjust aggressor. There is more reason to consider the mother an unjust aggressor, since she has put the fetus in the dangerous position it finds itself without any way of extricating itself from the danger. Nor can one argue that the life of the mother is more valuable without opening the door to killing any innocent person when the life of some more important person is at stake.

Craisson will not accept any argument that looks upon the fetus as part of a whole (the mother). The fetus is not part of the mother, and hence cannot be sacrificed like an ordinary organ or member of the body for the good of the whole. The argument that the fetus is going to die shortly under any circumstances will not justify the craniotomy any more than other arguments presented. It is not certain in the first place that the child will die. Experience shows that a large number of infants are able to be removed after the death of the mother and be baptized. Moreover, can anyone point to any other case where it would be permissible to kill a person who, one knows, is going to die in the near future; especially when death would deprive the person of such a necessary grace as baptism? Even if the precaution is taken of baptizing the fetus while still in the womb, the person baptizing must know of the doubt that surrounds uterine baptism. Craisson concludes that no reason could justify taking the life of a child in this way.

In a subsequent article in the same periodical the Abbe A. Eschbach, rector of the French seminary in Rome, took issue with Craisson's interpretation of the response of the

Sacred Penitentiary.[7] If the meaning of the response was
so clearly negative, the tribunal would not have used such
noncommittal language. He thinks the response can be
taken just as easily to mean that the question is being
disputed and that the Penitentiary does not want to decide
the issue at this time. Eschbach says that he actually
knows some theologians who teach the liceity of
craniotomy to save the mother when there is no other
means available. He then puts himself in the place of these
authors to examine with his readers the reasons they would
give to justify their positions.

In all Eschbach presents four arguments that might be
used to defend craniotomy. The first is drawn from an
analogy with classical cases already seen, such cases as,
killing a child used as a shield by an unjust aggressor and
trampling a child on a narrow bridge in escaping an unjust
aggressor. Is there not some analogy between these cases
in which the life of an innocent child is taken in just
self-defense and taking the life of a fetus when it proves an
obstacle to saving the mother? One might want to argue
that craniotomy involves direct killing, but does not St.
Thomas hold that the act is specified by the intention? The
intention here is to save the life of the mother, which is
certainly a good intention. The killing of the fetus is unintentional. Craisson would not allow the fetus to be considered an unjust aggressor. But were there not many
theologians who justified the direct abortion of an unanimated fetus on the grounds that it was an unjust aggressor?
If the unanimated fetus can be considered an unjust aggressor, why not the animated fetus? As for the possibility
of the fetus surviving the death of the mother, at least long
enough to be baptized, Eschbach quotes a certain Dr.
Hubert to the effect that for the fetus to survive is the
exception. Also, St. Alphonsus allows the acceleration of
the death of a child that might come from baptizing it with
cold water. Craniotomy would not involve any greater acceleration. Finally, Eschbach says that Craisson's citation
of the condemnation (Proposition 34) of Innocent XI is not

pertinent, since the condemned opinion was speaking of some extrinsic threat of death, not an intrinsic threat, such as is present here.

Although Eschbach differed with Craisson's interpretation of the response of the Sacred Penitentiary, he was actually in agreement with his position that craniotomy to save the mother was wrong. In a follow-up article he responds to the arguments presented above in favor of craniotomy.[8] But before responding he says that the case was presented too starkly. It is not sure at all that the mother will survive even if the craniotomy is performed, or that she will die if it is not. It is possible that the child will die first, and then the problem ceases. Also, a caesarean section would be a less radical solution in some cases, namely when it would certainly save the life of the child, and probably the life of the mother. Recourse to craniotomy would be the sole medical solution only in exceptional cases. But from a moral standpoint it would still be objectionable. Eschbach argues first from the danger of abuse drawing the familiar analogy with expelling semen. If craniotomy were ever permitted, it would open the door to all manner of abuse. But even prescinding from such consequences it would still not be permissible. He does not accept the argument of the defenders of craniotomy that this is an altogether new procedure which calls for an entirely new moral look. To Eschbach what the moralists of the past had to say would be quite pertinent to the problem. First, it is not all that new. Celsus spoke of the procedure, and so did Tertullian, back in the second and third century. Sanchez also spoke of *dilaceratio* as one of the methods of abortion aimed directly at the fetus. If one wants to know how moralists in the past would have responded to this case, all he has to do is see what they say about direct abortion of an animated fetus. They condemn absolutely any procedures aimed principally at removing the fetus, even to save the life of the mother. The only question that has to be raised today is whether there are any considerations that would allow departure from the judgment of theologians of the past regarding procedures involving a lethal attack on the fetus.

The defenders of craniotomy appeal to an analogy with medical abortion which Gury defended and which was also defended by an Antwerp doctor in the *Revue théologique* in 1857.[9] They also claim that the Holy Office when asked about medical abortion did not think it opportune to decide the issue, although many of the members of the congregation made no effort to hide their preference for the opinion that favored the mother. All of this support can be claimed for craniotomy as well. Eschbach simply denies the analogy between the two cases, showing that Gury only allowed medical abortion because it did not involve any attack on the fetus itself. In other words he did not consider it direct killing. Since craniotomy is an attack on the fetus itself, the arguments for medical abortion simply cannot be extended to it.

Eschbach then considers the argument from St. Alphonsus' statement that it is permissible to baptize a dying infant with ice water, even though it might hasten his death somewhat. He finds first that the analogy is defective; craniotomy is often neither necessary nor sufficient to save the mother's life or help the child. But even apart from this, theologians have always made a distinction between a procedure equally effective in achieving a good end as well as a bad end (shortening a life), and one aimed principally at a bad end (the destruction of the fetus). One cannot compare pouring water in a baptismal rite with craniotomy, since the latter is primarily a destructive procedure. The baptism, even in the circumstances of this case, is at least equally conducive to the welfare of the child.

Eschbach continues with a refutation of the argument that the fetus is an unjust aggressor. He admits that many serious authors used this argument to justify the abortion of an unanimated fetus to save the mother, but he adds that none applied this to the animated fetus. Some have argued, and with some truth, that they were inconsistent in this respect, but Eschbach feels that they were not entirely without justification. When these authors spoke of aggression, they were thinking in terms of the threat that a diseased part of the body presents to a person's health. Since in their opinion the fetus before a rational soul was infused was part of the mother, they could legitimately apply the principle that allowed one to amputate an arm or leg to save a person's life. But once the rational soul is infused, the fetus can no longer be considered a part of the mother. There is no longer question of the type of aggression they felt would justify abortion.

The defenders of craniotomy are willing to admit that the fetus is not an aggressor in the ordinary sense of the term; it is innocent. It would be wrong then to attack it with the intention of destroying it: this would be real assassination. What they intend is really to save the life of the mother. If the death of the fetus is a consequence of this, it is accidental and unintentional; just as it is in the case of the child used as a shield or the child trampled on the bridge by an escaping horseman. Eschbach finds a certain amount of confusion in this comparison. In dealing with these two cases theologians were speaking of an act that was by nature aimed at self-defense, but which ended in the death of an innocent person because of accidental circumstances. This, he felt, was clear in the case of the horseman fleeing the unjust aggressor. The case of the child used as a shield might not be so clear since it looks more like what happens in craniotomy or cephalotripsy. Eschbach admits that there would be a similarity between the two cases if the man defending himself had as the immediate object of his first act the destruction of the child. A second act, then, would be his real defense against the unjust aggressor. But this need not be the case. The supposition in legitimate self-defense is that the blow is aimed materially and immediately at the aggressor. The infant is struck only because it is accidentally in the path of the blow. In this situation there is no analogy with craniotomy.

Eschbach is heavily dependent on Lugo in his argumentation here. He ends the discussion with a lengthy quotation from the section where Lugo argues in favor of the act of self-defense which involves the death of a child used as a shield. He calls attention particularly to Lugo's insistence that a direct intention would include an intention of the means as well as the end. It is because craniotomy is an intended means that it cannot be justified. The fact that it is aimed at a good end, saving the life of the mother, will not justify it.

Eschbach concludes his treatment of craniotomy with the statement that if craniotomy were justified it would do great social harm by opening the door to abuse. Moreover, he finds nothing in the teaching of theologians or moralists that could justify it. Rather they are unanimously opposed to it, whether explicitly or implicitly.

When he wrote his first article on craniotomy, Eschbach said that nothing had appeared in print at that time in defense of the procedure. In fact, he himself had to present the defense for it. But shortly after he completed his own treatment, an explicit defense of the procedure appeared in an appendix to the *Acta sanctae sedis*.[10] Although the original article and the two succeeding articles on craniotomy were unsigned, it is generally agreed that they were the work of Pietro Avanzini, a diocesan priest, who was the first editor of this Vatican journal. Avanzini agrees that if the question is considered purely from the standpoint of past opinion, the answer is clear: the common opinion is against it. He concedes that it would be somewhat temerarious to go against an almost unanimous opinion unless, as Melchior Cano put it: *plane gravis et nemini observata ratio, aut auctoritas, sed clara et conspicua obstet.* Avanzini seemed to think that such a serious reason not previously noticed by theologians was available to challenge the common opinion against craniotomy.

Before mentioning this reason, Avanzini calls attention to the authors who, he says, in the past allowed the abortion of the animated fetus to save the mother. He is referring to the authors mentioned by Sanchez, namely Simon of Brescia, Socinus, and Felinus. His argument was that authors who allowed direct abortion to save the mother would also allow craniotomy, although they did not refer to it. The serious reason, not apparent to authors in the past, would seem to be the assumption that without the operation both the mother and the fetus would die. Authors in the past have put the emphasis on the fetus' right to life. Avanzini argues that since the fetus is going to die anyhow, it has already lost its right to life. The only right it has is to determine how it shall die. He concludes that it has no right to choose a method of dying which includes the death of its mother. Its only moral choice then is death by craniotomy.

After presenting this completely novel argument, he begins to attack the arguments of past authors. They argue, for instance, that killing an innocent person is intrinsically wrong, yet they justify killing a child on a narrow bridge in the path of a horseman escaping an unjust aggressor, bombing a convent in an attack on a city, and so on. Are not all these people innocent? If they allow this, why would they not allow craniotomy? Also, the fetus is not all that innocent; it is a material aggressor. The distinction between direct and indirect killing is not pertinent here, since if one holds that an unjust aggressor can be killed directly, so can the fetus. Also, according to St. Thomas this distinction refers to the intention rather than the material act. What is directly intended in craniotomy is to save the mother. The death of the child is only indirectly intended. By way of a supplementary argument Avanzini says that the procedure will allow for the baptism of the fetus.

The first theologian to challenge Avanzini was Eschbach himself.[11] Although somewhat surprised to find an article in defense of craniotomy in a journal under the supervision of the Sacred Palace, he advises that one should not overinterpret the authority of this journal. Apart from the intrinsic authority of the acts of the Holy See it publishes, the conclusions and opinions it presents are like those of any other review, only as valid as the reasons that support them.

Eschbach first checked on the authors cited by Sanchez as holding the liceity of abortion of the animated fetus
to save the mother. He finds that Felinus does no more than
mention the other two authors (Socinus and Simon of Brescia) without taking any position himself; he merely comments *cogitandum*. Socinus, after mentioning that Simon
of Brescia held this opinion, merely observed that this is a
question of great practical importance, but he did not want
to decide it at that time.[12] When he does return to it later,
he merely says that those responsible for such an abortion
are irregular. Eschbach was not able to uncover anything
about Simon of Brescia, but he does not think that one can
lean too heavily on a completely unknown author. Besides,
all these authors were talking only about abortion; they
make no mention of craniotomy. So, even if they can be
cited in favor of abortion to save the mother, they in no way
destroy the unanimity of the past against craniotomy.

Eschbach simply refuses to accept the argument that in
the case under discussion the child loses its right to life.
This is not a new case, but one that older authors were well
aware of. No moralist has ever said that a person loses his
right to life when it becomes impossible to prolong it.
Eschbach tries to exemplify his position with a case of a
boatman and his passenger. No one would say that in a
storm where both would die if they remained on the boat, it
would be permissible for the boatman to kill his passenger
by hitting him over the head, and then throw him overboard. And the passenger in this situation is really in a less
defensible position than the fetus. He entered the boat
freely and may well have foreseen the danger. The fetus is
not in his present predicament by his own choice.

Eschbach concludes that there is no theological authority at all in favor of craniotomy and that Avanzini has
produced no new argument that would weaken the unanimous opinion against it. He then begins to address the
practical issue, namely that the procedure has been commonly accepted by the medical profession of his time.
Eschbach shows that this acceptance in France occurred
over a period of thirty or forty years. In 1835 the statement

was made that embryotomy, to which English and German
doctors have recourse frequently, was not practiced in
France unless the fetus was certainly dead.[13] By 1870,
however, a statement made in the new dictionary of
medicine and surgery showed that the opposition to the
procedure in France was weakening.[14] The medical profession tended to justify the procedure by downplaying the
fetus, although for different reasons. Preference was to be
given to the mother, and even at a time when caesarean
section was becoming a less risky procedure. Surgeons
had no scruples about craniotomy in preference to caesarean section, because it was safer for the mother.

Theologians, according to Eschbach, tended to justify
the procedure, when they did, by classifying the fetus in
these circumstances as an unjust aggressor. Against this
argument he presents the objections of a certain Dr.
Hubert of the faculty of the University of Louvain. Briefly
Dr. Hubert argues that the fetus can hardly be considered
an aggressor, much less an unjust aggressor.[15] Aggression
implies some kind of action; passive aggression seems to
be a contradiction in terms. In the present state of our
knowledge it is impossible to say whether the fetus takes or
receives the food and space he has from the mother. But it
is not an inert body, since it enjoys a certain activity and
develops under its own power. If one wants to consider this
aggression, perhaps he can stretch the term enough to
include it, but it can hardly be considered unjust. Injustice
implies something on the part of the agent, and something
on the part of the object. It implies that the agent goes
beyond his rights, and the object suffers some injury there-
from. If one considers the fetus, he has to concede it the
right to live and to develop, so he can hardly say that the
fetus is going beyond his rights. Yet one has to consider the
mother's right to live as well. If the development of the
fetus threatens this right, cannot the mother defend herself
against the danger involved? Dr. Hubert responds that this
reasoning would be correct, if there was question of a third
party to whom the mother had no obligation. But in freely
conceiving the mother has entered into a quasi contract by

which she takes on certain obligations. One cannot say that the mother's commitment to provide for the fetus would not hold if it involved risk for her, for example, such risk as a caesarean section. This would imply that moral commitments hold only when it is easy to fulfill them. It would be like saying that a soldier who enrolled in the military voluntarily and was put in charge of defending a bridge could abandon his post whenever his life was in danger. And in this case there would be question only of omission; in craniotomy there is genuine commission. He adds that it is the mother herself who has put the fetus in this situation. The fetus could not refuse it, he cannot change it. She has created her own problem. Granted that the fetus is not going beyond his rights, and that consequently there can be no question of unjust aggression, one can hardly speak of craniotomy as legitimate self-defense.

In subsequent appendices Avanzini lists and responds to the objections to his position raised by Eschbach.[16] He admits that extrinsic authority is against him, but he says that all of these authors argue from the illiceity of direct killing of the innocent. This is not the question. It is rather whether the fetus has a right to choose a way of dying which also includes the death of his mother. He claims that authors have not treated the problem from this angle before, except, perhaps, for Theophile Raynaud. Actually, it will be recalled that Raynaud was dealing more with the problem of caesarean section when it would involve the death of the child, but he did argue that it would be permissible because the fetus was an unjust aggressor. Certainly, if the fetus can be considered an unjust aggressor, any procedure necessary to save the life of the mother would be permissible. But Eschbach had already given his refutation of this argument.

Avanzini does not really try to refute any of the intrinsic arguments Eschbach offered, but spends his efforts rather to find more extrinsic support, which turns out finally to be the support mostly of silence. He makes the claim that during the first ten centuries the Fathers condemned abortion stemming from maliciousness or lust. They never dealt explicitly with abortion to save the life of the mother. Since they certainly must have known of this problem, their silence must be interpreted as consent. He then makes reference to the passage in the *De anima* where Tertullian discusses embryotomy, assuming, too uncritically perhaps, that Tertullian is giving his approval to the procedure. According to Avanzini the controversy over aborting an animated fetus to save the mother did not arise until the sixteenth century when the question was raised by Simon, Marianus, and Felinus. In honesty, however, Avanzini would have to say that the attitude of theologians toward this question was quite clear and explicit right from the early fourteenth century when John of Naples raised the question regarding the unanimated fetus. Even those theologians who were willing to allow this stated quite clearly that it did not apply to the animated fetus. And from the cautious way they approached even this exception one would have to conclude that they were doing more than merely explicitating what their predecessors for the first centuries of Christianity had always understood.

Avanzini also finds some support for his position in the opinions of such jurists as Menochius and Tessaurus. It will be remembered that these authors questioned the whole idea of the death sentence for abortion, as well as a penalty for abortion to save the mother. Both felt clearly that there was an obligation in conscience not to perform such an abortion, so their question referred more to the punishment than the sin. Avanzini also claimed for his own side all those who would allow the abortion of the unanimated fetus to save the life of the mother, because the fetus is an unjust aggressor. If they are to be consistent, they have to accept his thesis. He claims, finally, that there is no difference between his case and *acceleratio partus*. Eschbach has already considered these claims in his previous articles.

After the death of Avanzini the defense of embryotomy was taken up by Daniel Viscosi, a professor at the seminary of Cerreto Sannita in Italy. He published in 1879 what is

undoubtedly the most exhaustive treatment of embryotomy ever attempted, running 331 pages.[17] After prefacing
the work with a brief history of the problem, he begins his
own defense of the practice, although he modestly admits
that his own thesis can be defended only as probable.

Accepting the general principle of theologians that direct killing of an innocent person is never licit, he sets out
to show that craniotomy or embryotomy in this case does
not involve direct killing.[18] In introducing his thesis he tells
his readers that the words *direct* and *indirect* can be taken
in two senses. They can refer to the physical act itself
which of its nature either aims at death or brings it about
accidentally. This will be recognized as the sense in which
Corduba made use of the distinction. Or they can refer to
the intention of the agent. If the agent intends death,
whatever the nature of the cause he places, the death is
direct. If he does not intend it (whatever the nature of the
cause), the death is not direct.

Viscosi opts for the approach that relates the distinction to the intention of the agent, and argues that if the
agent does not intend death, no matter what the nature of
the cause he places, it is indirect killing. Viscosi feels that
he finds support for this position in St. Thomas, especially
in his treatment of self-defense. The general principle
there is that an act gets its moral species from what is
intended, not from what happens accidentally. In self-
defense, what is intended is saving one's own life, not the
death of the assailant. It is on this basis that it can be
justified. From this Viscosi concludes that when something is not willed for itself but for some end to which it is
ordered, it is not directly willed. Also, when an act leads to
different ends, only that end is the real one (direct) which
the will has in view when it goes into action. What all this
adds up to is that it is basically the intention rather than the
nature of the cause that determines the morality of an act,
so that even if what was intended was only an accidental
effect from the standpoint of the nature of the cause, it
would be directly willed.

Viscosi then applies this to embryotomy. If it were viewed from the nature of the act, it would have to be considered direct killing, since the dissecting of the child is obviously and of its nature a lethal act. But if it is looked at from the viewpoint of the will of the surgeon, Viscosi claims that the killing would have to be considered indirect. What is directly willed is saving the life of the mother. The surgeon does not want the death of the fetus.[19] He does what he does only because he wants to save the mother. In fact, Viscosi says that it will be easier for the will of the surgeon to remain indirect regarding the death of the fetus than it will be for the person trying to defend himself not to want the death of his assailant. Since the latter is dealing with an enemy, human weakness may corrupt his will to want the death of his assailant. But no one has any reason to want the death of an innocent fetus.

Once he has satisfied himself that embryotomy is not direct killing, the next question to be faced is whether there is a sufficient reason to justify it. In arguing this point he appeals to the principle that one may choose the lesser of two evils.[20] Unfortunately, he does not always distinguish clearly between the principle for *counseling* the lesser of two evils and that for *choosing* the lesser of two evils. The former would apply even to moral evil, and is not really pertinent to this discussion. But it is not even clear how the principle of choosing the lesser of two evils applies. The burden of Viscosi's previous chapter seemed to be to show that the whole purpose of the embryotomy was to save the mother's life. In other words, the choice was not the death of the child but the life of the mother. If one were actually choosing the death of the child as a lesser evil than the death of both mother and child, he would be directly willing the child's death. It would seem that at this point in his argumentation what he should really be doing is showing that saving the mother's life, which is his direct intention, is a good sufficient to balance the death of the fetus, which is merely permitted. Otherwise, he is starting a whole new line of argumentation, and one which is hardly consistent with his stand that embryotomy is only indirect killing.

Be that as it may, Viscosi can come up with only three authors who mention the principle in connection with abortion. One of them, Simon of Brescia, actually rejects abortion to save the life of the mother, but merely presents the principle of choosing the lesser evil as a reason that might be given to justify it. The other two authors, Tessaurus and Menochius, as already seen, did use the principle, but not to explain away moral guilt. Sanchez used the principle when dealing with the use of a doubtful drug in a desperate situation. If certain death was the alternative for both mother and fetus, he allowed the use of a drug when it was doubtful whether it was *sanativa* or *mortifera*. His argument was that doubtful death is a lesser evil than certain death. Viscosi tried to show that he should have applied this even though the medicine was certainly *mortifera*, and therefore should have accepted embryotomy. The truth is, however, that Sanchez did not.

Viscosi goes on to say that the adversaries of embryotomy try to argue against this principle by quoting from St. Paul, "we may not do evil that good may come of it" (Rom 3:8). To Viscosi one can conclude nothing from the principle unless he can prove the minor, that is, that embryotomy or cephalotripsy is a *malum*. But this is precisely what is being questioned. After some exegesis of the text of St. Paul he concludes that he was speaking of formal evil, that is, intentional evil, and evil that was caused without any justifying reason. This does not apply to embryotomy. The death of the fetus is not intended, and there is a supremely important reason to place the cause, namely, to avoid a greater evil.

In his next chapter Viscosi tries to justify embryotomy by arguing that it fulfills the requirements of licit indirect killing of an innocent person.[21] He does this by comparing embryotomy to the three cases that have become classic among moral theologians, the case of the child on the narrow bridge, the child used as a shield by an unjust aggressor, and the case of killing innocent people in war time. In all three cases there is admittedly question only of indirect killing, because all the authors who allow this absolutely forbid direct killing of an innocent person.

Viscosi points out that if one merely considers the nature of the physical causes in these cases, he cannot deny that they aim at death. Who will deny, for instance, that the shoe of the horse landing on the child in the road will cause his death? Also, when an assailant uses a child as a shield, the same blow that kills him must kill the child first. What other justification is there for these actions except the fact that those who perform them do not intend death but only their own safety. The killing involved, however direct by reason of the cause, is indirect by reason of the intention of the agent. The same thing can be said for embryotomy. Even though the cause of the child's death is by nature aimed in that direction, the intention of the surgeon is to save the mother and the death of the child is indirect in this respect.

Viscosi actually argues that there are reasons to justify embryotomy that are not present in the other cases. For instance, the person attacked might have saved himself even without the death of the child; but the mother could not have been saved without the embryotomy.[22] The necessity of the latter, then, was greater. Also, the child on the road or the one used as a shield was in no way the cause of danger to the person trying to defend himself. But the fetus is the only cause of the danger to the mother's life. Is there not a stronger reason then to allow embryotomy, if one is willing to allow the death of the two children in these cases?

Viscosi then discusses an objection relating to the liceity of placing a cause of death. Even granted that the killing is not intended, that one has no other alternative, that there is a proportionate reason, the placing of the cause must be licit. One who does something illicit is responsible even for accidental affects. In the classical cases cited, the actions placed, such as escaping an unjust aggressor or self-defense against an unjust aggressor, were perfectly licit. One cannot say this about embryotomy; all the surgeon does is kill the child. Viscosi detects two false suppositions behind this objection; that one can judge an action to be licit or illicit prescinding from the end and circumstances, and that the surgeon in craniotomy does no more than kill the child. He denies both of them.

Against the first supposition he argues that many actions otherwise illicit can be justified by a proportionate reason. This s true not only of acts forbidden by positive law but also of those forbidden by the natural law. He gives as examples taking what belongs to another in extreme need, failing to make restitution of a sword to a person who wants to injure someone, and so on. Applying this to craniotomy, he argues that the circumstances make it licit. So there is no question of an illicit act; although it would be illicit apart from the reason behind it, it is licit when it is the only way to save the mother.

Viscosi simply denies that the surgeon does nothing more than kill the child; he extracts it from the womb. Killing the child will not achieve the surgeon's goal; this is accomplished only by removing it. Even if the child were dead, it would have to be removed. So it is not the life of the child that is the obstacle to the mother's health; it is its presence in the womb. All of the surgeon's acts are united by his intention to extract the fetus from the womb. In themselves they are incomplete acts.

In this discussion Viscosi is confronting Eschbach, so he treats at length a difficulty presented by him. Eschbach cites Lugo's discussion of the case of the innocent child used as a shield by an unjust aggressor. Lugo says that the act of the person assailed is aimed at killing the assailant, although here and now it cannot avoid killing the child used as a shield. If the act were aimed at the child himself, it would be unjust. Thus, if the purpose of the person defending himself was to kill the child first, to get him out of the way, and then kill the assailant, it would be unjust. In this approach the person assailed would intend the death of the innocent person as a means to his defense, and hence he would be intending it directly. It would be a separate act, and he would be defending himself in another act aimed at the assailant. Eschbach argues that this is precisely what happens in embryotomy, killing (dismembering) the fetus and removing it, the first of which is the means to the second.

Viscosi rejects this argument. He admits that the death of the fetus should be neither the means nor the end of the defense. But he says that this is all in the order of intention. If one foresaw, for instance, that with one arrow he could do no more than dispose of the innocent person, he would be allowed to do this, provided his ultimate intention was to defend himself. His intention would unite this act with a second act (the real self-defense) needed to immobilize the assailant. If this were not permissible, the right to self-defense in this case would be illusory. One could not use an arrow in self-defense unless he was sure he could get through to the aggressor with it. Who could be sure of this? Viscosi denies that Lugo holds that self-defense must be accomplished in one act to be permissible. All that is required is that all these acts be united by an ultimate intention that is justified.

This may be an oversimplification of Lugo. What seems to be essential in his thinking is that killing the child should not be a means to self-defense. This is clearer in the other example he gave. While he permitted the killing of innocent women and children in an attack on combatants in a war, he would not allow the attack itself to be made on women and children to demoralize the combatants and thus bring about their surrender. If the ultimate intention of self-defense can unite and justify all previous actions performed in its name, there seems to be no legitimate basis for this distinction. Yet Lugo made a distinction, and precisely because in the one case killing the women and children was a means and in the other it was not. It would seem to follow that according to Lugo more is required than an ultimate good intention. Killing the innocent non-aggressor should not be the means to achieve this intention. It should be added that he also explicitly ruled out abortion as a means of saving the mother's life.

In his next chapter Viscosi presents an argument in favor of embryotomy based on the assumption that the fetus is not just an innocent bystander, but an unjust aggressor.[23] He grants that the fetus cannot be considered a formal aggressor, but points out correctly that moralists have allowed self-defense even to the point of killing the aggressor where the aggression was only material. So this is the question: Can the fetus be considered a material aggressor? To support his thesis that it can, he goes back to the classic but disputed text in Tertullian, and argues that the craniotomy or embryotomy referred to was justified in the mind of Tertullian on the grounds of unjust aggression.[24] He then cites Theophile Raynaud, who also considered the fetus an unjust aggressor. Although he admits that Raynaud was singing *extra chorum* in holding this opinion, and that he had no followers, Viscosi thinks it should still be respected.

But his main argument depends on the many authors who allowed abortion of the unanimated fetus to save the mother, arguing that in this situation the fetus was an unjust aggressor. Viscosi quotes extensively from these authors. Since they have already been seen, there is no need to mention them here. Viscosi confronts an objection that St. Alphonsus and other theologians do not accept this opinion, at least in practice. He admits this to be true but claims that it is not because they do not admit that the fetus is an unjust aggressor. What they object to is the idea of expelling it *directa intentione*. He then quotes Busenbaum and Alphonsus asking why it is necessary to expel the fetus *directa intentione* when an indirect intention will suffice.[25] He concludes that these authors do not object to the use of means to expel the fetus, but only to the direct intention of expelling it. It is sufficient to use these means with the intention of saving the mother. They never deny that the fetus is an unjust aggressor, but only that it may be expelled *directa intentione*.

All of this says nothing explicitly about the animated fetus, that is, whether it can also be considered an unjust aggressor. This question, however, has already been raised in the form of an objection to Sanchez' opinion. If the unanimated fetus can be considered an unjust aggressor, there is even more reason to believe that the animated fetus in the same circumstances is one also. Viscosi claims that the authors who reject Sanchez' opinion on this score do not do so because they are opposed to expelling the unanimated fetus, but doing so *directa intentione*. So, presumably, they would not be opposed to expelling the animated fetus as an unjust aggressor. But what about Sanchez and his followers who explicitly rejected the expulsion of the animated fetus. Viscosi responds that they did not allow this, not because they did not consider the animated fetus an unjust aggressor but because they were concerned about its spiritual welfare. One might object that Sanchez could hardly have argued in this way since he says explicitly that it is *rarissimum* that the fetus will survive the mother and be baptized. Viscosi responds that no one ever forbade a person to tie a law to an hypothesis that would rarely or never be realized.

Besides their concern for the spiritual welfare of the fetus, theologians condemned abortion of the animated fetus to save the mother because they considered it direct killing.[26] They concluded this from the nature of the procedure itself. Viscosi asks why this must be considered direct killing when the killing of an unjust aggressor, or the child on the narrow road, or innocent people in wartime, can be considered indirect simply by reason of the intention of the agent? Such actions, Viscosi says, can be considered direct only in relation to their physical cause. His argument is that human actions should be considered direct or indirect by reason of the direction of the will, not by the direction of their physical causes. Killing an innocent person is forbidden in the sense that it may never be willed as an end or a means, not in the sense that given a proportionate reason one may never place a physical cause of death.

Viscosi's handling of the above problem is in no way based on assuming that the fetus is an unjust aggressor. If the fetus is looked upon as an unjust aggressor, it must be

admitted that a number of the classical authors allowed the
direct killing (direct intention) of the unjust aggressor. In
this they were departing from what was thought to be the
opinion of St. Thomas. According to Viscosi, all St.
Thomas ruled out was the direct intention of killing an
aggressor. To protect one's life, it is not necessary to intend
to kill the aggressor; it is sufficient to kill him with the
intention of protecting one's self. Viscosi presents this as
the opinion of Laymann. But granted that the fetus is an
aggressor, craniotomy or embryotomy would be permissible according to either opinion.

In his next chapter Viscosi takes up the objections of
Dr. Hubert to the opinion that the fetus is an unjust aggressor.[27] To be considered an unjust aggressor the fetus must
exceed his right and cause injury to the mother. Hubert's
argument was that the fetus was doing no more than exercising his own rights and developing according to the laws
of nature. He also argued that by reason of her own action
the mother entered into a quasi contract with the fetus to
protect him. Viscosi says that to find out whether a fetus is
developing according to the laws of nature, one has to see
whether he is developing in a manner calculated to achieve
nature's end. The purpose of generation is the good of the
species, the body politic, and the Church. If the fetus is
developing in such a way that it will not realize any of these
goals, it cannot be said to be developing according to the
laws of nature. In the case at hand, the fetus is developing
in such a way that it will not add to the species, and if it
causes the death of the mother, it will actually detract from
it. Can one say that the fetus has this right, and that it is
according to nature?

Viscosi admits that what the fetus does is ultimately
from nature, as Cangiamila protests, but while this removes responsibility from the fetus, it does not eliminate
the damage. It does no good to say that God is behind
nature. The defect is in the creature, not in God. To
Hubert's argument that the mother enters into a quasi
contract with the fetus to provide for it, Viscosi responds
that it would be quite impossible to prove any kind of

contract with a nonexistent being. Whatever obligations the mother has toward the fetus arise from nature and the marriage obligation. They do not arise from any contract with the fetus.

Viscosi then returns to Eschbach, particularly his contention that ordinarily the obstacle to normal delivery is the mother rather than the fetus.[28] If this is the case, embryotomy is wrong. Viscosi says that the most he can conclude is that it is wrong when the mother is the source of the difficulty. Eschbach's argument really was that since in spite of this fact no one ever considered the mother an unjust aggressor in the past, there is no more reason to consider the fetus an unjust aggressor when it is the source of the difficulty.

Viscosi denies first that the mother is an aggressor in these situations. A careful distinction should be made between aggression and defect. Aggression always implies some kind of action against the life of another. In cases of this kind the mother is passive. The pain she experiences is evidence of this. If her physical constitution is such that normal delivery is impossible, this must be considered a defect, not aggression. If this is the case, no one would allow an attack on the mother to deliver the child. This is clear from what theologians have held in the past about caesarean section on a live mother. If she were really considered an unjust aggressor, a caesarean section would be permissible, however lethal it might be. But theologians in the past have never allowed this. The same cannot be said of the fetus. Theologians in the past have considered at least the unanimated fetus an aggressor.

Viscosi accuses Eschbach of distorting the arguments whereby these theologians justified the abortion of the unanimated fetus. It will be remembered that Sanchez argued that this was licit to save the life of the mother because the unanimated fetus was a part of the mother and a kind of aggressor. Eschbach claimed that these theologians were really using only one argument, namely, that the fetus in these circumstances could be removed like any other diseased member of the body. Viscosi is making the

claim that these are two different arguments, and that the
only valid one is the argument from aggression. Eschbach
denied that they were arguing from aggression since they
allowed direct expulsion of the fetus.[29] But if they were
arguing from aggression, Viscosi could legitimately extend
the argument to the animated fetus. It will be recalled, of
course, that Sanchez and his followers refused to consider
the animated fetus an aggressor.

Viscosi simply denies the validity of the argument derived from the fact that the fetus is a part of the mother.
The fetus is not part of the mother, at least not in the sense
that the other members or organs of her body are. And if
one is going to accept the Stoic concept of the fetus, he will
have to admit that it remains a part of the mother until it is
born. To Viscosi, the fetus is a distinct human being, even
if only inchoatively, from the moment of conception.

Viscosi then tries to draw an analogy between medical
abortion which some recent authors have allowed, and
embryotomy, arguing that one who allows the former
should also permit the latter.[30] He relates Gury's *Pelagia*
case, but says that this is not the case that commonly
occurs. Ordinarily abortion is performed to prevent the
danger that would occur in a future delivery. Theologians
in the past have not permitted this. Viscosi, however,
accepts Gury's (second) solution of the case as he presents
it and argues from it to the liceity of embryotomy. He sees a
difference between Gury's case and embryotomy because
in the former the source of the danger to the mother is some
disease in her. In embryotomy the source of the danger is
the fetus itself. This makes embryotomy look better. But
he sees no other difference between *acceleratio partus* and
embryotomy. Gury and Ballerini did not consider *acceleratio* a direct attack on the fetus, but Viscosi considers
it just as homicidal as embryotomy. If you take a fish out of
water, you kill him. If you put a bird in a vacuum, you kill
him. If you throw someone into a fire, you kill him. The
same thing happens when you remove a nonviable fetus
from the womb, just as effectively as when you dissect it

with a knife. But this is permissible when there is unjust
aggression. Although Gury allowed taking a life in just
self-defense, he did not really appeal to this reason to
justify medical abortion.

Viscosi next turns to what he thinks is one of the more
valid arguments of the opponents of embryotomy; that it is
a violation of the rights of the child.[31] The violation would
arise from shortening the life of the child. Viscosi responds
that the abbreviation of the child's life is minimal and
provides the opportunity for doing a great good, saving the
life of the mother. If he was aware of the situation, would
not the child willingly make this little sacrifice? One might
object that the child has no right to shorten his life in this
way. To this Viscosi responds that people are always doing
this, and that theologians have actually praised sacrificing
one's life for a friend. Viscosi even argues that when the
damage is minimal and the advantage to another is great,
one might even be obliged to undergo it. Finally, since the
loss to the child is minimal, one could apply the principle:
parum pro nihilo reputatur.[32]

He goes on to draw an analogy between this case and
the familiar case of Alphonsus in which he allows the
baptism of a dying child with ice water even though it might
hasten the death of the child. This is permissible even
though it is the cold water itself that hastens the death of
the child. Viscosi does not accept the explanation that this
is licit because the act of its nature does not tend to the
death of the child but only to wash it, whereas in embryotomy the act of its nature tends to the death of the
child. Viscosi says that while it is not the nature of water to
kill, it is the nature of cold water in these circumstances to
kill. What makes the difference to Viscosi is the intention.
It is because the agent does not intend the death of the
child but its supernatural welfare that the act is licit.
Embryotomy should be licit for the same reason. The surgeon does not intend the death of the child. His intention is
ultimately to save the mother's life, and proximately only to
remove the child.

Viscosi will not accept as a difference between the two cases the fact that in the embryotomy case the life of the child is shortened by several hours whereas in the baptismal case there is question only of the length of time it would take to warm the water. Viscosi does not feel that one can make that accurate a time estimate in either case. When the danger is present, one administers the baptism and does not take the chance of waiting for warm water.

Viscosi responds to a twofold attack made on his position by Eschbach. Eschbach's first argument was that the supposition underlying Viscosi's position was false. Viscosi claimed that a brief shortening of the life of the fetus would insure the safety of the mother. Eschbach claimed this to be an imaginary case. Either the mother is close to death, as is the fetus, and the embryotomy will be nothing but a torment to her, as liable to hasten her death as save her. Or she is still in possession of her strength and will be able to survive the short time the fetus is expected to live. To be realistic Viscosi has to assume that the child could live for a considerable period of time. Viscosi responds that it is possible to conceive of a case between the two extreme situations which Eschbach presented, and in such a case embryotomy would be the realistic solution.

Eschbach also denied the analogy with the case of St. Alphonsus, and for three reasons. First, Alphonsus was not setting down a universal principle, but only dealing with a specific case of baptism. Secondly, he allowed the abbreviation of the child's life only because his supernatural end was at stake. Finally, the act of pouring the water on the child was of its nature an ablution rather than a death-bearing act. Viscosi spends most of his response on the second argument. His position is that if a supernatural goal will justify shortening a life, so will an important natural goal, like saving the mother's life. Or if there is really a question of killing, he quotes St. Thomas to show that even a supernatural goal will not justify it. He is speaking of the article in which St. Thomas outlaws a caesarean section on a mother even though it is the only way the child may be baptized. He concludes by saying that he has already shown that it is only the intention of the agent that makes pouring the water an ablution; it is not such by nature.

Viscosi admits that the weight of theological opinion is against his position but he leans heavily on the initial response of the Sacred Penitentiary to show that it is still an open question.[33] According to Viscosi if it was clearly illicit and a source of serious danger to the Church the Tribunal could not have been so noncommittal. It seemed clear to him that it did not want to give an authoritative solution to the problem precisely because it was doubtful. How then does one evaluate the common opinion of theologians against embryotomy? Viscosi says that this may be evaluated on the basis of the number of theologians holding the opinion, on the length of time over which it has been held, or on the reasons given to support it. He then discusses each of these possibilities.

He is least impressed by numbers as such, and cites many authors to confirm him in this respect.[34] He points out correctly that in the tradition one author *omni exceptione maior* (unequalled) can outweigh the authority of many. What is more important than numbers is the reason behind the opinion they support. According to Eschbach the reason behind an opinion that goes against a common opinion would have to be so convincing that the latter would be completely deprived of support. Viscosi feels that this is demanding too much. Such a reason would make the opinion supporting embryotomy certain. All that is required according to Viscosi is that the reason be weighty enough to make the opinion probable, leaving the common opinion with probability as well.

Eschbach claimed that there was a tradition of nineteen centuries against embryotomy. Viscosi counters that this is not a divine or apostolic tradition, or even an ecclesiastical tradition. It is rather a tradition of theologians. He raises a difficulty that this kind of tradition is built up simply by authors copying what their predecessors had to say on a

particular point, without examining it carefully themselves. There is no reason why such a tradition cannot give
way to a new opinion. An opinion, he agrees, can be new in
two senses; either because it goes against the traditional
opinion, or because the question was never considered by
theologians of the past. It would be easier to accept the
second than the first, and what is more important in such
acceptance is not time but reason.

Viscosi argues that the question of embryotomy was
never explicitly discussed in the past. If it was discussed, it
was rather under the heading of abortion. But Viscosi sees
a big difference between these two cases. In abortion a
fetus is expelled while it still has a right to remain in the
uterus. In embryotomy the fetus has come to term; it no
longer has a right to remain in the uterus. It is permissible
for the mother to expel the fetus at the end of term even
independently of any danger to herself. How much more is
it her right to expel it when it is threatening her life? If there
were authors from the time of Simon of Brescia who held
that it was permissible to abort a fetus to save the life of the
mother, it can be said that at least implicitly the opinion
allowing embryotomy is not a new one.

According to Viscosi, then, the older theologians dealt
with the question of embryotomy only implicitly, that is,
under the heading of abortion of the animated fetus to save
the mother.[35] The reasons behind their opposition to abortion he reduces to two: it is direct killing and the fetus is
innocent. Viscosi denies that craniotomy is direct killing.
In discussing the concept of direct killing he says that
theologians beginning with St. Thomas have traditionally
based this on the intention of the agent rather than on the
physical nature of the act. This was true of St. Thomas in
dealing with self-defense; it was true also of other theologians in dealing with taking the life of an innocent person.
As examples of the latter he cites the usual ones, that is,
the innocent child used as a shield, the child on the narrow
bridge in the path of a fleeing horseman. He then goes into
Lugo's understanding of the intention of the agent. He
agrees with Lugo that an intention is direct whether the

abortion is the end in itself or only a means to the end. He denies, however, that in embryotomy the death of the child is even a means to the end. It is not the death of the child but rather its removal that saves the life of the mother. It is not necessary then to intend the death of the child even as a means. Also, there is more reason to justify embryotomy than medical abortion, since the fetus is at term and no longer has a right to remain in the uterus. In final confirmation he refers to Gury's opinion that even medical abortion did not involve the direct intention of the death of the child.

In arguing that the fetus is not innocent in the case in question he directs most of what he has to say against Apicella.[36] Apicella said in so many words that it was ridiculous to consider the child an unjust aggressor. Viscosi admits this if one is thinking in terms of formal aggression, but against Apicella he argues that aggression can be unjust even if not voluntary. To Viscosi the fetus is the unjust aggressor, rather than the mother, because the threat to the mother arises from the efforts of the fetus to leave the womb which is imprisoning him. The acts of self-defense are reactions to these efforts. Apicella argued that since the fetus was in the womb by a voluntary act of the mother, she had no right to attack it. Viscosi replies that even though the mother became pregnant voluntarily, she did not thus lose her right to life. Nor did she have an obligation not to become pregnant, even though she might have known antecedently that this problem would occur.

In summary then, Viscosi offers what appear to be six arguments in favor of embryotomy. His major arguments, however, seem to be two, namely, that the fetus is an unjust aggressor and that embryotomy does not constitute direct killing. If he can prove that the fetus in these circumstances is an unjust aggressor, embryotomy can be justified without further argumentation. But it is precisely in proving the fetus to be an unjust aggressor that he meets his main challenge. The argument that it does not constitute direct killing, then, seems to be a backup argument. If the fetus has to be considered an innocent nonaggressor, it is only by reducing embryotomy to indirect killing that it can be justified. Although he is not entirely clear on this point, Viscosi seems to admit the traditional understanding of indirect killing of an innocent nonaggressor. To be indirect, it may not be either the end or the means to some other end, however justified this end may be. The fact that the embryotomy itself is not the end in view is not at all controversial. The issue is whether the death of the fetus is the means to the end. Viscosi claims that it is not. It is not the death of the child that achieves the goal of the operation, but its removal. Even if the child were already dead, this would have to be done.

It is precisely at this point that Viscosi's adversaries challenge his thesis. They argue that in the circumstances it is through the destruction of the child that the life of the mother is saved. While this could be justified if the child were an unjust aggressor, it can in no way be justified when the child is not an aggressor. Viscosi will argue that the destruction of the child in embryotomy is no different than the destruction of the child on the bridge or the child used as a shield. His adversaries respond that it is not by the destruction of the child on the bridge or the child used as a shield that the man who is unjustly attacked saves himself, but by the destruction of the assailant. So they deny any analogy.

Viscosi's argument from analogy with medical abortion will hardly impress the proponents of the latter, and probably does more to undermine their arguments for the liceity of this procedure than to strengthen his own thesis. The negative argument that embryotomy does not involve a violation of the rights of the fetus does not seem to be an independent argument, unless one holds with Avanzini that the child loses his right to life in these circumstances or that it is a right that the child can legitimately alienate. To take one or the other of these positions one would have to fall back on the argument that the fetus is an unjust aggressor, or that embryotomy does not constitute direct killing.

It would appear that the craniotomy issue in the nineteenth century arose from the increased use of this procedure on live fetuses to solve delivery problems. To what extent the noncommittal response of the Sacred Penitentiary may have contributed to the controversy is debatable. But the first author to defend it in writing was Avanzini. Although his thesis was presented poorly, his basic defense of craniotomy seemed to consider the child an unjust aggressor. After the death of Avanzini, Viscosi took up the defense of the procedure. Besides arguing that the fetus was an unjust aggressor, he tried to show that even if this was not the case the procedure could be justified as indirect killing for which the proportionate reason would be the life of the mother. The other arguments he used were really of secondary importance, and unable to stand by themselves.

CHAPTER THIRTEEN

Craniotomy Controversy
Continued: Pennacchi

A few years after Viscosi published his defense of craniotomy another Italian seminary professor took up the defense of the same procedure. The professor, Joseph Pennacchi, like Avanzini, was also an editor of the *Acta Sanctae Sedis*. In fact he tells his readers that he had originally intended to publish the present work in the *Acta*, but that the Master of the Sacred Palace did not think it prudent to publish it in the same periodical with the official acts of the Holy See. Since the question of craniotomy had been handed over by the Holy See to the study of qualified men, he felt that such a publication might prejudice the study.

Although the monograph is entitled *De abortu et embryotomia*, it spends very little time on abortion.[1] For the most part it discusses the ecclesiastical penalty attached to abortion. As for the morality of abortion, the author does no more than cite the condemnations of Innocent XI and Ballerini's annotations to Gury. So the monograph is devoted mainly to the morality of embryotomy. As proponents of this procedure the author names besides Avanzini, Ballerini, D' Annibale, Apicella, Viscosi, and a certain Victor

Constantini. As adversaries he names Ciarmadori, Eschbach, and Ciolli.[2] He then proceeds to summarize the
arguments for embryotomy given by previous authors. Although most of these have already been seen, it may be
helpful to list them. They are as follows.

1   The killing of the fetus in craniotomy is indirect.
2   Craniotomy is the lesser of two evils.
3   Indirect killing of an innocent person is licit.
4   It is licit to take the life of an unjust aggressor.
5   Craniotomy is not different from medical abortion.
6   Craniotomy does not violate the rights of the fetus.
7   In a conflict of rights the stronger right prevails.

The first six of these arguments will be recognized as
those of Viscosi. The seventh was used by Stephen
Apicella who in his defense of craniotomy argued from a
conflict of rights between the mother and the child. Both
have a right to life, that is, to the same thing, and it is
impossible for both of them to exercise their right simultaneously. When this happens, both rights cannot be real;
only one can be real, the other only apparent. The reason
behind this is that in nature there cannot be any real opposition between rights, any more than there can be real
opposition between one truth and another. Where there is
a collision or conflict, it must be said that the one right
either does not exist at all, or else it is subordinate to the
other. Consequently, in a conflict the stronger and more
evident right, to which the others are subordinate, ought to
prevail. Applying this to the conflict between mother and
child in a dangerous delivery, Apicelle argues that both
have a right to life, but the right of the mother is stronger
since it is connected with the domestic, social, religious,
and moral order. This cannot be said for the right of the
fetus not only because it has not yet been born, but also
because it will never be born under any circumstance.
Thus far Apicella.

After presenting Apicella's argument, Pennacchi goes
on to discuss the response that has been given to these
arguments, especially that given by Eschbach. The first

argument is taken from the consensus of theologians, who have always considered killing an animated fetus illicit and seriously wrong. Pennacchi responds with Viscosi that numbers are not as important as reasons. Numbers, moreover, can be outweighed by the authority of one important and respected theologian. Also, craniotomy to save the life of the mother is not considered direct killing by its proponents. And even if it was considered direct killing, many authors allow this when dealing with an unjust aggressor, and there are serious reasons for considering the fetus an unjust aggressor in this situation.

Pennacchi then devotes his attention to the case taken up by the Moral Academy of Rome on April 24, 1876.[3] The case, already referred to by Viscosi and others, was that of a surgeon, Titius. Faced with a delivery problem relating to his patient, Maevia, he feared that both mother and child would die shortly unless the child could be removed by craniotripsy. Some of Maevia's family opposed the surgery not only because of the physical welfare of the child but especially because of its spiritual welfare. Titius, however, said that the child could be certainly baptized in the womb. This was a partial solution to the problem, but Maevia, still hesitant, asked to consult her pastor. Having heard the case, and realizing that the woman and her relatives, fearing for her life, would not easily accept his judgment, the pastor asked for time to consider the case. Titius, however, afraid to delay the surgery, went ahead with it and without opposition from the mother. The pastor withdrew in silence.

Three questions were raised regarding the case: Is it permissible to take the life of the fetus, when both mother and child will otherwise die? Must one always speak out when an obligation is certain? What judgment should be made of the role the pastor played in the case? In answering the first question, the young man who was handling the case argued that it was not permissible to take the life of the fetus in these circumstances since it would be direct killing. His argument was based on the divine precept (Thou shalt not kill!), the principle that one may not do evil to achieve good, and the familiar axiom of St. Ambrose: If you cannot help one person without injuring another, it is better not to help him.

Pennacchi simply denies that taking the life of the fetus in this case constitutes direct killing, at least when looked at from the standpoint of intention. He would hold then that there are times when killing which is direct in a material sense only, and indirect by reason of intention, is not homicide. But even supposing that the killing is direct in every sense, he challenges the statement that it violates the fifth commandment. Pennacchi is not ready to present a firm conclusion on the point, but he discusses at some length reasons against including feticide under the prohibitions of the fifth commandment. His first argument is that the fifth commandment and the commandments of the second tablet in general, have to do with injuries to the neighbor. But one cannot be considered a *proximus* (neighbor) until he is born. The fetus has a relationship of filiation to the mother, but it is not a *proximus* to her. Indeed it would be difficult to apply any of the other commandments to a fetus. Pennacchi thinks that he finds confirmation in Josephus and Philo for his stand that the commandment against killing is aimed at protecting only those already *in societate*.

His greatest support, however, comes from the Hebrew text of Exodus, which punishes abortion only with a fine. If it were considered homicide, the punishment would be the death sentence. He admits that the Septuagint text weakens this argument, at least for the formed fetus, but since the Hebrew text has great authority behind it, the Septuagint reading could not establish without doubt the abortion of the formed fetus as homicide. He also points to the difficulty Origen had with applying the *lex talionis* to the fetus, especially the "eye for eye" and the "tooth for tooth" punishment.[4]

Pennacchi then responds to certain objections against his argument from the Hebrew text. The first is that it is not clear whether the *death* spoken of in the text refers to the mother or the fetus. Pennacchi seems willing to admit this,

but argues that the same difficulty could be raised against
the opposite opinion. Another argument might be that the
abortion was not punished with death because it was accidental. Pennacchi retorts that in the Old Testament own-
ers were punished with the death sentence even for
homicide caused by animals under their care, if there was
negligence. Finally, some might want to ascribe the lesser
penalty in the abortion case to the fact that the father has
full power over his children. Pennacchi responds that although the law gave the father power to sell children into
slavery, there is nothing in Hebrew law that would give the
father the power of life and death over his children. There
is also the authority of Philo that parents who abandoned
their children were held guilty of homicide. If they had
power of life and death, this indictment could hardly be
made. In all this argumentation, however, Pennacchi
makes it clear that the only point he is making is that killing
the fetus would not clearly fall under the fifth commandment. He is not arguing in any way that the fetus is not a
homo or that killing the fetus is not wrong.

Pennacchi then devotes himself to a defense of several
proponents of craniotomy attacked by Eschbach. The first
of these was Avanzini whose argument that the fetus lost
his right to life in this situation was challenged by Eschbach.[5] Pennacchi maintains that Avanzini's real argument
was that the fetus in these circumstances had no right to
prolong his life at the expense of the life of the mother.
Eschbach had used the example of the death of Saul to
illustrate his point. The fact that Saul was going to die soon
did not give the Amalekite the right to inflict a mortal
wound on him. He also argued that a man in a boat has no
right to kill and throw overboard a companion in the boat
when it treatens to capsize because of overweight. Pennacchi denies any similarity between these cases and
craniotomy. Saul was no threat to the Amalekite. If he was,
the action of the Amalekite would have been justified. It
was because it constituted a threat to the life of the mother
that Avanzini denied the fetus the right to prolong its life.

Also, the threat to the boatman did not come from the companion in the boat, but from the storm. So neither does this analogy seem valid.

He moves from Avanzini to a defense of Apicella and his argument based on a conflict of rights.[6] Apicella argued that in such a conflict the stronger rights should prevail, which would mean that in this case the rights of the mother would prevail. Eschbach is willing to admit the general principle, but denies that the prevailing right of the mother entitles her to take the life of an innocent person. So he denies that it can be applied to this case. In fact, he denies that there is a real conflict of rights here. Such conflicts exist when two people claim rights to the same thing, for example, the same piece of property. This would apply to two men on a raft that can hold only one. But what conflict of rights is there between mother and child? Each has a right to his or her own life. Does Apicella want to say that the mother has a right not to be attacked by the fetus? But he does not consider the fetus an unjust aggressor. Nor does anyone talk about a collision of rights in unjust aggression, since the aggressor has no right to attack. Does he want to say that the mother has a right to remove a cause of death even by destroying it if there is no other way? And that the fetus on the other hand has a right to life? Eschbach says that Apicella simply asserts that the mother has this right; he does not prove it. Eschbach also challenges the assumption that the mother has a stronger right to life. Everyone has an equal right to life. The strength of one's right does not depend on what might be called his grip on life.

Pennacchi does not see why Apicella cannot apply the general principle regarding a conflict of rights to the craniotomy case. If it is a general principle, it should apply. Or if there is some special reason why it does not apply, it is up to Eschbach to show this. The stronger right of the mother he says is due to the fact that the child is not yet born and never will be born. Also, the mother became pregnant with the hope that she would have a child, not that she would bring about her own death. But he promises to say more about this conflict of rights later.

Pennacchi also assumes the defense of Viscosi against the attack of Eschbach.[7] Eschbach claimed that Viscosi confused the concept of indirect killing with that of killing which was voluntary *secundum quid* (in a limited way). In the latter, although the willing is direct, it is nonetheless regrettable; an example would be jettisoning valuable cargo to lighten a ship. Pennacchi responds that even if Viscosi was in error in this regard, it makes no difference because the craniotomy case is just like killing an unjust aggressor, trampling the child on the narrow bridge, or killing innocent people in wartime. He then responds to Eschbach's argument that there is no unjust aggression in the craniotomy case. He admits that there is no formal aggression, but claims material aggression to be present. The argument from aggression cannot be as absurd as Eschbach claims, since many theologians in the past admitted it in the case of the unanimated fetus. Eschbach does not see how a fetus can be considered an aggressor if it is just trying to live that life which the mother gave it. Pennacchi admits that the fetus received its life from the mother, but not to threaten the mother's own life.

Pennacchi concluded with what seemed to be a conflict of rights argument. The fetus had no right to prolong life at the expense of the life of the mother for three reasons: the mother preexisted the fetus in time; even if she sacrifices her life for the fetus, it will be of no use since the fetus will die anyhow; the life of the mother is more valuable both for her family and for society. Eschbach denies that the mother has the right to kill the fetus, even if all these reasons were verified. As for the reasons themselves, he admits the preexistence of the mother. Pennacchi would want to conclude that the child therefore does not have a right to cause the death of the mother. If the mother cannot protect herself by taking the life of the child, the only alternative is the death of both. But who can prove that the Author of Nature wants both mother and child to die? To

Eschbach's objections to the argument that the life of the mother is more valuable Pennacchi would allow some validity, if the child were to survive. But the supposition is that the child will not survive.

Pennacchi's final target is Alexander Ciolli, a priest from Florence who also wrote against craniotomy.[8] Ciolli argued that craniotomy is direct killing, which includes even killing which is intended as a means. Pennacchi responds that even if it is direct killing, one could not conclude immediately that it was wrong. The argument that it is not direct killing is only one of the arguments used in support of craniotomy. It is really an accumulation of arguments that demonstrates the liceity of craniotomy, not just the one or the other. Pennacchi does not see either how Ciolli can argue from Ballerini that craniotomy is wrong, since Ballerini himself allows it to save the mother. Finally, he simply denies that the killing in craniotomy is direct. He argues from Ballerini that one may licitly place a cause of death not to bring about the death but to achieve some other equally immediate goal. According to Pennacchi this is exactly what happens in the case of craniotomy. The cause of the death of the fetus is placed to save the life of the mother, an equally immediate effect. Ciolli raises the objection that if it is permitted to destroy the fetus because of a dangerous delivery, it should also be permissible to do so to save the mother from some extrinsic threat as well. Pennacchi denies this because in the later case the fetus is not the source of the threat, but only the occasion. The source is the angry husband or father.

Pennacchi is not at all convinced by Ciolli's argument that the fetus is not an unjust aggressor. Ciolli used the familiar argument that the fetus is not active but passive. It was passive in its conception and passive in delivery, more of a victim than an agent. Pennacchi does not see how he can say that the fetus is not an aggressor in this case, when so many authors admitted that the inanimate fetus was an aggressor in a life-threatening situation. He denies also that the fetus is passive in delivery. The fact that it is forced by nature makes no difference. If one had to endure an evil simply because it came from nature, many absurdities would follow. Even if he were to admit that there is some kind of aggression, Ciolli would deny that it is unjust, since it is forced by nature. Pennacchi will not accept this conclusion, although he admits that this fact prevents the aggression from being formal. To Ciolli the fetus is not an unjust aggressor because it is simply using its right to life. Pennacchi retorts that the mother has a right to life also. This Ciolli concedes but he denies that it extends to bringing about the death of the fetus. Pennacchi has the same problem in seeing how the right to life of the fetus extends to threatening the life of the mother. Also, the mother is forced by nature as well as the fetus. This should justify unburdening herself of the fetus, and for a stronger reason, since the fetus will not survive anyhow.

Ciolli also argues that it is the mother who is the unjust aggressor. Pennacchi responds that even if it is admitted that the impediment to birth frequently comes from the mother, since she is made this way by nature, she ought to enjoy the same right not to be threatened by the fetus as Ciolli claims the fetus has not to be killed by the mother.

Pennacchi then takes up the defense of Apicella and his argument from a conflict of rights. Ciolli accepted none of Apicella's arguments to show that the rights of the mother should prevail in this situation. As an individual human being her right to life was no greater than that of the fetus. Nor did the fact of maternity give the mother any advantage in this respect. Finally, the mother's more important position in the order of nature does not give her a stronger right, since, first of all, it is accidental; secondly, the fetus must be treated like a child already born; and thirdly, the child may one day be more important than the mother.

Pennacchi concedes that Ciolli is not contending that the rights of the child should prevail, but only that his rights are equal to those of the mother. In answer to the individual reasons given by Ciolli he says that although as individuals the rights of mother and child are equal, the fact of aggression introduces a change in the balance. Here is where the conflict of rights comes in, and this is why the rights of the mother should prevail. Although Pennacchi appears to be talking in terms of a simple conflict of rights, his argument ultimately seems to be reduced to one of unjust aggression.

In response to Ciolli's second point Pennacchi insists that the parental relationship introduces inequalities into the relations between two individuals. Many theologians have admitted this in the past when they said that the mother has a stronger right to life than the fetus. He goes on to show that according to Taparelli the rights of the mother are superior by reason of generation. This is true even when the fetus is no obstacle to the life of the mother. How much more so is it true when the fetus is actually attacking the mother?

Pennacchi admits that the mother's more important position in the order of nature is accidental, but does not see how this makes a difference. He admits also that this position would not give her a right to take the life of the fetus without reason. But when the fetus becomes a threat to her life, it does give her this right. He does not feel that Ciolli's comment that in the eyes of the law a fetus must be considered as a child already born calls for a response. The law presumes that the child in question will be born, which is not the case here. To the objection that the child may grow up to be more important than the mother he responds that the supposition in the case is that the child is not going to survive at all. Also, the comparison is in the present, that is, to the present relative importance of mother and fetus. Finally, although a child may grow up to be more important than a parent, he may also grow up to be a prodigal or a thief.

Ciolli asks finally why, if it is permitted to perform a craniotomy to save the mother's life, it is not permissible at some earlier period to perform an abortion. Pennacchi simply responds that one cannot anticipate unjust aggression. Here again, although Pennacchi is speaking in terms of a conflict of rights, it is not clear that he is speaking of anything different from unjust aggression, at least in a material sense.

In what appears to be a final summary Pennacchi says that to prove the liceity of craniotomy it must be shown that the fetus is a *per se* cause of death to the mother and that the craniotomy is only accidentally ordered to killing the fetus. Some would say that proving the fetus a *per se* cause of the mother's death would be difficult, since the cause is really due to the smallness of the mother's organs or to some weakness or imperfection in her. Also, the killing of the fetus is intended as the *finis operis* of the act and gets its moral specification from this. The *finis operantis* will not take away the intrinsic morality of the act. It is clear then that the safety of the mother is not the object of the craniotomy, but an added circumstance.

For a fetus to be a *per se* cause of the mother's death it must of itself and directly produce this effect. To Pennacchi this seems obviously to be the case, since the operation of removing the fetus saves the mother's life. Also, it is the attempts of the fetus to escape the womb that cause the threat to the mother. Finally, if the fetus were not a *per se* cause of the mother's death, but something else, one should have to be able to point to another cause. But no one has been able to do this. Pennacchi will not admit that it is some defect in the mother that causes her death. This defect is always there. Since it poses a threat only in delivery, it seems clear that in itself it is not a cause.

Even if the killing of the fetus is directly intended as a *finis operis* its moral specification derives from the fact that death is inflicted on the fetus as a cause of maternal death.[9] This would not be wrong because the mother is more obligated to preserve her own life than that of the fetus, especially when the fetus can be baptized. He grants that a good *finis operantis* will not justify a bad *finis operis*,

but he maintains that killing the fetus in the circumstances
has not been proved wrong. He also denies that saving the
mother's life is only a *finis operantis*. The mother's life is
not saved by the intention of the agent, but by the operation
itself, which would make it the *finis operis*.

With this Pennacchi puts an end to his dissertation and
subscribes to the liceity of craniotomy. He feels that he is in
good company in doing this, claiming the support of a
Jesuit, Cardinal Tarquinius, who apparently urged Avanzini to defend his position. He also mentions some authors
previously opposed to craniotomy who changed their
minds, among whom was Pacifico Ciarmadori. But he does
hope that the medical profession will find some method of
saving both the mother and the child in these circumstances. In this connection he mentions that he has
heard that a famous surgeon at the University of Padua by
the name of Porro has perfected a method called uterotomy
that hopes to achieve exactly this goal.

He attaches to the end of his dissertation a set of
practical rules dealing with difficult pregnancy cases issued by Bishop Peter J. Baltes, Bishop of Alton (later
Springfield) in Illinois.[10] There is clear support for Pennacchi's position in these rules, three of which deal
explicitly with medical abortion and craniotomy. Rule 9
prescribes that when both mother and fetus are threatened
by death unless medicine is given which acts directly on
the fetus and causes an abortion, it may be given to save
the mother's life. Rule 11 states that if it is foreseen that a
caesarean section will cause the death of the mother but an
embryotomy will not, this second procedure must be used.
Finally, Rule 14 says that when it is certain that both fetus
and mother will die unless the fetus is removed from the
womb, if this cannot be done in any other way, one may
have recourse to craniotomy. It seems clear that these
rules imply an acceptance both of direct abortion and
craniotomy to save the life of the mother. They were published in 1879.

The name of Pennacchi must be added to those who defended embryotomy to save the mother's life. He takes his place beside Avanzini, Apicella, and Viscosi. Curiously, the practice did not seem to win any advocates among theologians in any other European countries. The strongest defense was certainly that of Viscosi. Apicella contributed only one argument based on a conflict of rights, but Viscosi, while admitting that Apicella favors embryotomy, seems to consider him more of an adversary because of his attack on the argument from unjust aggression. Pennacchi does not add any new arguments to the discussion, but merely takes up the defense of its proponents against Eschbach and Ciolli. He defends in order Avanzini, Apicella, and Viscosi. His final summary, however, does offer some material for reflection. He argues that saving the mother's life is not simply the *finis operantis* of embryotomy but the *finis operis* as well. It will be remembered that Lugo, when defending the killing of the child used as a shield or the killing of women and children in wartime, was satisfied that the act itself was aimed at legitimate self-defense. He would not have been satisfied if the act was aimed at the death of the child, or the women and children, even though the ultimate intention might have been self-defense. In these circumstances he would have considered the killing of the innocent parties a means to an end, and therefore immoral. Is Pennacchi trying to make the same point here? In other words, is he justifying the procedure because the *finis operis* is saving the mother's life? The answer to this question is not clear, since he also seems to justify the procedure as a response to unjust aggression. But apart from Pennacchi, it might be asked whether this fact (saving the mother's life is the *finis operis*) would justify killing the fetus. In other words, is this what Lugo is saying when he justifies killing the child-shield, that is, is he saying that it can be justified when the *finis operis* of the act is immobilizing the assailant?" Since Lugo did not use this terminology, translating what he said into it involves a certain risk. What does seem clear is that to Lugo, if killing the child-shield was a means to self-defense, it was not permissible. And he says explicitly that it would not be permissible for a mother to take a drug to save her life if it would do so only by causing an abortion. In other words if the abortion was the means of saving her life, it was wrong.

CHAPTER FOURTEEN

Craniotomy Controversy
Continued: Waffelaert

Shortly after the appearance of Pennacchi's monograph on abortion and craniotomy, there began in the *Nouvelle revue théologique* a series of articles refuting it by J.G. Waffelaert, professor of Moral Theology in the seminary at Bruges, Belgium. In the first article, after enumerating the seven arguments Pennacchi offers, he notes that there is considerable overlapping in these arguments.[1] In fact, if one, for instance, chooses the argument based on considering the fetus an unjust aggressor, he automatically cancels out the possibility of using the arguments presuming that the child is an innocent person (nonaggressor). It is only in the second article, however, that he begins his refutation of these arguments.[2] Since a number of these arguments apply the distinction between direct and indirect killing to the cases under discussion, he first addresses himself to a clarification of this distinction.

Pennacchi argues that craniotomy to save the mother can be justified because it involves only indirect killing of the fetus. Waffelaert denies this assertion and then tries to explain the distinction, at least as he sees it. As already seen, Pennacchi and Viscosi argued that the killing of the infant in craniotomy is indirect, maintaining that the distinction depends not on the nature of the cause which produces this effect, but rather on the intention. Even though the procedure is aimed at the death of the fetus, since the intention of the agent is primarily to save the mother, the killing cannot be considered direct, but only indirect. What is directly intended is to save the mother.

Waffelaert contends that this is not an adequate explanation of the distinction. To apply it accurately, one must consider not only the relation of the act to the intention, that is, the will of the end, but also its relation to the means. Direct willing applies not only to the end intended but also to the means chosen. To will directly, then, can mean two things; to have the intention of the end or to choose the necessary means. Whenever one places a cause that has two effects, he can place it with the intention of obtaining one of the effects (which will be directly willed). But it does not follow that the other effect will be willed only indirectly. A distinction has to be made. If the effects are equally immediate, and not subordinate one to the other, then the effect which is *praeter intentionem* will be only indirectly willed in placing the cause. But if the two effects are not immediate but subordinated so that one is the means to the end, then this effect is also willed directly; *directe eligitur tanquam medium ad finem directe volitum seu intentum* (it is directly chosen as a means to an end directly willed or intended). The will regarding the means can be called an *intentio* in a less strict sense, but the word is usually reserved to signify the direct will of the end. Waffelaert does not see how Viscosi and Pennacchi can escape the charge that they are using the Machiavellian principle that the end justifies the means when they justify craniotomy to save the life of the mother.

Waffelaert supports his interpretation of the distinction between direct and indirect by appealing to St. Thomas' example of taking bitter medicine. The intention of the person taking the medicine is to recover his health. Taking the medicine is the means to achieve this. The bitter taste of the medicine is *praeter intentionem;* he is not taking the medicine because it is bitter. But if the medicine cured him precisely because it was bitter, although it would still be *praeter intentionem*, it would be *directe volita* as a means to recovering his health.

Waffelaert then turns to the difficult passage in St. Thomas on self-defense. The defenders of craniotomy interpret it in a way that would be favorable to craniotomy. St. Thomas says that acts receive their moral species from the intention behind them, not from what happens unintentionally, since this is accidental. In self-defense, although the sword causes the death of the aggressor, his death will be accidental since it is *praeter intentionem*. What is intended is the safety of the person attacked. Similarly, the surgeon who dissects the child in the womb, does not intend the death of the fetus but only the health of the mother. The death of the fetus must be considered *praeter intentionem* that is, indirect.

Waffelaert advises his adversaries that if they want to use St. Thomas, they should take his teaching in its entirety. When St. Thomas says that acts receive their species from their intention, he is not telling the whole story of the morality of acts. Certainly, the intention must be good, if the act is to be morally good. But this is not enough. It is also necessary that the object and circumstances be good. Even in regard to self-defense St. Thomas is not satisfied with a good intention; there must also be a proportion between the means used and the requirements of defense. Waffelaert says that if his adversaries will show that craniotomy is good in reference to its object and circumstances, he will readily admit that the intention will make it completely moral.

But what does St. Thomas mean when he says that acts receive their moral species from what is intended, not from what is *praeter intentionem?* Waffelaert says that the term "species" here refers only to the species derived from intention—the last and essential species of the act—and not the material species which comes from the object and circumstances. In self-defense there is question of killing an unjust aggressor, which, according to Waffelaert, everybody admits may be directly willed. This must be kept in mind when applying what is said here to a case (like craniotomy) where an effect may be willed only indirectly. He calls attention to what he has already said about *intentio*. To be in the intention in the strict sense, an effect must be the end of the act. Any other effect, even though a means, although directly willed, can be said to be *praeter intentionem*.

Whenever two effects do not follow immediately from an act, but are subordinated, one may have two intentions, one properly so-called, and the other in a less strict sense, which is rather a direct will than a direct intention. But if the two effects follow immediately from the act, there will be only one intention and only one of the effects will be directly willed. He goes on to say that St. Thomas in the article on self-defense is not at all concerned with the subordination or nonsubordination of the effects, since this is not at issue. What is at issue is the intention. St. Thomas is arguing that self-defense is legitimate as long as the final intention of the defendant is to save his life and not to kill the assailant. The latter intention would be legitimate only in the case of punishment by a public authority. But St. Thomas does not deny that the death of the aggressor may be willed directly as a means of safety for the defendent when it is deemed necessary.[3] As long as his intention is to defend himself, the death of the adversary may be directly willed when a necessary means. From all this Waffelaert says that it should be clear that he is not speaking of a case where there are equally immediate effects.

It is somewhat hazardous to apply what St. Thomas says in dealing with self-defense to cases where there is no unjust aggression, or at least to arguments where this is not appealed to. Yet this is what Pennachi and Viscosi seemed to be doing. Whatever one may say about the importance of a good intention in self-defense, it may not be sufficient to justify killing outside of this context. But Viscosi and Pennacchi were also able to appeal to those cases, which had become classical, where according to them the killing of completely innocent people was justified as indirect killing because it was not intended. They are speaking of the frequently cited cases where an innocent child is used as a shield by an unjust aggressor, or where an innocent child is playing on a narrow bridge in the path of horseman fleeing an unjust aggressor, or where innocent people are killed in an attack on a legitimate military target.

Waffelaert challenges their explanation of these cases as inadequate. A good intention is not enough to justify killing an innocent person (nonaggressor). It is also necessary that there be no subordination between the bad effect and the good effect, but that both be equally immediate. Waffelaert feels that this condition is fulfilled in the classical cases mentioned above. It is not by killing innocent bystanders that one defends himself against combatants in battle, but by killing the combatants. Nor is the death of the child in the path of the horseman the means to his safety; it is the flight itself that saves him. Finally, it is not the death of the innocent child used as a shield that saves the man attacked, but the death of the assailant. In none of these cases, then, is the death of the innocent person the means to the end. But in craniotomy, although the intention is to save the life of the mother, which would make the death of the child indirect in this sense, the destruction of the child is directly willed as a means to this end. It differs in this sense from the cases mentioned above. The death of the child in craniotomy could be justified only if it could be considered an unjust aggressor.

Since he does not accept medical abortion, Waffelaert bypasses Pennacchi's argument drawn from this analogy. He does, however, criticize the use of the term *acceleratio partus* to name this procedure. A distinction should be made between abortion and premature delivery. Abortion has to do with a nonviable fetus; premature delivery only with a viable fetus. The two should not be confused by using the same terminology. He proceeds then to Pennacchi's argument that the fetus is an unjust aggressor.[4] In analyzing the concept of unjust aggression, Waffelaert argues that one can violate the rights of another in two ways; by a positive act which one has no right to place and which causes injury to one's neighbor which he has a negative right not to undergo; or by omitting an act which one has a duty to place in justice, if by the omission the neighbor is deprived of something he has a positive right to demand. In the situation calling for craniotomy there is certainly no question of omission of an act prescribed by justice. Such an obligation could arise only from a contract of some kind, which does not exist. Neither is there any positive act of injustice on the part of the fetus. It is customary to say that the mother has a right to life. It would be better to say that she has a right not to be unjustly deprived of life or those goods which follow upon life. No one has a positive right to life, but everyone has a right not to be unjustly deprived of life.

So it is only by placing a positive act which deprives another unjustly of life that one becomes an unjust aggressor. In the case of the fetus, of course, the aggression could only be material, since the fetus is incapable of a deliberate act. But is there any aggression at all? Where is the positive act that causes injury to the mother? Is it the attempt of the fetus to escape the uterus? Is it the fact that the fetus is feeding on the mother? According to Waffelaert everyone knows that in all this it is the mother rather than the fetus who is active. The cause of the danger in the craniotomy case is really only the presence of the fetus. Even if the fetus were dead (and in no sense active), the danger to the mother would be the same. But if it is purely passive presence that causes the danger, where is the aggression? How can one speak of aggression in reference to purely passive presence?

If two shipwrecked people are on a raft that will hold only one, can either be considered an aggressor merely by his presence on the raft? One could hardly eject the other, then, on this basis, and the same would hold for the fetus. The only reason for ejecting such a person would be that his very presence on the raft (in the womb) involved some injustice. Waffelaert then asks whether there is any reason for considering the presence of the fetus in the womb unjust.

For the presence of the fetus to be unjust, it is not enough that its presence be a source of harm to the mother, but it must be a source of unjust harm. This could happen in two ways. Either the fetus had no right to introduce itself into the uterus, or it ought to vacate by reason of a positive right acquired by the mother. He dismisses the second hypothesis as ridiculous, since no one acquires a positive right to the act of another except by contractual agreement. Nor is the first hypothesis any less ridiculous. The fetus was not introduced into the uterus by any action of its own, but by an action of the mother. The fetus, then, can hardly be said to be violating any right of the mother by its mere presence in the uterus. Waffelaert then appeals to Capellmann's argument from the viewpoint of medicine that the obstacle to delivery for the most part is the mother herself. Also, the activity in delivery is on the part of the mother. So, if the fetus is in the uterus because of the mother and the active agent is the mother, how can there be question of injustice or unjust aggression by the fetus?

Waffelaert next treats the argument from theological authority offered by Pennacchi. He dismisses the argument from Tertullian, who was speaking explicitly of craniotomy, for reasons already seen. Before taking up the theologians cited by the adversaries in favor of their position, Waffelaert feels that he must clarify the state of the question. It is not concerned with indirect abortion, which most authors allow, using the principle of the double effect. It concerns, rather, direct abortion and craniotomy. To conclude to the liceity of these, the adversaries must prove that the fetus is an unjust aggressor, since theologians in the past held that direct killing of an innocent person was not permissible. The adversaries have to show that theologians considered the fetus an unjust aggressor. To do so, they cite the theologians who held that direct abortion of the unanimated fetus is permissible to save the life of the mother, since the fetus in these circumstances is an unjust aggressor.

After chiding Pennacchi for misrepresenting certain authors, he goes on to give the fruits of his own research. He concludes from his study of about fifty authors of the past that most reject direct abortion absolutely. Of those who allow direct abortion of the unanimated fetus, only seven or eight speak of unjust aggression. All the others argue precisely from the fact that the fetus is not yet animated, a reason which could not be used if the fetus was animated.

Proponents of the craniotomy thesis maintain that if those authors who allow the abortion of the unanimated fetus to save the life of the mother were consistent, they would have to allow craniotomy. In other words, they would have to admit that the animated fetus in a similar situation is also an aggressor. But only one does this, namely Raynaud.[5] Waffelaert concedes that Viva and Mazzotta may be interpreted in this way, but neither is quite as explicit as Raynaud. The other five theologians, however, explicitly reject direct abortion of the animated fetus, since the fetus is an innocent person.

Apicella argued in favor of craniotomy on the basis of a conflict of rights.[6] The conflict was not real, but only apparent, since in the presence of a stronger right, the so-called conflicting right has to be considered subordinate. In the craniotomy case Apicella claimed that the right of the mother was stronger. So the right of the fetus would have to give way, and craniotomy would be licit. In responding to this argument Waffelaert analyses the rights involved. He states first that the mother's right to life is not a positive right; it is rather a negative right not to be deprived unjustly of the use of life. One who deprives the mother unjustly of life does an injury both to God, who is the sole master of life, and then to his neighbor. The same would have to be said about the child's right to life. In other words both mother and child have a right not to be unjustly deprived of life, and therefore the right to defend themselves against unjust aggression. Since, however, Apicella agrees that there is no unjust aggression in the case at hand, the mother can claim no right to take the child's life on this score.

Waffelaert continues his argument with the statement that the mother's right to life implies the right to use all honest and legitimate means to preserve her life, and consequently the right not to be unjustly deprived of these means. This right of the mother even implies an obligation to use means necessary to preserve her life, at least up to a point. But the right in question may be violated by a positive act on the part of the child. If this act is unjust, the infant would be an unjust aggressor (which Apicella denies). If the child has the right to place the act, there would be a conflict, and it would be necessary to determine which of the rights was only apparent. But where is this positive act that prevents the mother from exercising her right to life? There is no evidence of such an act. Nor does the mother's right to life impose on the child a positive duty in justice of furnishing her with the means to preserve her life, so that it would be guilty of culpable omission. No one has such a duty in justice apart from a contract or quasi contract. So it is difficult to see how the mother's right to life will justify craniotomy.

According to Apicella a craniotomy decision would have to involve the public authority. He has to have recourse to such authority because the traditional position has always denied to the private individual the right to take the life of another, at least outside of unjust aggression. He argues that the public authority does authorize craniotomy because it never prosecutes surgeons who perform this operation. Waffelaert responds that the failure of the state to punish craniotomists need imply only toleration, not positive approbation. Also, he does not see how the public authority can make legitimate what would otherwise be illegitimate. If the child is innocent, as Apicella seems to admit, the state has no authority to take his life. The state has no general right over life and death, but may impose the death sentence only where some crime has been committed. So, there is no way in which the intervention of the state, even if it were clear approval, could justify this destructive type of surgery.

At the end of this installment Waffelaert takes up the familiar analogy (introduced by Eschbach) with the boatman who takes on a passenger. If a storm blows up and the boat begins to sink because of the weight, the boatman may not simply throw his passenger overboard. Pennachi had denied the comparison with the craniotomy case because the passenger in the boat case was not the cause of the danger, but the storm. In the craniotomy case, the source of the danger is the child. Waffelaert responds that this would make a difference if the child were an unjust aggressor; but it is not. Moreover, as he has shown from Capellmann, the source of the danger comes more from the mother than the child.

In another installment Waffelaert takes up the charge of Viscosi and Pennacchi that the number of theologians supporting an opinion is really not all that important; what is important is their reasons.[7] The two authors are relying on Melchior Cano in taking this position. But Waffelaert denies that Cano ever argued that *only* the reasons counted. Waffelaert concedes their other argument that the authority of one author can be such as to outweigh many ordinary theologians, if he is *omni exceptione maior*, but adds that if such an author exists he will certainly have a following. Viscosi and Pennacchi, finally, tried to detract from the weight of the common opinion against their position by charging that many of these authors do no more than copy and follow one another like birds and sheep (*ad instar avium et ovium*). Waffelaert simply refuses to accept this charge against the classical moralists. The fact that authors agree on something does not necessarily mean that they did no more than uncritically copy one another.

What is to be done when cases of difficult and dangerous delivery present themselves?[8] Waffelaert is presuming here that it is too late for premature delivery (not in the sense of medical abortion). On the medical side he quotes Dr. Hubert who recommends that if a forceps delivery will not solve the problem, the passage may be enlarged by an episiotomy or symphysiotomy. If even this will not be sufficient, a caesarian section may be called for. But if the mother refuses the caesarian section, the only alternative is to await the death of the fetus and then remove it.

Historically, caesarean section on a live mother was considered a lethal procedure. St. Thomas would not allow it even to provide for the baptism of the child. In the seventeenth century Comitolus still considered it murder and called those doctors who had recourse to it "butchers." Waffelaert says that in his time it is not necessarily, or even certainly, fatal. Given the development that has taken place, it is not so clear any more that a mother might not be obliged to undergo it even to save the life of the child. But he feels that in practice, if the woman shows real opposition, no mention should be made of such surgery.

What about the obligation of the priest or confessor in a dangerous delivery situation? In Waffelaert's opinion, if the doctor is a craniotomist, it will be frequently useless for the priest to say anything. In any case he should be careful not to cause greater evils. Waffelaert is following here the pastoral norms for leaving a penitent in good faith. But if the doctor asks the priest whether it is permissible to take the life of the child to save the mother, he should respond that he does not see how this can be licit. If the mother, anxious about her own life, asks the advice of the confessor, he shoud be very prudent because of the difficulty of the decision for her. Often it may be prudent to give no more than an evasive response, telling her to ask the doctor to do everything he can to save the child. These norms will be recognized as following the same lines that were set down earlier by Kenrick. [9]

In his final discussion of Pennacchi, Waffelaert focuses on his position regarding medical abortion. [10] Since in dealing with this problem Pennacchi does no more than follow Ballerini, Waffelaert turns his attention to the rather lengthy note 11 appended to Gury's treatment of abortion where Ballerini presents his own observations. It will be remembered that Ballerini allows what he calls *acceleratio partus* (medical abortion) to save the life of the mother. Ballerini had distinguished between direct and indirect *acceleratio* in two different ways: the nature of the means used and the intention of the agent. Even though the means used were of their nature aimed at *acceleratio partus*, the procedure would be licit as long as the intention was to save the mother. The death of the fetus would be *preater intentionem*.

Waffelaert finds the distinction between direct and indirect based on intention (which is key to Ballerini's position) rather ambiguous. The reason is that the word intention can be taken in two senses. If it is taken in the strict sense, that is, *intentio finis*, something can be *praeter intentionem* and still directly willed, since it can be directly willed as a means to the end. If you take the word *intentio* to apply to willing the means as well as the end, an abortion willed as means would not be *praeter intentionem*. To eliminate the ambiguity Waffelaert sets down six propositions which he says ought to be accepted by everyone:

1 Direct killing (in any sense) of an innocent person is intrinsically wrong.
2 Direct killing (direct intention in the strict sense) of anyone is wrong.
3 Direct killing (not a direct intention, but a direct will, that is, means to an end) of an unjust aggressor is licit.
4 Indirect killing (no direct intention, but a direct will) of an innocent person is wrong.
5 Indirect killing (no direct intention, no direct will) of an innocent person may be licit.
6 Indirect killing (in any sense) of an unjust aggressor may be licit.

Waffelaert says that Ballerini is really trying to justify abortion by direct means (number 4 above). The distinction he uses besed on intention, which allows him to say that the abortion is indirect since the intention is to save the life of the mother, is not pertinent. Killing which is indirect only in this sense is justified only in unjust aggression. Actually,

Ballerini has no need of this distinction, since what he really tries to show is that direct abortion does not constitute direct killing.

Ballerini reduced the whole question of medical abortion to the question of the mother's obligation to preserve the life of the fetus. Waffelaert simply denies that this is a valid position. It is not just a question of the mother no longer supporting a pregnancy by not preventing an abortion. The abortion takes place as the result of a positive act placed by the physician. The text from Lugo, which puts the issue in terms of prolonging the life of the fetus, referred to indirect abortion, so it is not pertinent to this situation. Waffelaert can see no distinction between direct abortion and direct killing.

W affelaert attempts a refutation of the arguments in favor of craniotomy, especially the argument that the killing of the fetus is indirect and that it constitutes self-defense against unjust aggression. He feels that these authors, especially Pennacchi, are misusing St. Thomas to defend their position. Since the latter was speaking of self-defense, he was satisfied that killing of the aggressor was *praeter intentionem* in the sense of the ultimate goal of the act. He was not concerned whether it was the means. But when the life of an innocent nonaggressor is at stake, killing him must be excluded not only as an end but also as a means. Whether this is a legitimate interpretation of St. Thomas on self-defense is questionable, but certainly he was speaking in the article only of self defense. Waffelaert maintains that when one is sheaking of indirect killing of a nonaggressor, the killing must be excluded not only as an end but also as a means. The implication is that Pennacchi and Viscosi did not exclude the killing as a means. In justice to both of these authors it must be said that they claim to have excluded the death of the fetus as a means to saving the mother's life. The real question is whether the exclusion was really valid.

Waffelaert also attacked the argument that the fetus is an unjust aggressor. In doing so he analyses the right to life as a negative right, that is, the right not to be unjustly deprived either of life or the use of means necessary to preserve life. He denies that the fetus is doing either, and consequently that it can be considered an unjust aggressor.

Waffelaert finally refutes Ballerini's argument in favor of medical abortion. Since Ballerini is not as clear as he might be on this point, Waffelaert can be excused for not reading him accurately. He seems to think that Ballerini justifies medical abortion because the intention is indirect, namely, to save the life of the mother. This was not precisely Ballerini's position. It was rather that direct abortion is not necessarily direct killing, which goes against the ordinary presumption. To Ballerini direct abortion would be wrong only if the mother had an obligation to continue to support the child. He denies that such an obligation exists when such support would endanger her life. Given these circumstances abortion would be wrong only if it involved direct killing. If the procedure is mere *acceleratio partus* it does not constitute a direct attack on the fetus and therefore cannot be considered direct killing.

CHAPTER FIFTEEN

Resolution
(1884-1950)

In his introduction Pennacchi mentioned that the question of the morality of craniotomy to save the mother, according to the Master of the Sacred Palace, had been handed over to a group of reputable men for their study.[1] And when Waffelaert was about half way through his series of articles refuting Pennacchi's position he announced that the Congregation had come out and said that craniotomy could not be safely taught in Catholic schools.[2] The statement to which he referred was a response to a question proposed to the Holy Office by D. Caverot, Cardinal Archbishop of Lyons. Here is the way it reads: "May it safely be taught in Catholic schools that craniotomy is permissible when otherwise both mother and fetus will perish, but with the operation, although the child will perish, the mother's life will be saved?" The response, signed by Cardinal Monaco (May 31, 1884), was given only after long and careful study, which took into consideration the opinions of experts on the subject. It stated simply: "This cannot be safely taught." The Cardinal goes on to say that the Holy Father confirmed this response in an audience held on the same day.[3]

Once the response was given, the question was raised whether it was to be considered a doctrinal and definitive response, or only disciplinary and prudential. Eschbach says that it was immediately observed that the form of the response was similar to that used by the Holy Office in 1861 regarding the errors of ontologism.[4] At that time there were some in Belgium who argued that the response forbade only the teaching of ontologism; it did not forbid one to hold it. When this was brought to the attention of the Holy See by the bishops of Belgium, Cardinal Patrizzi in the name of the Holy Father wrote and expressed some surprise that such doubts had arisen. Moreover, they were not such as to warrant a new interpretation and declaration of something already quite definite. They could be resolved completely by appealing to the response itself. On the basis of this response from the Cardinal the bishops of Belgium advised those concerned that the question was decided definitively, and that it was the will of the Holy Father that *sublatis erroribus* (abandoning error) all should be in agreement. This put an end to the controversy over ontologism. When he published the second edition of his *Disputationes* Eschbach was able to say that the same thing happened to the controversy over craniotomy. The response of the Holy Office condemned the opinion that it could ever be licit.

Although the response of the Holy Office solved the controversy over craniotomy, it did not touch, at least explicitly, a whole host of other pregnancy problems and surgical procedures. The question arose, especially among the professors of the Catholic faculty of Lille, whether these other procedures were also condemned. Six sets of cases were drawn up and submitted by the Bishop of Cambrai to the Holy See for solution. The cases generally dealt with procedures in which either the life of the mother or the fetus was at stake, or at least in danger. The cases were presented in 1886, but no response came until 1889. The response, again signed by Cardinal Monaco, did not attempt to deal with the individual case, but set down a general principle.[5] After calling attention to the previous response regarding craniotomy, it said that this applied to any surgical procedure directly lethal *(directe occisiva)* either to the mother or the fetus.

Shortly after the first response of the Holy Office condemning craniotomy M. Matharan, S.J., took up the defense of Ballerini against a charge made by Eschbach that he was teaching craniotomy.[6] Eschbach charged that Ballerini in his annotation of Gury taught that to save the mother it was permissible: to remove a fetus (nonviable) from the uterus by suitable means; to kill it immediately (for example, in craniotomy), as long as the death of the fetus was not intended directly. He also charged that in both Ballerini was departing from the teaching of Gury himself.[7]

The charge that he was teaching craniotomy was based on a note Ballerini made to Gury's statement that it was not permissible to kill the fetus to save the mother.[8] Ballerini says that this statement must be understood *sensu in praecedenti nota exposito* (in the sense of the preceding note). In that note Ballerini says that one may not directly will the death of the fetus. He adds that if the death of both mother and fetus is certain, the mother is not bound to undergo a death that will not save the fetus. He then refers to those authors mentioned by the *Salmanticenses* who said that in certain circumstances the fetus was like an unjust aggressor whose death, according to St. Thomas, resulted only indirectly from self-defense.

The confusion seems to have arisen primarily over the use of the words *directly will*. Matharan insists that in the preceding note, to which Ballerini referred when he made this statement, he extends direct willing to include even the means to the end.[9] One may not place an action which is the cause of death to the infant, even if the death of the infant is not the end desired but only a means to the end. In either case the death of the child is willed directly. Eschbach seems to be charging that Ballerini is satisfied as long as the death of the child is not the end of the procedure. Matharan insists that this is not a correct interpretation of Ballerini. To prove his position he also refers to the part in the notes where Ballerini is distinguishing between procedures aimed at the death of the fetus and those aimed at the mother's health. Craniotomy would certainly have to be classified as one of the former, which Ballerini clearly ruled out.

Another cause for the confusion was Ballerini's reference to the theologians who considered the fetus an unjust aggressor where the life of the mother was at stake, and therefore according to St. Thomas could be killed as long as the intention was to save the mother. These theologians were not, of course, speaking of the animated fetus, so the reference may not be pertinent to the craniotomy case, but it must be admitted that the reference introduces a note of ambiguity in the discussion. Matharan insists that Ballerini is appealing to these authors because they justify medical abortion on these grounds. The difficulty is that in this note Ballerini is talking about killing the fetus rather than abortion.

Matharan then takes up a defense of medical abortion, and denies first that Ballerini departed from Gury's teaching in this regard. He quotes from the sixteenth edition of Gury's *Compendium*, published in 1865, in which Gury made allowance for this kind of abortion. This was a year before his death in 1866. The second edition of his *Casus*, in which he changed his solution to the Pelagia case, was also published in the same year. It seems clear, therefore, that Gury changed his opinion from earlier editions.

Matharan defends the use of the term *acceleratio partus* against Eschbach's charge that it causes confusion with a procedure that can be perfectly legitimate: premature delivery of a viable fetus. Matharan argues that the term abortion is a generic term which can cover violent as well as nonviolent means. The term *acceleratio partus* refers to the type of abortion that does not attack the child. Matharan admits that older authors condemned abortion, but this was because they identified it with killing the fetus. This was probably because of the methods used. Unless this is the reason, it is hard to explain why they condemned abortion even during the last months of pregnancy.

Matharan also tries to explain away the distinction made by authors in the past between procedures aimed at curing some disease in the mother and procedures aimed at abortion. This distinction was adequate because they were concerned with some malady in the mother that needed treatment. Could it not be that the total source of the danger would be the fetus itself? If so, would it not be permissible to procure an abortion by means which would not attack the child itself? Perhaps the older theologians were not aware that such a case could exist; or perhaps they did not know of any procedure for delivering such a fetus without directly attacking it. He seems to feel that Voit was the first theologian to have considered and allowed this case a century ago.

Matharan defends *acceleratio partus* as an act which is not intrinsically evil. The death of the child is not due to the extraction itself but to the unfavorable circumstances in which the child finds itself after delivery. It is unlike a procedure which involves a direct attack on the child. In comparing it with the case of the child used as a human shield, he finds that the extraction is much less a cause of death than the javelin of the person defending himself in the latter case. Other authors, however, have not been impressed with the argument that *acceleratio* does not involve direct killing. They compare it to taking a dying man from his bed and throwing him into a river. Matharan finds this comparison strange. What kind of reason could one have for such monstrous conduct? He finds a better comparison in the case of the mother in a shipwreck with a child in her arms, when her means of support in the water will not sustain both child and mother.

In a response published in a later issue of the *Revue* Eschbach insists that Ballerini must have taught craniotomy since his name was mentioned in this connection in the *Acta Sanctae Sedis* in 1873 and 1884, and there was no protest on his part.[11] In dealing with the question of medical abortion he accuses Matharan of using arguments to defend medical abortion just as though there was no ban on craniotomy. Matharan had said that the fetus, although innocent, was an aggressor on the mother's life. He then argued that if it was even permissible to kill an innocent child used as a shield by an unjust aggressor, it should be permissible to remove a fetus whose presence is a source of danger to the mother. Eschbach does not see how Matharan can escape the conclusion that craniotomy could be justified on the same grounds. He seems to be leaning especially on Matharan's statement that the fetus is an aggressor.

Later issues of the *Revue* carried a second exchange between Eschbach and Matharan.[12] The latter takes up the charge that his arguments for medical abortion would justify craniotomy. He admits that he used the word aggressor of the fetus, but only by way of comparison with the innocent child used as a shield. He was not arguing that the fetus could be considered an aggressor from a moral viewpoint, but only that it was the source of the mother's problems. In the other case the child was not the source of the danger to the man defending himself, but the unjust aggressor. Matharan would not allow the fetus to be killed as an unjust aggressor. As an innocent person he may not be killed directly. It is precisely because medical abortion does not involve this that he permits it. The same could not be said of craniotomy. The cephalotribe achieves only the death of the fetus. In this respect it differs even from the bullet or javelin that penetrates the human shield and the unjust aggressor at the same time.

Matharan returns to the dispute about Gury's opinion. Eschbach, referring to the first solution of the Pelagia case, said that this is not the language of a man in doubt. Also, the Ratisbon edition, published in the same year as the second Lyons edition, retained the original solution. Eschbach maintains that information he has at hand makes him doubt that the second Lyons edition was published *par les soins* by Gury. Nor was the second solution of the Pelagia case retained very long. An edition published ten years later contained the original solution of the case.

Matharan is not impressed by the argument that Gury did not change his opinion drawn from the Ratisbon edition. He says that Gury really never bothered about editions of his work published outside of France. He denies also that the second edition of his *Casus* was not published under his supervision. When Gury published the two editions of the *Casus*, Matharan says that he was teaching with him at the Jesuit philosophate at Vals and saw him going over the proofs of the manuscript. He claims that not a page, not even a line, of this second edition went to the publisher without his approval. To allay any suspicion Eschbach's somewhat cryptic statement about the publication of this edition might give rise to, Matharan testified to the fact that Gury was in full possession of his faculties until he died, which was almost a full year after he completed the manuscript for the *Casus* and the *Compendium*.

Finally, to sharpen the area of dispute, Matharan sets down two norms within which he works. The first is that any abortion procured by an act which ends directly in the destruction of the fetus is homicidal and never licit. The second is that an abortion procured by an act which of its nature is not lethal or destructive of the fetus but only removes it from the womb is licit if necessary to save the life of the mother.

In his final response Eschbach charges that Matharan has taken a position that goes against all past teaching without giving any proof.[13] He simply states that removing the fetus from the womb is not a lethal act. Eschbach proceeds to show him that it is a lethal act. He does this more by example than by direct argument. For Eschbach death does not have to follow immediately to prove an act lethal. He gives the example of a lethal dose of poison. It will be effective, but it may work slowly. More important than the immediacy of the effect is the clear connection with the cause. He gives the example of a bird enclosed in an hermetically sealed container. Gradually it uses up all the oxygen and dies. Also, if you remove a fish from water, however carefully you do it, and leave it on a table, it will die. All of these acts are lethal, and everyone, whether

philosopher or ordinary person, would admit this. Eschbach admits that there are two kinds of cause-effect relationships: necessary and accidental. He gives the example
of a person who causes slight injury to another person. If
the second person neglects to take care of himself and dies
as a result, his death cannot be imputed to the person who
causes the injury. The injury did not cause the death, but
the neglect. But this is not the case in medical abortion.
The death of the fetus follows necessarily from its premature removal from the uterus, and without the intervention
of any other cause.

The responses of the Holy Office condemned
craniotomy and all other procedures involving direct killing of the fetus, but did not speak, at least explicitly, to the
question of medical abortion as defended by Ballerini and
others. It was precisely because they did not think this involved direct killing of the fetus that they argued it could be
defended. To get an authoritative answer to the specific
question of medical abortion Archbishop Sonnois of
Cambrai presented such a case to the Holy Office. It was
the case of a doctor who was dealing with a pregnant
woman in danger of death where the sole cause of the
danger was the pregnancy itself. The only way to save the
mother was to remove the fetus. Since it was not viable, it
could not possibly survive outside the uterus. But the
means used to remove the fetus involved no direct attack
on it. Rather, every effort was used to deliver the fetus
alive, even though it would certainly die after delivery. It
was obviously the classical case discussed and defended
by Ballerini and others. After reading the response of 1889,
the doctor on the case was in a state of doubt about the
liceity of this procedure.

The Holy Office responded July 24, 1895, that the procedure in question could not be safely used, in accord with
the decrees of 1884 and 1889.[14] What it was saying practically was that a medical abortion involved direct killing and
therefore could not be justified any more than craniotomy
or other procedures of this kind. These responses resolved
on the level of authentic teaching the controversies of the

second half of the nineteenth century. Since the theologians involved, such as Viscosi and Pennachi, were arguing only in favor of the probability of their opinions and only until such time as the opposite opinion should become clear or church authority should settle the issue, it must be presumed that these responses were accepted by them. Some of the protagonists, however, such as Avanzini, Ballerini, and D'Annibale, were already dead by the time the responses appeared, so there is no way of knowing what their reaction might have been. But Lehmkuhl, who lived on into the twentieth century did retract his previous position in later editions of his *Theologia moralis*.[15] After presenting the arguments he made in favor of medical abortion he says that in truth the reasons he gave were specious rather than truly convincing. The truth is, he continues, that the fetus is primarily and *per se* the object of attack, just as a person whom another might strike with a mortal blow. To tear asunder violently the membranes and tissues which connect the fetus to the mother is nothing else than to inflict a fatal wound on him. What is done to the fetus involves direct killing and is intrinsically evil.

In the first half of the twentieth century no further questions were raised about either craniotomy or medical abortion. The authors of the period argued almost unanimously against both. There were still a few who would insist that the response of the Holy See did not include the case where both mother and fetus would otherwise die, but little or no evidence could be brought forth to support this position. The period saw a proliferation of manuals which went into many editions and were frequently carried on by successors after the deaths of the original authors. The most prominent of these manuals were authored originally by Noldin, Sabetti, Genicot, Vermeersch, Marc, Wouters, Merkelbach, and Prummer. For the most part, however, they did no more than present the traditional position with the arguments in favor of it. The earlier authors would go more or less into detail arguing specifically against craniotomy and medical abortion.

Due to progress in medical science the problem of craniotomy and medical abortion was solved on another level. As caesarean section became a safer procedure, there was less pressure to resort to craniotomy to solve delivery problems. Several other procedures were also available to solve such problems, and without endangering the mother's life. As medical science learned how to handle complications of pregnancy, the indications for direct abortion also became less and less frequent. In fact toward the end of this period maternity hospitals were able to claim that such indications were almost nonexistent.[16] The whole issue of craniotomy and direct abortion to save the life of the mother was reduced largely to the realm of speculation.

No other official reference to abortion came from the Church until the publication of *Casti connubii* by Pius XI.[17] Although this encyclical was preoccupied with the problem of contraception, it touched briefly on abortion, even though little was being said at that time about abortion as a method of birth control. The encyclical speaks of an attack on the fetus in the womb as the gravest kind of wrong, commenting at the same time that there are some who would leave this to the wish of the parents. Others consider it wrong except for very serious reasons, which they refer to as medical, eugenic, and social. These also want the civil law to recognize these indications.

Most of the attention of the encyclical is given to abortion for medical indications, that is, where the life or health of the mother is at risk. While showing the greatest sympathy for the pregnant mother whose health or even life is being threatened, the encyclical asks: What reason could ever justify direct killing of an innocent person? The Pope goes on to say that such killing either of the fetus or the mother is forbidden by the commandment: Thou shalt not kill! Both lives are sacred, and not even the civil authority could ever have the power to destroy them. The *ius gladii* (power over life and death) is limited to those who are convicted of some crime. And one cannot appeal to a right of self-defense against an unjust aggressor. Who would ever call an innocent little child an unjust aggressor? Nor can one appeal to a right to take the life of the fetus because of extreme need. Rather it is the duty of the doctor to save the life of both mother and child. Anyone who under the pretext of medicine or out of false mercy woule take the life of either would prove himself unworthy of his noble profession. The encyclical concludes the treatment of abortion with the statement that eugenic or social reasons are no more valid than the medical reason already mentioned.

The reader will recognize in this brief statement abbreviations of arguments made by proponents of craniotomy and abortion. Statements of this kind are never meant to be theological treatises, so one cannot expect to find in them full and complete argumentation. In spite of the clarity of the statement, however, a well-known Italian physician still claimed that it did not cover the case where the mother and child would otherwise die, and that therefore an abortion in this situation was morally permissible. Dr. Pestalozza, the physician making the claim, was arguing that abortion in this case did not involve direct killing, since the purpose was to save the life of the mother.[18] The argument, of course, was not a new one, and it was immediately challenged by P. Gemelli, rector of the Catholic University of Milan.[19]

The distinction between direct and indirect abortion would still give rise to difficulties in judging individual cases. It will be remembered that Dr. Capellmann argued in favor of puncturing the amniotic sac where this was necessary to reduce the size of the uterus, even though it would cause the danger of abortion.[20] In Capellmann's opinion the abortion, if it occurred, would be indirect, since it was not the abortion as such that solved the mother's problem, but reducing the size of the uterus by draining off amniotic fluid. Benedict Merkelbach, a Dominican theologian, in a monograph dealing with pastoral questions related to embryology took issue with Capellmann on this case.[21] Merkelbach argued that this would be direct killing, since the doctor in puncturing the sac intended to remove the amniotic fluid. He becomes a little vague at this point arguing first that the fluid is necessary for the survival of the fetus and then that the procedure involves the danger of abortion. Ultimately, it seems to be the danger of abortion that concerns him most, since he seems willing to allow the puncture if the danger is absent. But, given the danger, he considers the puncture a lethal action. Merkelbach was, however, willing to allow the puncture if this was the only way the fetus could be baptized. The difference between this case and the one he rejected was that in the baptismal case no removal of amniotic fluid was intended, since this was in no way necessary for baptism. Presumably, the danger of abortion would also be less in this case, at least in Merkelbach's judgment. Otherwise it would have to be condemned. But these cases are only of speculative interest today, since progress in medical science and technique has made amniocentesis a relatively safe procedure.

Another controversy arose over the removal of a cancerous but pregnant uterus. It was initiated by a statement made by the Dr. Pestalozza mentioned above. It will be recalled that he did not think the encyclical *Casti connubii* outlawed an abortion to save the mother when otherwise both mother and child would die. On a later occasion he repeated this statement and offered two examples by way of illustration: the removal of a cancerous but pregnant uterus and the removal of the fetus in a case of *hyperemesis gravidarum*.[22] In arguing for the hysterectomy in the cancerous but pregnant uterus he appealed to the authority of Arthur Vermeersch, a Belgian Jesuit teaching at the Gregorian University in Rome. The judgment of the *hyperemesis* case was apparently his own.

There is no doubt that Vermeersch considered the procedure in the hysterectomy case an indirect abortion, but not for the reason given by Pestalozza.[23] If the distinction between direct and indirect abortion depended solely on the intention of the agent, Pestalozza's assessment of both cases would be correct. Eventually, Vermeersch would clarify his own position, but in the meanwhile Gemelli took issue with Pestalozza not only on the *hyperemesis* case but also on the hysterectomy.[24] In opposing his solution of the hysterectomy case Gemelli admitted that he was departing from accepted opinion. Gemelli considered the hysterectomy in this case a direct abortion because it brought certain death to the fetus.

It was at this point that Vermeersch entered the controversy with an article in *Periodica* in which he pointed out that there are three ways of approaching the distinction between direct and indirect causality.[25] The first way puts the whole burden on the intention of the agent (this is the way of Dr. Pestalozza). The second looks not only to the intention of the agent but also to the nature (*finis operis*) of the act. According to this approach, for an abortion to be indirect it is not sufficient that it is not intended as an end. It must not be willed even as a means. This is Vermeersch's own approach. The third approach is that of Gemelli. Causality is direct or indirect according to the certainty of the effect. If the death of the fetus is certain, the causality is direct; if it is less than certain the causality is indirect or *per accidens*. Vermeersch goes on to say that the first way of distinguishing is no longer accepted. The third way, which makes the distinction depend on the certainty of the effect, was never accepted. The only approach that is traditional and makes sense is the second approach.

Gemelli took occasion to respond to Vermeersch in the *Nouvelle revue théologique*.[26] He began by repeating his argument that the abortion was direct because the death of the fetus was certain, even more certain than saving the life of the mother. Also, one could hardly think of a more direct abortion since the first part of the operation consists in cutting off circulation between the mother and the fetus by ligating the arteries that supplied the blood. The fetus is deprived by this procedure of his source of life, and is therefore killed; it does not just die. Gemelli argued too that the death of the fetus cannot be considered accidental when it follows necessarily. Nor in his opinion can it be called accidental since it is accidental that the uterus is pregnant; this is what the uterus is for. Gemelli does not agree either that the abortion is not voluntary, at least *in causa*, since the doctor wants to perform an operation which of its nature and of necessity brings certain death to the fetus. If abortion is licit in this case, it should also be permissible in a case of serious *hyperemesis gravidarum*.

Vermeersch responded to these arguments one by one. He denies first that the good effect must be as certain as the evil effect to make the abortion indirect.[27] The distinction between direct and indirect does not depend on the certainty of the effect. Nor does the good effect have to be as immediate as the evil effect in the chronological order. All that is required is that the evil effect should not be the means of achieving the good effect. Cutting off the circulation does not in itself make the death of the fetus direct, since it is the arteries of the mother that are ligated, not the arteries of the fetus, and each has its own circulatory system. It is true that oxygen and nourishment are thereby cut off from the fetus, but the fetus itself is not immediately touched by the surgery. Also, it does not die immediately, but is delivered alive. If it were viable, it would live. The abortion occurs *per accidens*, since the same operation would be performed whether the mother was pregnant or not.

To Gemelli's argument that the abortion is not accidental because the uterus is by nature destined to carry a pregnancy. Vermeersch responds that, even though this is true, it is not by nature pregnant; there are times when a uterus is empty, and some uteri are never pregnant. To the argument that the abortion is *voluntarium in causa* he responds that the death of the fetus is neither willed nor chosen as an end or as a means. It arises from the concurrence of another cause which the agent cannot and is not bound to prevent. He denies, finally, the parallel between this case and abortion to solve a problem of *hyperemesis*. Separating the placenta from the uterus involves the fetus directly, since the placenta belongs to the fetus. Even if one wants to distinguish between a part of the placenta which belongs to the mother and a part which belongs to the fetus, they are so joined together that it is impossible to affect the one without affecting the other. Moreover, the problem of the mother is not solved by removing the placenta, but by removing the fetus.

Benedict Merkelbach, the Dominican theologian already mentioned, agreed with Vermeersch's solution of the problem of the cancerous but pregnant uterus.[28] He presents a number of reasons to show that the mother's life is not saved by removing the fetus. His first reason is that the danger to the mother does not come from the fetus but rather from the cancer. The danger to the mother would be present even if she were not pregnant. It follows that the mother's life is not saved precisely by removing the fetus but rather by removing the uterus. It is achieved in exactly the same way it would be achieved if the mother were not pregnant. Terminating the pregnancy in itself has nothing to do with saving the mother's life. If the diseased uterus were left in place, the life of the mother would still be in danger. So the removal of the fetus is in no way a means to saving the mother's life. The abortion, consequently, is indirect.

With Vermeersch, Merkelbach argues that the fact that damage is done to the fetus chronologically prior to saving the mother's life is not pertinent. It is the mother's arteries that are being ligated, not those of the fetus. Nor does the fact that the damage to the fetus follows *per se* make any difference, since it is not the means of achieving the good effect.

Vermeersch and Merkelbach had many followers even in the medical profession. But a Franciscan by the name of Mancini was still not convinced.[29] He argued that the uterus belongs to the fetus as well as to the mother. It belongs to the mother in so far as it is a part of her body. It belongs to the fetus since it is destined to sustain fetal life. So one cannot conceive of an action directed against the uterus which does not directly affect the fetus. The abortion, therefore, cannot be indirect.

Mancini also argued that although there is no difference between a hysterectomy performed on a pregnant woman and on one who is not pregnant from the standpoint of the surgery performed, there is from the standpoint of ethics. There is no subject of rights present in an empty uterus. In the pregnant uterus there is a fetus present whose rights must be respected. Also, an abortion is indirect when the surgery does not terminate in organs essential to the life of the fetus but in other organs not necessary to sustain the life of the fetus. He does not think that one can validly distinguish in this type of case between surgery directed at the placenta and surgery directed at the uterus. The distinction would be valid only if one could consider the mother and the fetus as two totally distinct beings. But this cannot be done, since the life of one is meshed in with that of the other, as nature planned it. The fetus has a right to the normal functions of the uterus, which would make it wrong to interfere with these functions.

Vermeersch again responded, and this time was joined by A. Janssen, a professor at the University of Louvain.[30] Both deny that the organs of the mother belong to the fetus in any proper sense. Mother and fetus are two distinct beings with their own organs and vital functions. There is a relation of dependence on the part of the fetus, but there is only extrinsic union between the two, a union of the container and the thing contained. The uterus belongs to the mother. It can be said to be destined for the good of the fetus in the same way as food and a house are destined for the good of man. But it is not an organ of the fetus. It is only an external good of the fetus, whereas it is an internal good of the mother. The fetus has a right to the use of the uterus, but the mother has a prior right since it pertains to her intrinsic good. As a part of her body, it may be disposed of, just as any other part, when the good of the whole body demands it.

The fact that no action on the uterus will not have some effect on the fetus as well only shows that such actions have two effects. It does not prove that a subsequent abortion will be direct. The surgery in this case directly touches the uterus, and only accidentally the fetus. Nor does the benefit to the mother come from the abortion, but only from the removal of the uterus. So the abortion cannot be direct.

Vermeersch admits that the presence of the fetus in the uterus adds an ethical dimension to the surgery. The fetus certainly may not be injured directly. Also, removing a pregnant uterus calls for a more serious reason than removing an empty uterus; it may not be done unless there is no other way to save the mother's life. Yet the presence of the fetus does not interfere with the mother's right to use licit means to save her life. It does not prevent the removal of the uterus in this case even though indirectly and accidentally it causes harm to the fetus. The fetus does not have an absolute right to life, but only a right not to be directly attacked.

Vermeersch objects also to the definition of direct abortion used by his adversary. For an abortion to be direct it does not suffice that it terminate in organs necessary for the life of the fetus. It is required that the abortion be the only immediate effect of the act, or if there is a good effect, that the abortion be the cause of the good effect. But this is not the case in the surgery under discussion.

Finally, if there is a real distinction between mother and fetus, an act can touch one without touching the other. If it terminates in the placenta, it touches the fetus; if it terminates in the uterus, it touches the mother. Vermeersch, however, admits that the placenta is a common organ, a concession he will not make regarding the uterus. He denies finally that the distinction between direct and indirect abortion depends on the certainty of the effect.

Mancini continued his discussion of the case in further articles in *Palestra del clero*, but did not add significantly to arguments already made.[31] It is not clear that he was ever convinced of the liceity of a hysterectomy in the case, but after him it ceased to be a controversial issue. There was general acceptance of the procedure by moral theologians.

Another case that became controversial was that of the ectopic pregnancy. Most of the discussion centered around the tubal pregnancy, which is the most common type of ectopic. The initial problem in dealing with ectopics was one of diagnosis. It was very difficult to decide before surgery whether the problem arose from a pregnancy or some other kind of growth or tumor. When the doubt could not be solved otherwise, some theologians allowed surgery for the removal of the "cyst." They were arguing on the presumption that a pregnancy would be in the proper place, so that a growth elsewhere would more likely be a cyst or tumor and could be removed if the mother's life was in danger.

The more important issue, however, had to do with the morality of removing what was certainly an ectopic pregnancy to save the life of the mother. The *American Ecclesiastical Review* beginning in 1893 carried a running discussion of the problem.[32] The discussion involved both theologians and members of the medical profession in their respective roles. The three theologians contributing their opinion were Augustine Lehmkuhl, a German Jesuit, Joseph Aertnys, a Dutch Redemptorist, and Aloysius Sabetti, an Italian Jesuit teaching in an American Jesuit theologate at Woodstock in Maryland.[33] Lehmkuhl argued for the removal of the ectopic pregnancy in much the same way he argued in favor of abortion to save the mother. He did not consider it direct killing if it did not involve an attack on the fetus itself. It will be remembered that he retracted this position after the response of the Holy Office (1895) condemning medical abortion. Sabetti also allowed the direct removal of the fetus, and without the limitations set by Lehmkuhl, since he considered the fetus in an ectopic pregnancy an unjust aggressor. To Sabetti the ectopic pregnancy differed from the uterine pregnancy in this respect; the fetus was not where it should be. It could be removed, then, as an unjust aggressor.

The third consultant, Joseph Aertnys, would not allow the removal of the pregnancy. To him such removal constituted direct killing, and he refused to consider the fetus an unjust aggressor. Oddly enough, while Lehmkuhl and Sabetti allowed the removal of the ectopic fetus, neither admitted the argument of the other. Sabetti refused to allow direct removal if the fetus was innocent, since he considered this direct killing. Lehmkuhl from his corner refused to consider the fetus an unjust aggressor.[34] The fact that it was not in the right place did not impress him as an argument. The fetus had nothing to do with this. His present condition was the result of the action of his parents and natural causes, and the defect was parental as well. Even if one wanted to call the fetus an aggressor in some sense, there was no injustice about it.

In 1898 the question of removing a tubal pregnancy was brought to the attention of the Holy Office.[35] It was worded as follows: "Is it permissible to do a laparotomy when the pregnancy is extrauterine or ectopic?" The Holy Office responded that in a case of urgent necessity it would be permissible to do a laparotomy for the removal of ectopic conceptions, as long as serious provision is made, as far as possible, for the life of both the fetus and the mother.

This first response of the Holy Office was not as clear as it might have been, and hence left some doubt whether provision for the life of the child ruled out the removal of an ectopic pregnancy before viability. As a result a second response was issued in 1902. The question referred precisely to the removal of an ectopic fetus before the expiration of the sixth month. The Holy Office responded that this could not be done and referred back to the decree of 1898, and particularly to the clause which demanded that serious and opportune provision be made for the life of the fetus and the mother.[36] What became clear from this response was that direct removal of a nonviable fetus was no more acceptable when the pregnancy was ectopic than when it was uterine.

Some years later an American Jesuit, T. Lincoln Bouscaren, in a book entitled *Ethics of Ectopic Operations* explored the whole issue to see if other alternatives offered themselves.[37] While he opposed direct removal of the fetus, and whatever arguments had been used to try to justify it, he was able to show convincingly that the condition of the tube itself in these cases became dangerously pathological. He argued then that the pregnant tube could be removed. He did not think that the analogy between this case and that of the cancerous uterus was perfect. While the fetus was the cause of the pathology in the tube, in no sense was it responsible for the cancer. But even though it caused the pathology in the tube, as long as the tube was pathological, and endangering the life of the mother, it was the tube that was the object of the surgical procedure, not the fetus. The abortion then would be indirect. Bouscaren argued then that where the mother's life would be otherwise in danger, it would be permissible to remove the pregnant tube. Theologians generally accepted the conclusion of Bouscaren. There might have been differences of opinion regarding details, but there was general agreement that the tube might be removed as a pathological organ when necessary to save the life of the mother.

T his was the last major controversy in the abortion issue during the first half of the twentieth century. Individual cases would continue to present themselves for solution, and questions would continue to be raised, but the general guidelines for the solution to these cases were available, even though their application might not always be easy. It was not until the beginning of the second half of the century that the tradition regarding the morality of abortion began to be questioned. Although most of this questioning came from outside the Roman Catholic community, it was bound to offer a challenge to the tradition. But it is beyond the scope of this book to pursue this challenge in any way. Indeed it would take another book of at least the same proportions to do so.

CONCLUSION

───────────

The Christian tradition from the earliest days reveals a firm antiabortion attitude. There is no reason to believe that this was a Christian innovation. Strong evidence points to a continuity between this attitude and that of the Jews especially the early Jewish communities of pre-Christian times. But it contrasts markedly with the attitude and practice of the Roman world where the frequency of abortion, and particularly of infanticide, was noted even by pagan writers.

Early condemnations of abortion were generally associated with similar condemnations of infanticide, an indication that in the minds of the early Christians the two were closely related. The condemnation of abortion did not depend on and was not limited in any way by theories regarding the time of fetal animation. Even during the many centuries when Church penal and penitential practice was based on the theory of delayed animation, the condemnation of abortion was never affected by it. Whatever one would want to hold about the time of animation, or when the fetus became a human being in the strict sense of the term, abortion from the time of conception was considered wrong, and the time of animation was never looked on as a moral dividing line between permissible and immoral abortion. As long as what was aborted was destined to be a human being, it made no difference whether the abortion was induced before or after it became so. The final result was the same: a child was not born.

The current debate regarding abortion departs notably from the past in this respect. Many of those who argue in favor of abortion make the primary issue one of hominization. If the fetus is not yet a man, or a human being, or a person, or whatever terminology is used, it is entitled to less consideration. For many the time of hominization is the general dividing line between moral and immoral abortion. In the Christian tradition the distinction between the formed and unformed fetus (animated and unanimated) played no more than a secondary role, at least in reference to abortion. It was mainly used for purposes of legal classification and the grading of penances relative to the reconciliation of sinners.

Although the question when life begins, or when human life begins did not play a decisive role in determining the morality of abortion, it was of great interest to the ancients. What seems to be the more primitive approach held that the fetus did not become a human being until it was born. This was the judgment of the Jews in early biblical times. The Stoic philosopher associated life with breath and held that the fetus did not come alive until it began to breathe. Before it was born the fetus was considered to be part of the mother, and its development was explained in this way. The Aristotelian philosopher moved the beginnings of life back into the fetal period. In fact, the strict Aristotelian held that life began at the moment of conception (or perhaps even before, in some sense). But it was not human life at this stage. The human soul was not infused until the fetus was formed in the mother, and this occurred after forty days in the male fetus, ninety days in the female fetus. Aristotle also said that movement would be detected in an aborted fetus at the same times. According to the strict Aristotelian the fetus, before it was formed, had initially a vegetative soul, then a sensitive soul. But not all accepted this succession of souls. Some simply held that before the human soul was infused, the fetus was part of the mother. Others explained the growth and development of the fetus in the womb by the presence of a formative force in the semen. But there were a number of early Fathers who held the human soul was present right from the beginning. This was true not only of the traducianists, who maintained that the soul was transmitted in the semen just like the body, but also of some creationists, who held that the human soul was created when it was infused.

The question when life began was of decisive importance in classifying abortion as homicide. There is no evidence that early Christians ever associated the beginning of life with birth and therefore did not consider abortion at any time homicide. For centuries, however, the beginning of human life was associated with the formation of the fetus, an association which had its origin in the Septuagint as well as in Aristotle. In this context homicide was limited to the abortion of the formed fetus. Church practice in dealing with irregularities took this limitation into account, and spiritual penances were often graded according to whether the fetus was formed or unformed. But even though abortion of the unformed fetus was not considered real homicide, it was looked upon as anticipated homicide, or interpretive homicide, or homicide in intent, because it involved the destruction of a future man. It was always closely related to homicide.

It was not until the fourteenth century that the distinction between the formed and unformed (animated and unanimated) fetus was used as a basis for an exception to the general condemnation of abortion. A Dominican theologian, John of Naples, was the first to allow abortion of an unanimated fetus if necessary to save the mother's life. The basic reason for the allowance was precisely the fact that the unanimated fetus was not yet a human being. Some later authors questioned whether he was really advocating induced abortion or merely allowing treatment aimed at curing some maternal ailment. There is less ambiguity about authors such as Thomas Sanchez who argued that the fetus was a part of the mother, and in these circumstances, an unjust aggressor. If true, these arguments would justify induced abortion. In many respects the argumentation paralleled that used in the Hebrew tradition to justify dismembering the fetus at the time of delivery to save the mother's life. The only difference was that the dividing line was placed at term rather than at the time of formation.

The exception made by John of Naples had a respectable following, but it also met with opposition. The opposition stemmed from the objection that the arguments used would justify exceptions which no one wanted to make, such as, abortion of the animated fetus to save the mother, and abortion of the unanimated fetus, for other reasons. For a number of reasons, chief among which was the general acceptance of immediate animation, the whole issue of aborting the unanimated fetus to save the mother became obsolete.

Although some of the early church Fathers held immediate animation, theories of delayed animation formed the basis of church practice for many centuries. In the early seventeenth century a Belgian physician, Thomas Fienus, argued in favor of early animation. The argument was based on the need for a formative principle in the embryo right after conception. After ruling out other possibilities, Fienus concluded that this had to be a soul. It also had to be the same soul that was present in the fetus at the end of the developing process, since a succession of souls made no sense to Fienus. The opinion met initially with considerable opposition, but in the course of the next three centuries replaced the theory of delayed animation as the common opinion. It met with great favor from the medical profession, although the issue was more one of philosophy than of medicine. It was accepted in church practice in 1869 when Pius IX removed the limitation set in 1591 by Gregory XIV on excommunication for abortion. Even after immediate animation with a rational soul was commonly accepted there were still a few Aristotelians who continued to hold a succession of souls.

Some have seen in the doctrine of the Immaculate Conception a confirmation of the theory of immediate animation. Although this belief has a long history in the Church, it was not defined until 1854, a few centuries after the opinion was introduced by Thomas Fienus. A few theologians before that time saw in the dating of the feasts of the Immaculate Conception (Dec. 8) and the Nativity of the Blessed Virgin (Sept. 8) an implication regarding immediate animation. But even if one could draw some conclusion from this data, it would pertain only to the Blessed Virgin. But the dating of church feasts does not imply church teaching. Nor did the definition of the Immaculate Conception say anything about the time when the human soul was infused into the Blessed Virgin. All that was defined was that her soul was free from any taint of original sin from the moment of infusion, whenever that took place. The only opinion the Church has ever condemned was that which identified animation with the time of birth. It has never taught immediate animation. Even the fathers of Vatican II resisted efforts to elicit such a teaching statement in connection with its condemnation of abortion. And the most recent declaration (1974) on abortion from the Sacred Congregation for the Doctrine of the Faith made a similar bypass of the question.

Quite as meaningful historically as the issue of deliberately induced abortion was that of accidental abortion. In fact, there is good reason to believe that the case in Exodus was one of accidental abortion. During the Christian era the question of accidental abortion was resolved along the same general lines as accidental killing. The initial legislation freed anyone who was engaged in some necessary activity from responsibility for accidental killing, as long as there was no neglect. Soon the norm became the liceity of the person's act rather than its necessity. If the person was doing something licit and there was no neglect, he would not be responsible for a resulting death. The reader will remember the case of Placidus, and more particularly, that of the Carthusian monk, although in the latter case the more basic issue was that of animation. Initially, theologians and canonists held an individual responsible if the killing resulted from an action which was illicit for any reason. As the subject was more thoroughly considered, they demanded that there be more of a connection between the act and its liceity, and the resulting death. If the illicit act was not the actual cause of the death, or if the reason it was illicit had nothing to do with the danger of causing death, the death would not be imputed to the agent. The reader will recall the case of the cleric on horseback who was struck by another cleric and died from falling off his horse rather than from the blow itself. He will also recall the case of Placidus. The fact that he had stolen the horses (done something illicit) would not in itself make him responsible for the subsequent abortion.

The above reasoning may sound somewhat legalistic, but there is a realism underlying it which admits that not all killing can be reasonably avoided, and courageously confronts the issue of imputability. In the earlier description of accidental killing, the danger of causing death was not foreseen except perhaps in a confused sort of way. Eventually, however, cases arose in which it was quite possible to forsee clearly at least the danger of causing death. Would deaths in such cases be imputable? The question came up in the abortion discussion in connection with the use of remedies such as bloodletting, purgatives, and even bathing, which were prescribed for their therapeutic effects but which carried with them the danger of abortion if the woman was pregnant. The danger of causing an abortion was foreseen quite clearly when prescribing these remedies. Antonius de Corduba was the first theologian to maintain that since such remedies were by nature principally salutary, they could be prescribed when necessary to save the mother's life. But if they were principally lethal, they could not be prescribed. Later authors allowed the use of remedies even if they were only *equally* salutary. The Corduban distinction introduced a new dimension into the abortion discussion, but the distinction met with immediate acceptance. Eventually, it would become known simply as the distinction between *direct* and *indirect* abortion.

The claim is frequently made that the concern of the Catholic Church for the fetus was related chiefly to the question of baptism, that is, the eternal welfare of the fetus. History certainly testifies to the concern of the Church for the spiritual welfare of the fetus, but it testifies with equal clarity that the prior concern was with the taking of fetal life. It was because abortion constituted the taking of fetal life that it was condemned. If the one responsible for the abortion was also to blame for allowing the child to die without baptism, this was an additional fault. But even if the fetus could have been baptized after the abortion, the Church would not have condoned it. It is quite true that interest in baptism was primary in those cases where the abortion was considered accidental, and therefore indirect. If the fetus would have had an opportunity otherwise to be baptized, even accidental abortion to save the mothers' life was not acceptable. Only a few theologians considered privation of baptism a primary barrier in abortion deliberately induced to save the mother's life. These were the theologians who held that it could be justified as self-defense against unjust aggression. If it prevented the baptism of the child, they would not allow it even in this case. Some nineteenth-century theologians offered as a reason for what they called *medical abortion* the fact that it would allow the child to be baptized. But again this was a secondary consideration. It was only after they had justified medical abortion as indirect killing that they offered this additional reason for allowing it. They would not have allowed direct killing to provide for the baptism of the child.

One of the most important controversies that arose was over craniotomy or embryotomy to save a mother's life. Those who argued in favor of these procedures maintained that the fetus in these circumstances was an unjust aggressor, even if only in a material sense. If this argument could be made, these procedures could be justified as legitimate self-defense. It will be remembered that St. Thomas and his followers did not allow an intention of killing the aggressor even in self-defense; only the state had this right. But he was satisfied that a private individual could achieve his goal of self-defense without intending to kill the assailant. The killing could be an accidental effect of the self-defense, and therefore *praeter intentionem* (unintentional). The proponents of craniotomy and embryotomy contended that all this would apply to these procedures, and that the killing of the fetus would be an unintended effect. But the adversaries refused to consider the fetus an unjust aggressor in any sense. If the proponents of these procedures wanted to convince this group, they would have to justify it apart from a premise of unjust aggression.

No one in the tradition had ever justified intentional killing of an innocent (nonaggressor) person. But accidental killing even of a nonaggressor was not under certain circumstances imputed to the person who placed the act from which it resulted. The key question was whether it was sufficient that the killing of the fetus be *praeter intentionem* in the way St. Thomas required in reference to killing an unjust aggressor in self-defense. Some of the proponents of craniotomy wanted to extend St. Thomas' norm to cover a case where there was no aggression and allow acts of violence directed against an innocent person. The tradition, however, took a different approach to this case. It was more related to what St. Thomas and his predecessors had to say about accidental killing of an innocent person (2-2, q. 64, a. 8). What is clear is that when Corduba took up the question of abortion to save the mother's life he would not allow the type of act that might be proper in self-defense. Even though one might be able to claim that according to St. Thomas the killing even in this case was *praeter intentionem*, it was not permissible if the victim was a nonaggressor. If the act was *principaliter mortifera* it could not be condoned. Some of Corduba's successors qualified his principle somewhat, but none would allow action against a nonaggressor that was *principaliter mortifera*. One cannot get the kind of clarity about this issue he would like since there are at least three interpretations of the meaning of St. Thomas' article on self-defense. But it seems safe to say that the tradition allowed less when the victim was a nonaggressor than when there was unjust aggression, even though in both cases one might claim that the killing was *praeter intentionem*.

What is noteworthy is that none of these authors, with the exception perhaps of Apicella, tried to justify abortion or embryotomy to save the mother's life as an exception to the prohibition against direct killing of an innocent person. And even Apicella, admitting that a private individual did not have this right, felt that he had to introduce the state into the case to justify it. The rest all tried to justify it as accidental in some sense. It was undoubtedly their failure to do this convincingly that led to the condemnation of their opinions. It may be difficult in many cases to know where to draw the line between accidental and deliberate killing, but church authorities apparently felt that these theologians had gone over the line. And this seems to coincide with a common sense approach to the case. This may be the reason why theologians today who want to allow for induced abortion or embryotomy to save the mother's life are more inclined to argue for an exception to the general prohibition of direct killing of an innocent person.

This brings to a conclusion this study of the development of the Roman Catholic perspective on abortion. Curiously enough, the Church today finds itself in a position quite similar to the one which prevailed at the beginning of the Christian era. In those days it was surrounded by a society in which abortion (and infanticide) was practiced frequently. For the first one hundred and fifty years of its existence the Church had no support from the civil law in combating this evil. During the next eighteen hundred years this support was provided in the form of laws penalizing abortion. At the end of the nineteenth century Dr. Carl Capellmann credited Christian civilization with the achievement of almost eradicating abortion. Today, unfortunately, the trend has been reversed. The movement in the western world is toward liberalizing abortion legislation. In the United States laws protecting the fetus against abortion decisions by the mother have actually been declared unconstitutional. And in our present society the frequency of abortion is far greater than anything the Roman or ancient world ever knew or dreamed of. The early Church (together with the Jews) was able to present a common front against abortion in the pagan world. Can a divided Christianity repeat the performance of the early Church? Perhaps one can only respond, although hopefully, with the worlds of Hamlet: "Tis a consummation devoutly to be wished."

ABBREVIATIONS

AAS   *Acta Apostolicae Sedis*
ACW   Ancient Christian Writers
AER   *American Ecclesiastical Review*
ASS   *Acta Sanctae Sedis*
CSEL *Corpus Scriptorum Ecclesiasticorum Latinorum*
CSSL *Corpus Scriptorum Series Latina*
D   *Digestorum seu Pandectarum Justiniani*
DTC   *Dictionnaire de Théologie Catholique*
LCL   Loeb Classical Library
Mansi *Amplissima Collectio Conciliorum*
NRT   *Nouvelle Revue Théologique*
PG   *Migne, Patrologia Graeca*
PL   *Migne, Patrologia Latina*

NOTES

CHAPTER ONE   The Jewish Background

1   H. H. Ploss and M. Bartels, *Woman* (1935) cited David N.
    Feldman, *Birth Control and Jewish Law* (New York, 1967) 268.
    Feldman ascribes the Christian doctrine on abortion to the teach-
    ing on the entry of the soul into the body and the requirement of
    baptism. This reason would hardly explain the traditional con-
    demnation of abortion before the infusion of the human soul when
    theories of delayed animation prevailed.
2   *Jerome Biblical Commentary* (New Jersey, 1967) 3:52-53. For a
    study of the Code of the Covenant and its relation to near eastern
    codes see Henri Cazelles, *Études sur le Code de L'Alliance* (Paris,
    1946).
3   Exodus 21:22-25. All bible quotations are from *The New American
    Bible* unless stated.
4   Casuistic law is distinguished from apodictic law, such as is found
    in the Decalogue. The former deals with specific cases rather than
    general prohibitions.
5   Deuteronomy 25:11-12
6   Code of Hammurabi, nn. 209-14; Assyrian Code, nn. 21, 50-53;
    Code of Hittites, nn. 17-18, James B. Pritchard, *Ancient Near
    Eastern Texts*, 2nd Ed. (Princeton, 1955) 175; 181, 184-85; 190
7   Exodus 21:18-19
8   Exodus 21:20-21
9   Exodus 21:12-24. In early Israel the "avenger of blood" was the
    nearest of kin.
10 Deuteronomy 19:1-7

11   See Cazelles, *Études sur le Code de L'Alliance*, 131-45, for a more complete discussion of penal law in the Code of the Covenant.

12   See Genesis 4:23-24.

13   Code of Hammurabi, nn. 209-14, Pritchard, *Ancient Near Eastern Texts*

14   See Feldman, *Birth Control and Jewish Law*, 253 ff.

15   Ibid., 254

16   Moral treatises on justice still follow the same principle. It is epitomized in the axiom: *partus sequitur ventrem* (the offspring follow the womb).

17   Assyrian Code, n. 53, Pritchard, *Ancient Near Eastern Texts*

18   Genesis 9:6

19   See Feldman, *Birth Control and Jewish Law*, for a discussion of this question, 259-62.

20   Mishna, Oholot, 7, 6, cited by Feldman, ibid., 275

21   In his code Maimonides allows dismemberment because the fetus is like a *pursuer* of the mother. Theoretically this is a tighter reason than the prenatal status of the fetus and would not open the door to abortion in other situations. The stand that the fetus is not a human person would, at least in theory, give broader scope to abortion. But if one allows dismemberment of the fetus because it is a *pursuer*, there is no reason for a distinction based on the delivery of the head. One may defend himself against an unjust aggressor even if he is fully born. Maimonides did not allow the destruction of the fetus as a *pursuer* once the head had emerged.

22   Some despaired of ever determining who was moving against whom in this case, and therefore, of deciding who was the assailant and who the victim, Feldman, ibid.

23   Exodus 20:13

24   *The Septuagint Version of the Old Testament and Apocrypha* (Zondervan Publishing House Ed.), Christian Classics (Westminister, 1975).

25   John T. Noonan makes a rather incoherent statement about abortion in the Old Testament, first stating that it had nothing to say on the subject, and then showing how the Septuagint translation departed from it. And even this comparison is quite incomplete and misleading [*The Morality of Abortion* (Cambridge, 1970) 6].

26   Some have tried over the centuries to explain this difference as a mistaken translation. If this were the only difference between the Hebrew and Septuagint texts, the explanation would be reasonable, but it is generally admitted that the Septuagint departs frequently from the Hebrew text. Moreover, even in regard to this difference it would be difficult to explain the coincidence with certain lines of Greek thought as a pure accident.

27   *On the Generation of Animals*, bk. 2, 3, W. D. Ross, *Works of Aristotle Translated into English* (Oxford, 1908-53) 5:736

28   Not all who identified the time of infusion of the rational soul with formation accepted Aristotle's succession of souls. Some maintained that the fetus was supported by the soul of the mother before the rational soul was infused. Others held that a formative power in the semen was responsible for the development that took place prior to the infusion of the rational soul. See Thomas Aquinas, *De potentia*, q. 3, a. 9.

29   *On the History of Animals*, bk. 7, 3, *Works of Aristotle*, 4:583. Aristotle also says in this passage that movement can be detected in a male fetus aborted at forty days, but not in the female fetus until after ninety days. While most theologians will relate the time of animation to formation, some will link it to the presence of movement in the fetus. Since they both occur at the same time according to Aristotle, either criterion would be acceptable. But if a formed fetus is aborted and movement is present, it is a clear sign that it is still alive. If no movement can be detected, even though the fetus may have been previously informed with a human soul, it may already be dead. This question will be treated again in Chapter 7, p. 108.

30   bk. 3, 19, 108-09, F. W. Colson, *Philo*, (LCL, 1929-) 7:544-45

31   bk. 4, 8, 33, H. St. J. Thackeray, *Josephus*, (LCL, 1927-) 4:608-11

32   bk. 2, 24, ibid., 1: 372-75

CHAPTER TWO   The Roman Background

1   *Digest* (Justinian) 11, 8, 2. *Spes animantis* is a technical expression and difficult to translate. It might be translated freely by the expression "future man." For the explicit statement that the fetus cannot be considered a man, see D. 25, 2, 9, 1: *Partus nondum editus homo non recte fuisse dicitur* (Before the fetus is born, it cannot properly be called a man).

2   D. 25, 4, 1, 1. Translation: Before it is born, the fetus is part of the mother's body.

3   D. 28, 6, 10, 1

4   Tertullian, *De anima*, 25, 2, CSEL 20: 340-41

5   D. 1, 5, 7; 22; 26. Also D. 37, 9, 1, 11; D. 38, 16, 7

6   See Joseph Palazzini, *Ius fetus ad vitam* (Urbaniae, 1943) 22-34.

7   E. A. Westermarck, *Origin and Development of Moral Ideas* (London, 1906) 1:409 ff. See also, DTC, s.v. "Infanticide," 1718-19.

8 *De ira*, 1, 15, John W. Basore, *Moral Essays* (LCL, 1928) 1:145
9 Palazzini, *Ius fetus ad vitam*, 23
10 *Dictionnaire d'Archeologie Chretien*, s.v. "Infanticide"
11 *Ad Atticum*, 14, 20, E. O. Winstedt, *Letters to Atticus* (LCL, 1912-)
    3:280-81
12 *Amores*, 2, 14, 5; 35, T. Grant Showerman, *Heroides et Amores*
    (LCL, 1947) 422-27
13 *De consolatione ad Helviam matrem*, 16, Basore, *Moral Essays*
    (LCL, 1928) 2: 472-73
14 *Annales*, 14, 63, H. Furneau, *The Annals of Tacitus* (Oxford, 1891)
    2:467
15 *Satyrae*, 6, 386; 2, 32-33; 6, 594-97, G. G. Ramsey, *Juvenal and
    Persius* (LCL, 1917) 114, 20-21, 132-33
16 *Domitianus*, 22, J. C. Rolfe, *Suetonius* (LCL, 1914) 2:382-83
17 Tertullian, *Apologetica*, 9, 8, CSEL 64:25
18 *Encyclopedia of Religion and Ethics*, s.v. "Foeticide"
19 *Romulus*, 22, Bernadotte Perrin, *Plutarch's Lives* (LCL, 1948)
    1:162-63
20 *Historia naturalis*, 7, 9, H. Rackham, *Pliny: Natural History*
    (LCL, 1945) 536-37
21 *Pro Cluentio*, 2, 32, H. C. Hodge (LCL, 1927) 254-55. This case
    appears in Justinian's *Digest* (48, 19, 39) and is known in the
    literature as the law *Cicero*.
22 D. 48, 19, 3; D. 1, 5, 18
23 D. 48, 8, 1, 1
24 D. 48, 8, 3, 1 and 2
25 *Sententiae Iulii Pauli*, 5, 23, 13
26 D. 48, 19, 38, 5. See also *Sententiae*, 5, 23, 8. Translation: If
    anyone gives another a love potion or an abortion potion, even
    without an evil intention, since it is a source of bad example, he
    will be condemned to work in the mines if he belongs to the lower
    classes. If he belongs to the upper classes, he will be exiled and
    part of his property confiscated. But if the woman or man *(homo)*
    dies, he will be punished with a capital sentence.
27 D. 47, 11, 4. It is referred to as the law *Divus*.
28 D. 48, 19, 39
29 D. 48, 8, 8. Translation: If it is established that a woman has done
    violence to herself to cause an abortion, the prefect of the prov-
    ince will send her into exile.

CHAPTER THREE   The Early Christian Era
(to 300)

1   Galatians 3:1-6. See also Apocalypse 9:2; 21:8; 22:15. Noonan suggests the connection between *pharmakeia* and abortion, *Morality of Abortion*, 9.
2   J. P. Audet, *La Didachè, Instructions des Apôtres* (Paris, 1958) 188-89
3   Didache, 2, 2, Tr. J. A. Kleist, S. J., ACW, 6 (Westminster, 1948) 16
4   Ibid., 5, 2, Kleist, 18. See also note 43.
5   *Epistle of Barnabas*, 19, 5; 20, 2, Kleist, ibid., 62, 64. See also note 190.
6   Audet, *La Didachè*, 188-89
7   35, 1, PG 6:967-70
8   *Paedogogus*, 2, 10, 84, PG 8:511-14
9   *Philosophoumena*, 9, 12, PG 16:3387-88
10 B. Poschmann, *Penance and the Anointing of the Sick* (New York, 1964) 39-41
11 9, 8, CSEL 64:25
12 The ancients knew nothing about the female ovum, and hence nothing about fertilization. Conception occurred when the semen (they knew nothing either about the existence of sperm in the semen) was planted in the uterus. The most common opinion, that of Aristotle, considered the semen the active agent in generation. The *catamenia* (menstrual blood) of the woman provided the matter of generation. *On the Generation of Animals*, 1, 19-20, *Works of Aristotle*, 5:727-28
13 *De anima*, 37, CSEL 20:363
14 On this point see J. H. Waszink, *Tertullian, De Anima* (Amsterdam, 1947) 425, 2.
15 *De anima*, 25, 4, CSEL 20:341-42
16 *De virginibus velandis*, 14, PL 2:958
17 *Octavius*, 30, 2, CSEL 2:43
18 Ep. 52, 2-3, CSEL 3:619. *Novatus* should not be confused with *Novatianus*, after whom the heresy was named.
19 *Divinae institutiones*, 6, 20, CSEL 19:558-59
20 *De opificio Dei*, 12. See also 17. CSEL 27:11; 43-44
21 *Praeparatio evangelica*, 8, 8, PG 21:614. See Chapter One, p. 20.

CHAPTER FOUR   Early Legislation and
Patristic Thought (300-600)

1   *Concilium Eliberitanum*, c. 63, Mansi 2:16
2   Ibid., c. 68
3   Poschmann claims that there were eighteen such penances imposed by the Council, *Penance and the Anointing of the Sick*, 94.
4   *Concilium Ancyranum*, c. 21, Mansi 2:514
5   See Poschmann, *Penance and the Anointing of the Sick*, 94.
6   c. 22
7   Ep. 188, c. 2, PG 32:671
8   c. 8, PG 32:678
9   *Commentarium in epistolam S. Basilii canonicam primam*, c. 2, PG 138:589-90. Balsamon also admits that less social damage is done in abortion.
10   *De adoratione in spiritu et veritate*, 8, PG 68:545-46
11   *Quaestiones in Exodum*, 48, PG 80:271-74
12   *Constitutiones apostolicae*, 7, 4, Mansi 1:489-90
13   *Ambiguorum liber*, PG 91:1339-42. According to the ancients it was commonly thought that conception took place when the semen was received into the uterus (matrix).
14   *Commentarium in librum tertium sententiarum*, d. 3, q. 5, a. 2
15   1, 9, *De avaritia*, PL 11:326-27
16   Ep. 22 *Ad Eustochium*, 13, CSEL 54:160
17   It may be difficult for one with a modern understanding of the generative process to grasp the meaning of this statement. It has to be related to a context in which the existence of the female ovum was unknown and the male semen generally considered the only active agent in generation.
18   Ep. 123 *Ad Genuchiam*, CSEL 56:75
19   See note 16.
20   Ep. 121 *Ad Algasium*, 4, CSEL 56:16. The pertinent passage in this text became known as the *Sicuti semina* from the introductory words.
21   1, 17, CSEL 42:230
22   *Contra Iulianum*, 6, 14, 43, PL 44:847
23   *De civitate Dei*, 22, 13, 40, PL 41:776
24   *Enchiridion*, 85, PL 40:272
25   Ibid., 86
26   *QQ in heptateuchum*, 2, 80, CSEL 28:146. This text became known in the literature as the *Quod vero*.
27   *QQ veteris et novi testamenti*, 23, CSEL 50:50. This text is generally referred to in later literature as the *Moyses*.

28 *De diversis quaestionibus octaginta tribus liber unus*, 56, PL 40:39. See also *De trinitate*, 4, 5, PL 44:819.
29 *Sermo* 51, CC SL 103:229
30 *Sermo* 52, ibid., 231
31 *Concilium Ilerdense*, c. 2, Mansi 8:611
32 *Capitula Martini, Concilium Bracarense III*, PL 84:584
33 *Concilium Trullanum (Quinisextum)*, c. 91, Mansi 11:982
34 *Collectio Prisca*, PL 54, 754
35 *Collectio Dionysiana*, 40, PL 67:155-56
36 *Collectio Quesnelliana*, c. 3, PL 56:441
37 *Breviatio canonum Fulg. Furandi*, c. 152, PL 67,597
38 *Concordia canonum*, c. 103, PL 88:881
39 *Collectio hispana*, PL 84:308-09
40 *Syntagma canonum*, 13, 10, PG 104:919-23

CHAPTER FIVE   Private Penance and
                Abortion (600-c. 1100)

1 Poschmann, *Penance and the Anointing of the Sick*, 91-93
2 Ibid., 104-05. He traces this tradition back to Pastor Hermas, *Mandatum IV*, 3, 1-7, Joseph M. F. Marique, S. J., Apostolic Fathers (New York, 1947) 262
3 Poschmann, *Penance and the Anointing of the Sick*, 105
4 See *Caesarius of Arles, Sermo* 258, 2, PL 39:2222.
5 *Canones Hibernenses*, 1, F. W. H. Wasserschleben, *Die Bussordenungen der abendlandische Kirche* (Graz, 1956) 136-38. McNeill and Gamer, *Medieval Handbooks of Penance* (New York, 1938) 118-22
6 McNeill and Gamer, *Medieval Handbooks, 119*
7 According to Aristotle nothing seemed to happen to the semen during the first week, at least if it was not retained in the uterus *(On the History of Animals*, bk. 7, 3). He is not too clear on the time program for development after that. Augustine, however, offered a very precise time program (See Chapter Four, p. 58). It is not certain whether c. 6 refers only to the early days of conception or includes the blood stage as well. All that is clear is that it recognizes a liquid stage prior to the time flesh appears and takes on spirit. The latter stage may include a period of figuration as well.
8 McNeill and Gamer, *Medieval Handbooks*, 119
9 *Old Irish Penitential, De ira*, c. 6, McNeill and Gamer, *Medieval Handbooks*, 166

10 The *Canones* imply, at least if taken literally, that animation takes place as soon as flesh appears. The present canon seems to allow for an interval during which the flesh exists without spirit. It may be that although the *Canones* are less explicit, they are saying the same thing.

11 *Penitentiale Vinniae*, 20, Wasserschleben, *Die Bussordenungen*, 112

12 *Penitentiale Columbani*, c. 6, ibid., 356

13 *Penitentiale Cummeani*, 3, 23; 6, 3, 11, 21; 7, 2, ibid., 473, 478, 480-81

14 *Penitentiale Bigotianum*, 4, 2, 2-4, ibid., 453-54

15 *Penitentiale*, 14, 24; also 27, ibid., 199-200

16 *Penitentiale*, 13, 4, ibid., 197

17 *Penitentiale Bedae*, 4, 12, ibid., 225

18 Fournier-Le Bras, *Histoire des collections canoniques en occident* (Paris, 1931) 1:31-84

19 Poschmann, *Penance and the Anointing of the Sick*, 123; also 135

20 Third Council of Toledo (589) c. 11, Mansi 9:995

21 Council of Chalon, c. 8, Mansi 10:1091

22 Fournier-Le Bras, *Histoire des collections*, 1:91

23 A. M. Stickler, S.D.B., *Historia iuris canonici latini* (Turin, 1950) 107-08

24 Council of Tours (Third) c. 22, Mansi 14:86

25 Council of Chalon (Second), c. 25, Mansi 14:98. The objection to the penitential books was that they contained many errors and that their authorship was uncertain.

26 Council of Paris (Sixth), c. 32, Mansi, 14:559

27 See note 25 above.

28 *Penitentiale Romanum, Incipit sextus; Incipit praefatio*, H. J. Schmitz, *Die Bussbucher und die Bussdisziplin der Kirche* (Graz, 1958) 290; 266

29 5, 2, Wasserschleben, *Die Bussordenungen*, 367

30 2, 16, ibid., 366

31 7, 2, ibid., 369

32 Fournier-Le Bras, *Histoire des collections*, 1:127-83

33 Ibid., 2:22

34 *Capitulare secundum*, Mansi, 13:1013

35 *Praefatio Gildae*, 1, Wasserschleben, *Die Bussordenungen*, 105

36 *Penitentiale*, 1, 12, 4, ibid., 196

37 Poschmann, *Penance and the Anointing of the Sick*, 143-44

38 *Penitentiale Pseudo-Gregorii*, 17, Wasserschleben, *Die Bussordenungen*, 542

39 *Penitentiale*, 8-9, PL 110:474

40 P. Hinschius, *Decretales Pseudo-Isidoreanae et Capitula Angilramni* (Leipzig, 1863) 360

41 *Capitula Angilramni*, 20, PL 96:1037

42 *Capitula*, 41, PL 119:723

43 *Concilium Moguntinum*, c. 25, 1-3, Mansi 14:909

44 · *Concilium Wormatiense*, c. 35, Mansi 15:876

45 *Libri synodales*, 2, PL 132:279

46 Ibid., c. 89. *Si aliquis causa explendae libidinis vel odii meditatione ut non ex eo soboles nascatur homini aut mulieri aliquid fecerit vel ad potandum dederit ut non possit generare out concipere ut homicida teneatur*, PL 132:301

47 c. 7

48 c. 8

49 *Praeloquiorum libri sex*, 2, 3, 6, PL 136:193-94

50 See Fournier-Le Bras, *Histoire des collections canoniques en occident*, 2:326.

51 *Decretum*, 17:51, 52, 54, 57, 60, PL 140:951-54; 19 *(Corrector)* 5, PL 140:972

52 Although initiated by Leo IX, it is known as the Gregorian reform. See Fournier-Le Bras, *Histoire des collections*, 2:4 ff.

53 *Opusc.*, 7, 3, 10 ff., ibid., 2:6

54 Ibid.

55 *Decretum*, 10, 55-58, PL 161:706-07

56 See Chapter Four, p. 55.

57 See Chapter Four, p. 57 and notes 20, 26, and 27.

58 *Panormia*, 8, 12-14, PL 161:1307

CHAPTER SIX   Canonical Development
from Gratian to 1300

1 Gratianus, *Concordia canonum discordantium*, Ae. Friedburg, *Corpus iuris canonici*, Pars prior, (Leipzig, 1879)

2 *Decretum*, Pars 10, cc. 55-58; *Panormia*, lib. 8, cc. 12-14. Gratian uses the same passages from Augustine and Jerome, viz, the *Aliquando*, *Quod vero*, *Moyses* and *Sicuti semina*. See Chapter Four, p. 55 and notes 20, 26, and 27.

3 *Concordia*, c. 7, C. 32, q. 2

4 Ibid., cc. 8-10

5 Ibid., c. 20, C. 2, q. 5

6 Palazzini, *Ius fetus ad vitam*, 119

7 *Concordia*, c. 48, d. 50

8 *Glossa Cod. Ph. Berol.*, 1742. Cf. S. Kuttner, *Kanonistische Schuldlehre (Studi e Testi, 64)* (Citta del Vaticano, 1935) 237, note 2

9 *Glossa Stuttgartensis*, ibid., 236, note 2

10 *Glossa ordinaria a Ioanne Teutonico confecta*, ibid. Response of Nicholas, *Concordia*, c. 39, d. 50

11 Kuttner, *Kanonistische Schuldlehre*, ibid.

12 F. Thaner, *Summa M. Rolandi* (Innsbruck, 1874) 167

13 H. Singer, *Die Summa decretorum der M. Rufinus* (Paderborn, 1902) 482-83

14 Ibid., 483

15 The provision for some penance as a precaution may be based on the assumption that even though the abortion was not deliberate there may have been some negligence.

16 *Glossa ad* c. 20, C. 2, q. 5

17 The Aquilian law dealt with damage done to another's property. See *Digest*, 9, 2, 27, 22.

18 *Glossa ad* c. 9, C. 32, q. 2

19 Bernardus Papiensis, *Compilatio I*, Lib. 5, t. 10, Ae. Friedburg *Quinque compilationes antiquae*, (Leipzig, 1882) 57-58

20 E. A. Laspeyeres, *Summa decretalium*, 5, 10, 2 (Ratisbon, 1860) 348-49

21 A. Potthast, *Regesta Romanorum Pontificum* (Berlin, 1874-75) 472, n. 4312

22 *Compilatio IV*, 4, 5, 6, Friedburg, *Quinque compilationes*, 148

23 *Decretales Gregorii IX*, Lib. 5, t. 12, c. 5, Ae. Friedburg, *Corpus iuris canonici*, Pars Altera (Leipzig, 1879)

24 See Chapter Five, p. 80.

25 The original decree of Regino dealt more explicitly with sterilization than abortion. The version in the Decretals seems to aim just as explicitly at abortion. It reads as follows: *Si aliquis causa explendae libidinis vel odii meditatione homini aut mulieri aliquid fecerit vel ad potandum dederit ut non possit generare aut concipere, vel nasci soboles, ut homicida teneatur.* Compare with text in Chapter Five, n. 46. The underlined words account for the difference.

26 *Decretales*, Lib. 5, t. 12, c. 20. Throughout the history of the Church priests have been removed from the ministry after certain serious sins. For the priest this was the equivalent of exclusion from communion for the lay person, and was part of the penitential discipline of the Church. But even apart from penitential discipline the Church set up certain standards of conduct for her ministers. If one failed to meet these standards, he would not qualify for the ministry. Thus one could be excluded from the ministry because of certain crimes, or even because of certain defects. Eventually the word *irregularity* began to be used to cover those crimes or defects which would exclude one permanently from the ministry. It is defined as a permanent impediment

forbidding the reception of orders, as well as the exercise of orders already received. An irregularity is not a punishment in any sense of the term. This is obvious when it arises from some defect in the person. But it is also true when it results from the commission of some canonical crime. It is not because the Church wishes to punish the crime but rather because she wishes to exclude the unworthy from the ministry and protect its sanctity that she attaches an irregularity to certain crimes.

27 *Summa de penitentia*, Lib. 2, 1, 4

28 *Summa in titulos Decretalium* (Venice, 1586) 205

29 *Divina in V libros Decretalium commentaria* (Venice, 1570) 612

30 *Glossa in Lib. 5, t. 12, c. 5, Decretales Gregorii IX* (Venice, 1605)

31 *In librum V Decretalium*, t. 12, c. 5, *Decretalium aurei commentarii* (Venice, 1588)

32 *Summa aurea hostiensis*, Lib. 5, *de homicido voluntario et casuali* (Lyons, 1568) 358-59

33 *Rosarium seu in Decretorum volumen commentaria*, C. 32, q. 2 (Venice, 1577)

34 *Speculum iudiciale, de dispensationibus* (Venice, 1566) 105

35 *Pandectarum*, III, *Glossa in Divus* (D. 47, 11, 4) (Lyons, 1575). For the *Lex Pompeia* see D. 48, 9, 1.

36 Bartolus a Saxoferrato, *Commentaria Digestorum*, 47, 11, 4 (Venice, 1615)

37 *Lectura super I et II parte Infortiati* (Lyons, 1529) f. 55. Also *Consiliorum sive responsorum* (Frankfort, 1589) Cons. 390. Cited by Palazzini, *Ius fetus ad vitam*, 142.

38 Sir Henry Bracton, *De legibus et consuetudinibus Angliae*, f. 120-21 Ed. G. E. Woodbine (Cambridge, 1968) 2:341

39 H. G. Richardson, *Bracton, the Problem of His Text* (London, 1965) 130-31. See also Schultz, *Law Quarterly Review*, 61, 286-92. The text in Raymond will be found in his *Summa de penitentia*, Lib. 2, 1, 6.

CHAPTER SEVEN   Beginnings of Theological Discussion (1200-1500)

1 *Libri sententiarum*, Lib. 4, d. 31

2 *Commentarium in L. IV*, d. 31, a. 18, *Opera omnia* (Paris, 1890-) t. 30

3 Ibid., *Expositio textus*. Freely translated, the verses say that the semen once conceived remains a milklike substance for the first six days. During the next nine days it changes into blood, and then

during the following twelve days it solidifies into flesh. In the course of the next eighteen days it takes on the shape of a human being. The rest of the period is taken up with growth.

4   *QQ super libris de animalibus*, Lib. 9, qq. 16-17, *Opera omnia* (Westphalia, 1955) t. 12

5   See note 7 below.

6   *On the History of Animals*, bk. 7, 3, *Works of Aristotle*

7   *De animalibus*, Lib. 9, t. 1, c. 3, *Opera omnia* (Paris, 1890-) t. 11

8   Aristotle simply remarks that movement can be detected in a male fetus aborted after forty days.

9   *QQ super libris de animalibus*, Lib. 9, qq. 16-17

10 *Commentarium in librum IV Sententiarum*, d. 31, dub. 4

11 *Commentarium in librum IV Sententiarum*, d. 31, *Expositio textus*

12 *Commentarium in librum III Sententiarum*, d. 3, q. 5, a. 2, Solutio.

13 *Williams Obstetrics*, 14th Ed., (New York, 1971) 200

14 *Commentarium in librum III Sententiarum*, d. 3, q. 5, a. 1

15 *Summa theologiae*, 1, q. 92, a. 1, ad 1

16 Ibid., 2-2, q. 64, a. 8

17 Ibid., ad 2

18 Ibid., 3, q. 68, a. 11, ad 3

19 *In quintum librum Decretalium novella commentaria*, t. 12, c. 20 (Venice, 1581)

20 *Commentaria super V libros Decretalium*, Lib. 5, t. 12, c. 5 (Lyons, 1518)

21 *In quintum librum*, t. 12, c. 5

22 The reference is probably to the *poculum amatorium* of the *Qui abortionis*. It will be recalled that the one giving a person a love potion was penalized even though the intention may not have been bad because of the bad example. But the death penalty was not imposed unless the other person died. The *Si aliquis* goes beyond the *Qui abortionis*, and Andrea seems to agree here that giving a *poculum amatorium* should be classified as homicide if it causes an abortion or sterilization.

23 Ibid., c. 20

24 See Chapter Six, p. 91.

25 *Super Decretorum volumine*, c. 11, q. 5, n. 1 (Venice 1578)

26 *Commentaria in V libros Decretalium*, Lib. 5, t. 12, c. 20 (Venice, 1588)

27 *In causarum decretalium secundam partem commentarii*, c. 8, C. 32, q. 2 (Venice, 1578)

28 *Summa theologica*, Pars 2, t. 7, c. 8, para. 2, Quarto

29 Antoninus seems to be the first to use the eighty-day computation for the formation of the female. Some later authors will relate the

forty- and eighty-day computation to the purification requirements of Lv 12:1-5. The justification for this, if any, is not at all
clear, although some basis for it may be found in Hippocrates [*De
natura puerorum, Magni Hippocratis omnia opera* (Leipzig, 1825)
1:392-93]. Antoninus was certainly aware of the Aristotelian and
Augustinian computation. See Pars 1, t. 1, c. 6.

30   Ibid., Pars 2, t. 7, c. 2, para. 2
31   *Quodlibeta* (unpublished) q. 10
32   *Commentaria in primam partem libri V Decretalium*, t. 12, c. 5
     (Venice, 1593)
33   Simon de Brixia (Borsano) *in Clement.*, 1, *eodem titulo*
     (unpublished)
34   Marianus, *Commentaria*, ibid., c. 20
35   *Commentaria in libros V Decretalium*, Pars 3, Lib 5, t. 12, cc. 5
     and 20 (Venice, 1574)
36   *Summa rosella*, s.v. "homicidium" iii (Venice, 1495)
37   Ibid., iiii
38   *Summa angelica*, s.vv. "aborsus," "homicidium" (Venice, 1511)
39   *Summa tabiena*, s.v. "homicidium" (Bologna, 1517)
40   *Summa sylvestrina*, s.vv. "medicus," "aborsus," "homicidium"
     (Venice, 1578)
41   *Summa armilla*, s.v. "aborsus" (Venice, 1596)
42   *Manuale confessariorum*, c. 15, n. 14; c. 25, n. 62 (Rome, 1573)

CHAPTER EIGHT   Discussion of Therapeutic
                Abortion (1500-1600)

1   Antonius de Corduba, *Quaestionarium theologicum*, q. 38, dub. 3
    (Venice, 1604)
2   *Dilaceratio* can be translated literally as tearing apart or tearing to
    pieces. In the context it seems to refer to an attack on the fetus,
    such as occurs in craniotomy or embryotomy, but it may include
    an attack made apart from a delivery problem and prior to it.
3   *Summa*, s.v. "homicidium," ii, q. 26
4   *Summa theologiae*, 2-2, q. 64, a. 7
5   *De ablatorum resititutione*, Lib. 2, c. 3 (Brescia, 1605)
6   *Opuscula moralia, De restitutione*, Lib. 3, par. 1, dub. 7, n. 27
    (Lyons, 1631)
7   Ibid., par. 2, dub. 6, n. 23
8   *Institutiones morales*, Pars 3, lib. 2, c. 3, *Vigesimo secundo*
    (Rome, 1610)
9   Ibid., c. 4

10   *Clavis regia*, Lib. 7, c. 12, n. 19 (Venice, 1615)
11   *De matrimonio*, Lib. 9, d. 20, n. 6 (Antwerp, 1620)
12   Ibid., d. 17, n. 15.

CHAPTER NINE   Further Legal and
Theological Developments

1   Menochius, *De arbitrariis iudicum*, Casus 357 (Venice, 1590)
2   Ibid.
3   Tessaurus, *Novae decisiones S. Senatus Pedemontani*, Dec. 12 (Turin, 1590)
4   c. 9, C. 32, q. 2. As pointed out earlier, the text is not really Augustinian. See Chapter Four, p. 58.
5   For the law *Cicero* see D. 48, 19, 39 (Chapter Two, p. 28).
6   See Chapter Six, p. 102.
7   *Fleta*, 2, 60-61 (Selden Society Ed., 1955)
8   Sir Edward Coke, *Third Part of the Institutes of the Laws of England*, Chap. 7, (3rd edition, 1660)
9   See Chapter Six, p. 102.
10   Local councils held at Lille (1288), Avignon (1326), and Lavaur (1368) attached an excommunication to the act of causing death or abortion by giving someone poison, or the like. Mansi, 24:961-2 (c. 14); 25:754-55 (c. 18) 26:537 (c. 116)
11   *Bullarium diplomatum et privilegiorum*, 9:39-42
12   See Chapter Six, p. 97.
13   *Bullarium*, 9:431
14   *Responsa moralia*, Lib. 4, q. 13 *de abortu* (Rouen, 1709)
15   See Chapter Eight, p. 130.
16   *De iustitia et iure*, Lib. 2, c. 9, d. 10 (Antwerp, 1612)
17   *Aphorisms*, Fifth Sect., 29 and 31, W.H.S. Jones, Hippocrates (LCL, 1943) 4:166-67
18   *Gynecology*, bk. 1 (Baltimore, 1956) 66-67
19   *De natura pueri*, C. G. Kuhn, *M. Hippocratis opera omnia*, Tom. 1, p. 392 (Leipzig, 1825). Since the authenticity of many of these works is doubted, they are frequently referred to simply as hippocratic writings.
20   *Quaestionum moralium*, Tr. 29, c. 6, q. 1. n. 99 (Lyons, 1626)
21   Similar statements will be made later by Busenbaum (Chapter Ten, p. 180) and Alphonsus (Chapter Eleven, p. 210).
22   *De sacramento matrimonii*, Lib. 10, c. 13, n. 2 (Venice, 1645)

23   Pontius is referring here to St. Thomas' article on self-defense (2-2, q, 64, a. 7). To get a complete picture of St. Thomas' understanding of the determinants of the moral act one would have to fill in from other parts of his work. Pontius' purpose is to criticize him only in what he has to say about the intention of the act. He simply denies that if a death is only indirectly willed the person causing it is not culpable. St. Thomas would agree, but he takes up this question in the next article (a. 8). He is not dealing with it in a. 7.

24   *Theologia moralis*, Lib. 3, t. 3, p. 3, c. 4, n. 2, q. 2 (Lyons, 1681)

25   *De ortu infantium*, Cap. 9, *Opera omnia* (Lyons, 1665) 14

26   Ibid., nn. 1-9

27   Ibid., nn. 10-20

28   Raynaud's contemporaries simply deny this statement if applied to killing a nonaggressor, and many will deny it even in reference to self-defense.

29   *De ortu infantium*, nn. 21-28

30   *Epitome delictorum*, Lib. 2, c. 43, n. 10

31   *Opus morale*, Lib. 5, c. 1, dub. 4 (Venice, 1690)

CHAPTER TEN   Discussion Continued
(1600-1700)

1   *De formatrice fetus liber* (Antwerp, 1620)

2   Ibid., *Conclusio undecima*, p. 199

3   Since nothing was known about the female ovum, it was thought that the membrane was a cover for the semen. The ancients claimed that it was formed by heat, much as crust is formed around bread in an oven.

4   *De formatrice fetus liber*, *Conclusio nona*, p. 161

5   Ibid., p. 209 ff.

6   It is quite true that the Septuagint does not speak of animation, at least explicitly. But it speaks of formation or perfection rather than *motus et sensus*. These criteria are more Augustinian or Aristotelian than scriptural.

7   *Quaestionum medicolegalium*, Lib. 1, t. 2, q. 9 (Lyons, 1701)

8   Ibid., Lib. 9, t. 1, q. ultima

9   It is impossible to translate this expression literally. The meaning is simply that the writers of the Septuagint exercised considerable freedom and independence in writing their version.

10   For the *Qui abortionis* see Chapter Two, p. 29 and note 26.

11 Aristotle said that movement could be detected in a male fetus aborted after forty days. But the pregnant woman will experience fetal movements only at a much later date (after about four months).

12 Zacchia's puzzlement is valid against what seems to be the thought of Aristotle and the scholastics who used movement (or formation) as the criterion for the presence of the rational soul. It would not be as valid against Augustine who was simply trying to determine when life began in the fetus. Spontaneous movement could well be a sign of life. Before this time the fetus has already manifested other signs of life, such as growth, but these were usually explained by the fact that the fetus was part of the mother. It was growing like any other member of her body. Augustine did not want to close the door on animation (or the presence of life in the fetus) before movement could be detected. See Chapter IV, p. 57.

13 Ibid., Lib. 7, t. 3, q. 1, *Digressio de semine femineo*

14 *Resolutiones*, Pars 5, t. 6 (Lyons, 1667)

15 Ibid., *Res.* 43

16 Ibid., *Res.* 44

17 *Disputationes Scholasticae*, Vol. 6, d. 10, s. 5, n. 131 ff. (Paris, 1868)

18 See Chapter Eight, p. 137.

19 Ibid., n. 125

20 See Chapter Eight, p. 131.

21 *Medulla theologiae moralis*, Lib. 1, t. 4, c. 1, dub. 1

22 Busenbaum, like Lessius and Filliucius, seems to be thinking of a case where the life of the pregnant woman is threatened by some disease in her. The remedy then is medicine or treatment aimed at curing the disease, not an abortion. An abortion would neither be necessary nor sufficient.

23 *Theologia fundamentalis*, Tom. 1, nn. 1622-27 (Lyons, 1657)

24 Ibid., Tom. 4, *Theologia praeterintentionalis*, nn. 2795-2804 (Lyons, 1664)

25 *Crisis theologica*, Tr. 1, d. 14, c. 3 (Lyons, 1670)

CHAPTER ELEVEN   Theological Debate
(1679-1869)

1 *Resolutiones morales*, Pars 5, t. 6, *Res.* 44

2 *Bullarium diplomatum et privilegiorum*, 19:147. The condemnation took place at a session of the Holy Office before Innocent XI (March 4, 1679).

3 *Theologica trutina* (Padua, 1737) Prop. 34 and 35
4 See Chapter Nine, p. 164.
5 Sanchez' concern was not the danger of consent, but the danger of abuse. In other words he was not as worried about the danger to the individual as the danger to the moral order itself. If any autonomy was given to the individual in the use of sex outside the marital act, the intense pleasure connected with it would lead to frequent violation of the moral order.
6 *Theologica trutina*, p. 269
7 *Collegii Salmanticensis cursus theologiae moralis*, Tr. 13, c. 2, p. 4; Tr. 25, c. 1, p. 3 (Venice, 1764)
8 *Theologia moralis*, Lib. 3, p. 1 (Cologne, 1716)
9 See Chapter Ten, p. 172.
10 *Theologia moralis*, Tom. 3, p. 4, c. 4 (Venice, 1731)
11 *Universa theologia moralis*, Tr. 11, c. 3, q. 3 (Venice, 1753)
12 *Theologia christiana*, Tom. 10, 1. 2, d. 4, c. 9, 21-22 (Rome, 1773)
13 *Theologia moralis*, Tr. 7, q. 4 (Linz, 1751)
14 *Theologia moralis*, Tr. 4, d. 2, q. 3 (Bologna, 1754)
15 *Embryologia sacra*, Lib. 1, cc. 1-12 (Venice, 1763)
16 Ibid., Cap. 3
17 Ibid., n. 6
18 Ibid., Cap. 4
19 Ibid., Cap. 5
20 Ibid., Cap. 6
21 Ibid., Cap. 7
22 Ibid., Cap. 8
23 Ibid., Cap. 9
24 Ibid., Cap. 10
25 Ibid., Cap. 11
26 These scientists confused the follicle with the ovum itself. The mistake was not corrected until von Baer made the real discovery of the ovum in the early nineteenth century [J. H. Needham, *History of Embryology* (New York, 1959) 162-3].
27 *Theologia moralis*, Lib. 3, t. 4, c. 1, n. 394. Gaude Edition (Rome, 1905)
28 *Quaeritur* 3
29 Lib. 6, t. 1, c. 1, dub. 4, n. 124
30 *Compendium theologiae moralis*, Tr. 10, c. 2, a. 3, q. 1. See also note a (Ratisbon, 1851).
31 *Theologia moralis universa*, Lib. 2 (Milan, 1869) 490 ff.
32 *Théologie morale*, (Paris, 1874) 1:278
33 *Theologia moralis S. Alphonsi*, Vol. 1 (Benziger, 1880) 210-11
34 *ASS*, 5, 298
35 *Codex iuris canonici*, c. 2350, par. 1. The same change was made in the canon on irregularity, c. 985, par. 4.

36   See Chapter Nine, p. 146.
37   *Theologia moralis*, nn. 668-71 (Ancona, 1841)
38   *Compendium theologiae moralis, De quinto praecepto*, art. 3, p. 2 (Lyons, 1853)
39   *Revue théologique*, 2 (1857) 267 ff.
40   *Casus conscientiae*, 1, *De quinto praecepto*, cas. 10 (LePuy, 1862)
41   *Compendium theologiae moralis, De quinto praecepto*, art. 3, p. 2, Seventeenth Edition (Lyons, 1866)
42   *Casus conscientiae*, 1, *De quinto praecepto*, cas. 10, Second Edition (Paris, 1867)
43   *Compendium theologiae moralis P. Ioannis Gury ab auctore recognitum et annotationibus locupletatum, De quinto praecepto*, art. 3, p. 2, Annotationes (Rome, 1874) 382-3
44   *Theologia moralis*, Pars 1, l. 2, d. 3, t. 2, c. 3
45   *Medicina pastoralis*, (Aachen, 1901) 17

CHAPTER TWELVE   Craniotomy Controversy: Craisson, Eschbach, Avanzini, Viscosi

1   Capellmann, C., *Medicina pastoralis* (Aachen, 1901) 20
2   *Craniotomy* is defined as the cutting to pieces of a fetal head to facilitate delivery. It differs from another procedure called *cephalotripsy* in which the fetal head is crushed for the same purpose. *Embryotomy* is the dismemberment of the fetus to facilitate delivery. All of these procedures are destructive of the fetus.
3   Cappellmann was arguing from statistics that included fetal as well as maternal deaths. Since craniotomy always meant death for the fetus, a procedure like caesarean section, which might frequently save the fetus, would show a lower total death rate, and therefore be safer. But the maternal death rate alone would not be lower, and so caesarean section would not have been safer for the mother at that time.
4   *Theologia moralis*, Tr. 3, c. 9, n. 128 (Mechlin, 1860)
5   *De l'avortement medical. Peut-on sauver la mere par la mort certaine de l'enfant? Revue des sciences ecclésiastiques*, 25 (1872) 451
6   Ibid., 451-53
7   *L'embryotomie au point de vue moral*, ibid., 563-68
8   Ibid., 26 (1873) 194-201:298-304
9   See Chapter Eleven, p. 214. Cited by Eschbach, *Revue*, 299
10   *Questio moralis de Craniotomia seu de occisione fetus in utero matris ut mater a certa morte servetur*, ASS, 7 (1872) 285 ff.
11   *Revue des sciences ecclésiastiques*, 27: 274-52; 364-74

12   For the discussion of these authors see Chapter Seven, p. 116.
13   *Revue*, 27:369
14   Ibid., 370
15   Ibid., 371
16   Ibid., 460-64; 516-28
17   *L'embryotomia nei suoi rapporti colla morale cattolica*
       (Naples, 1879)
18   Ibid., Capo 3
19   Although he does not say it explicitly here, Viscosi will not allow
       the death of the fetus to be intended even as a means. Both the
       proponents and opponents of craniotomy accept the principle that
       evil may not be intended either as an end or a means. The
       difference between the two would seem to be that the proponents
       of embryotomy consider only the effect (the death of the fetus)
       evil. Their opponents look upon the act itself (the embryotomy) as
       evil. The proponents of embryotomy, then, are satisfied if the
       death of the fetus is not intended either as an end or a means.
       Their opponents will not allow the embryotomy itself as an in-
       tended means. The proponents of embryotomy rely on St.
       Thomas' article on self-defense to support their position, although
       St. Thomas was discussing only unjust aggression. Even though
       Viscosi in the present chapter considers the fetus an innocent
       bystander, he seems satisfied with the requirements St. Thomas
       sets down for dealing with an unjust aggressor.
20   *L'embryotomia*, Capo 4
21   Ibid., Capo 5
22   Even if the child on the road or the child used as a shield had
       survived the blow, the defense would have been successful as long
       as the horseman escaped or the aggressor was immobilized. But
       the mother would not have survived without the embryotomy.
       Viscosi's adversaries use the necessity of the embryotomy as
       proof that it is a means to saving the mother's life, and therefore
       intentional.
23   *L'embryotomia*, Capo 6
24   For Tertullian's position see Chapter Three, p. 41.
25   Both Busenbaum and Alphonsus seemed to be talking in terms of
       the Corduban distinction. Both also dealt with the case under the
       heading: Direct killing of the innocent.
26   *L'embryotomia*, Capo 7
27   Ibid., Capo 8
28   Ibid., Capo 9
29   A number of theologians allowed direct killing of an unjust aggres-
       sor, so Eschbach's argument would not be valid against them. If
       they considered the fetus an unjust aggressor, they would have no
       problem with direct expulsion.

30 *L'embryotomia*, Capo 10
31 Ibid., Capo 11
32 This axiom can be translated: Minimal amounts can be ignored.
33 *L'embryotomia*, Capo 14
34 Ibid., Capo 15
35 Ibid., Capo 16
36 Ibid., 284

CHAPTER THIRTEEN   Craniotomy Controversy
                    Continued: Pennacchi

1   *De abortu et embryotomia* (Rome, 1884)
2   Ibid., *Articulus secundus*, 31
3   Ibid., 48
4   Hom. 10 in Exodum, PG 12:370. Origen can hardly be used to
    support Pennacchi's argument here, since he had difficulty also
    with applying the *lex talionis* to the mother.
5   *De abortu et embryotomia*, 69
6   Ibid., 73
7   Ibid., 76
8   Ibid., 82
9   The distinction between *finis operis* and *finis operantis* is that
    between the purpose of the work and the purpose of the worker.
    They may be the same, but the purpose of the worker may go
    beyond that of the work. For example, the *finis operis* of a watch is
    to tell time; the *finis operantis* (the watchmaker) may be to make a
    living.
10 *De abortu et embryotomia*, 107-08

CHAPTER FOURTEEN   Craniotomy Controversy
                    Continued: Waffelaert

1   *De abortu et embryotomia*, NRT, 16 (1884) 94-106
2   Ibid., 160-79
3   There are at least three interpretations of St. Thomas' article on
    self-defense. Not all agree that he limits his use of the word
    intention to a willing of the end or goal of the act. In other words,
    not all admit that he would allow a direct willing of the death of the
    assailant as a means to the goal of self-defense.
4   NRT, 16 (1884) 293-321

5   Waffelaert does not mention Caramuel, perhaps because Pennacchi failed to mention him. It will be remembered that Caramuel was very hesitant about proposing his view that the fetus in some cases could be considered an unjust aggressor.
6   NRT, 16 (1884) 377-85
7   NRT, 17 (1885) 60-68; 200-10
8   Ibid., 369-80
9   For Kenrick's pastoral advice see Chapter Twelve, p. 225.
10 NRT, 17 (1885) 528-50

CHAPTER FIFTEEN   Resolution
(1884-1950)

1   *De abortu et embryotomia*
2   NRT, 17 (1885) 60
3   ASS, 17 (1884) 556
4   *Disputationes physiologico-theologicae*, Pars Tertia (Paris, 1884) 251-2
5   ASS, 22 (1888-90) 748
6   *La doctrine du R. P. Ant. Ballerini sur l'embryotomie et l'avortement*, NRT, 17 (1885) 410-34
7   *Disputationes*, 341
8   *Compendium theologiae moralis*, n. 403, par. 2, note b
9   NRT, 17 (1885) 410-34
10 See Chapter Eleven, pp. 214-219 for Gury's and Ballerini's opinion.
11 *Lettre de R. P. A. E. au R. P. Matharan, S. J.*, NRT, 17, 551-62
12 *Reponse du R. P. Matharan au R. P. Eschbach*, NRT, 18, 283-91
13 *L'avortement est-il toujours occisif de sa nature?* NRT, 18, 434-9
14 ASS, 28 (1895-96) 384
15 Twelfth edition, I, n. 1007-8
16 Kelly, Gerald, S. J., *Medico-moral Problems* (St. Louis, 1958) 75-83
17 AAS, 22, 539-92. The encyclical was published Dec. 31, 1930.
18 *Dopo l'enciclica sul matrimonio cristiano: La parole della scienza*, l'Osservatore Romano, Jan. 22, 1931. Dr. Pestalozza's statement would not go unnoticed since he was a personal friend of Pius XI and it was published in a Vatican organ.
19 *Dopo l'enciclica sul matrimonio cristiano. Necessarie precisioni*, l'Osservatore Romano, Jan. 28, 1931
20 *Medicina pastoralis*, (Aachen, 1901) 17
21 *QQ de embryologia et sterilizatione* (Liege, 1937) 40-46

22 See A. Janssen, *L'Hysterectomie pendant la grossesse, Ephem-erides Theologicae Lovanienses*, 11 (1934) 528-30.

23 *Catechismo del matrimonio* (Rome-Turin, 1931) 78

24 NRT, 60 (1933) 584

25 *De causalitate per se et per accidens, seu directa et indirecta, Periodica de re morali, canonica, liturgica*, 21 (1932) 101*-116*

26 *Application a l'avortement des notions de causalite per accidens et de causalite per se*, NRT, 60, 500-27; *De l'avortement indirect, 577-99; Encore l'avortement indirect*, 687-93

27 *Avortement direct ou indirect*, NRT, 60, 600-20; *Une courte con-clusion*, 694-95

28 *QQ de embryologia et sterilizatione*, 29-40

29 *In questione di isterectomia, Palestra del clero*, 13 (1934) 361-65

30 *De hysterectomia in mulierem gravidam exercita*, Periodica, 33 (1934) 193*-196* *L'Hysterectomie pendant la grossesse, Ephemerides Theol. Lovanienses*, 11 (1934) 554-60

31 *De hysterectomia terapeutica utero pleno, Palestra del clero*, 14 (1935) 5-9. Responded to by A. Janssen, *Ephemerides Theol. Lovanienses*, 12 (1935) 337-49.

32 R. J. Hollaind, S. J., *A New Moral and Physiological Problem, American Ecclesiastical Review*, 9 (1893) 331-42. *The Discussion of a New Moral and Physiological Problem*, ibid., 10 (1894) 12-60

33 *De conceptis ectopicis seu extrauterinis*, ibid., 9 (1893) 343-60

34 *Excisio foetus atque eius directa occisio*, ibid., 10 (1894) 67

35 ASS, 30 (1897-98) 703-04

36 Lehmkuhl, *Theologia moralis*, Vol. 1, n. 1010

37 *Ethics of Ectopic Operations*, (Milwaukee, 1933)